Tahir M. Nisar

Smartphone and App Implementations that Improve Productivity

Tahir M. Nisar

Smartphone and App Implementations that Improve Productivity

—

ISBN 978-1-5474-1665-3
e-ISBN (PDF) 978-1-5474-0054-6
e-ISBN (EPUB) 978-1-5474-0056-0

Library of Congress Control Number: 2018960086

Bibliographic information published by the Deutsche Nationalbibliothek
The Deutsche Nationalbibliothek lists this publication in the Deutsche Nationalbibliografie;
detailed bibliographic data are available on the Internet at http://dnb.dnb.de.

Published by Walter de Gruyter Inc., Boston/Berlin
Printing and binding: CPI books GmbH, Leck
Typesetting: MacPS, LLC, Carmel

www.degruyter.com

Acknowledgments

This book is based on work that I did as part of a research project on digital apps and smart workplaces. The project was funded by a grant from Southampton Business School, and I thank Frank McGroarty and Yehuda Baruch for their continued support throughout this project. I wish to express my gratitude to my doctoral student assistants, Khurrum Siddiq and Dina Al-Ghamdi, for helping me with data collection and report writing. Finally, I am grateful to Jeffrey M. Pepper and Jaya Dalal for their excellent editorial work.

Tahir M. Nisar
Southampton Business School
University of Southampton

DOI 10.1515/9781547400546-202

Contents

Preface

In the last decade, significant developments in information and communication technology have been achieved leading to substantial changes in the way companies operate and create value. Specifically, in order to adapt to the new digital era following the "dotcom-era" of the early 2000s, both established and nascent firms have started exploiting new technologies such as smartphone/tablet applications, which were derived from technology advances that allowed greater performance capability of computing, storage and connectivity. There are estimated to be 2.53 billion smartphone subscriptions globally today and 2.87 billion smartphones will be sold through 2020. With the sheer number of smartphones available worldwide and the powerful capabilities available on them through applications ("apps"), it is no surprise that usage is set to increase in the workplace. In recent years, the security fears in IT that slowed smartphone and tablet use as work devices have been replaced by the benefits derived from their flexibility and portability. The opportunities available through apps to workplaces and managers have already been undertaken in a variety of decision making situations and competitive environments. Apps can aid employees in a number of capabilities but with one common characteristic: they all make things easier.

"Apps," self-contained programs designed to fulfill a specific purpose on a mobile device, such as a mobile phone or tablet and interoperability with a computer, are divided into two categories: apps crafted for personal use and apps aimed at a business level. Apps for increasing personal productivity such as agendas and time management tools are less impactful compared to apps that enrich the workplace environment as a whole. The main purposes in which companies utilize apps at a corporate level can be related to many distinct management and organization functions such as: supply-chain, sales force automation (SFA) and customer relationship management (CRM). Such technologies have essentially reformed business operations as they permit work to be carried out in a coordinated way across boundaries of time, distance and function. Many businesses are further exploring the use of these apps as part of their technology solutions and automation of otherwise time consuming business tasks. Furthermore, social media and enterprise related apps have completely changed the patterns of communication in the workplace: a message now takes the form of "content." Employees spend less time searching for task-related information, significantly reducing the time spent on a searchable record of knowledge. Knowledge sharing leads to better decision making as faster access to more experts or relevant documents increases the chance that better decisions are made. Consequently, workers will likely seize any productivity improvement opportunity by accessing information expeditiously.

DOI 10.1515/9781547400546-204

This book will first provide information on how new technologies can increase the effectiveness of mobile applications in the workplace. Moving on, the benefits of mobile applications in workplace environments through the use of plentiful examples will be discussed and we conclude by stating why mobile applications are beneficial rather than harmful to organizations, considering the information provided. The book analyzes the advantages of increased collaboration, mobility, rewards, in addition to simplification of task structures and training in the work environment with the help of applications. Also, the potential benefits of productivity and efficiency that accrue to small and large organizations will be discussed. The use of apps in workplace environments and for work activities has revealed many opportunities for businesses to save both human and physical resources.

What You Will Learn

In this book, the use of mobile/tablet apps and their relative benefits for these categories within workplace environments will be thoroughly examined in order to formulate an answer to the question: why are companies using mobile apps to streamline their work processes? Technological change is a dynamic force, with impact on every business, forcing them to adapt and modify the way they conduct their activities, collaborate with their employees and interact with their customers. We will analyze these changes within the broad framework of organizational and institutional changes and their impact on productivity. The introduction of apps into businesses has revolutionized the way employees and managers carry out their jobs while also benefiting them socially. This book will look at the benefits apps are having in the workplace. In the process, we will introduce academic perspectives that link prospective advantages with practical commercial examples. Correspondingly, analysis will be structured into chapters that include not only principles but real-world application. At the same time, each chapter will critically assess implied benefits of the new app technology and draw out the main findings and conclusions. These conclusions will be combined into a final account which summarizes the overall beneficial magnitude of apps in the workplace and points out any potential issues that must be dealt with in conducting business in this fashion.

Chapter 1
New Innovative Business Services

Throughout the twenty-first century, technology has led to a new era of enhanced facility in human life, and improved productivity, thus higher profitability in enterprises. As the latest trend in terms of consumer electronics, smartphones and tablets undoubtedly revolutionized the way people do things and enabled firms to gain a competitive advantage. Through word of mouth and social media, it would be very difficult to overlook the expansion of the apps market over recent years. The number of smartphone users worldwide was estimated at 2.53 billion in 2018 (Statista, 2018) underlining the surge of growth of these devices, which support the market of software applications (see Figure 1.1). Given the importance of smartphones and tablets, mobile applications are what creates the distinctive value and sets them apart from other consumer electronics. There is thus no doubt that significant changes have taken place with respect to the workplace environment (Campbell, 2007). These technologies, with such importance, would not only influence the employees individually, but also can benefit the organization as a whole by the ease of use and improved efficiency. This can be seen from the experience of Uber, a mobile technology-based organization.

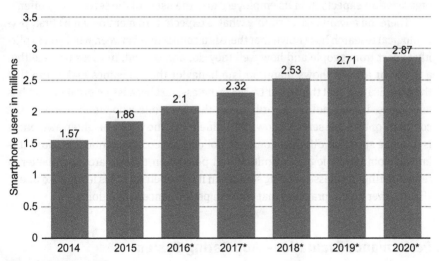

Source: Statista, 2018

Figure 1.1: Use of Smartphones

DOI 10.1515/9781547400546-001

Uber: A Mobile Application-Based Business

A number of pioneering companies have fully embraced the potential of mobile apps and have turned it into their unique selling point. *Uber* is an international transportation company that developed and operates the Uber mobile app (www. uber.com); Uber both coordinates with their employees, or drivers, and communicates directly with their customers through their mobile application. Through powerful marketing and an exceedingly stable infrastructure, Uber has successfully developed a business model that requires no great amount of fixed assets or office-based employees: instead they are able to earn a relatively high profit margin while maintaining low costs through their mobile application. With a proposed market valuation of $50 billion dollars (Forbes, 2014), Uber's focus on mobile applications shows the benefit of fully realizing the potential of apps to benefit, not just separate departments, but companies. One of Uber's goals is to *make every ride a great experience*. In order to achieve their goal, Uber has put forward different management and incentive policies that aim to motivate their drivers. However, they do also have incentive policies that concern both the drivers and the riders, such as their Community Guidelines, which outline standards for accountability, respect, and courtesy. The guidelines are a classic example of a technology-based management policy that explicitly states what the organization expects from its employees and the users of the service they offer.

There are advantages of stating what is expected. To mention a few; first, psychological research has shown that there is a connection between what you explicitly expect from people and how well they do, and second, in cases where either a driver or a rider shows inappropriate behavior the guidelines make sure that the organization "got things right." Nevertheless, just because an organization has guidelines, it does not necessarily mean that everyone who either works in the company or uses the service knows the guidelines. One way to heighten awareness is to make sure that different company policies are complementary, because it is known from psychology of cognition and perception that we are much better at remembering the message being sent when it is "coherent." This leads us to one of Uber's other digital practices that concern performance evaluation.

Performance Evaluation—App Rating System

Uber has developed an app where the driver and the rider can rate the experience they had using Uber. This can not only reinforce appropriate behavior, but it also makes it possible to indirectly "monitor" the behavior of the drivers, and for example, get an idea of whether they truly represent the values of the company or not. Hereby it also makes it possible to correct the behavior of employees who do not live up to the expectations. The app can also be considered a screening device, making it more likely that people who apply for a driver position behave in accordance with Uber's values. However, it is important that the drivers do not feel that the only reason for having the app is to monitor their behavior, because then it can have adverse effects, for example, demotivate the drivers. Overall, the app has several advantages that align with the goal of making each ride a great experience, but it is necessary to be aware of possible challenges related to the use of the app.

The Drivers—Not Employees but Partners

One thing that is prominent when looking at Uber's operations is that they do not call their drivers *employees*, but *partners*. By calling their drivers partners, they indicate that they are independent contractors and underscore a more equal relationship. This makes it more likely that the drivers feel ownership, which is known as one of the best ways to motivate a worker. In addition, it is likely to create intrinsic motivation, that is, motivation that arises from within. In other words, if you take on a discursive point of view, language creates reality, and you could say that calling the employees *partners* is one way of creating a reality where the workers are valued as not only employees, but as partners and all it connotes. Being a partner does often include a high degree of flexibility, and this is exactly one of the things Uber offers, which will be elaborated on in the following.

Flexibility—A Key Word in Uber's Digital Practices

When looking at Uber's operations, it stands out that being an Uber partner involves flexibility, and that it is one way the company tries to "compete" with other companies offering similar services, for example, about good quality workers. You can drive your own car, set your own schedule, and get paid instantly up to five times a day. The flexibility fits well with calling their drivers partners. It can also motivate the drivers, for example, because the partners decide themselves how much to work, and thereby how much to earn. However, it is important to remember that this is not necessarily always true, because there might be periods where partners are not "hired" for jobs even though they are willing to work. One important advantage of the flexibility Uber offers is that flexibility in work-life is less likely to create stress, which then leaves more space for fulfilling the goal of Uber—*to make each ride a great experience.*

What it All Comes Down to

It appears that Uber has different management policies and practices that aim to fulfil their goal of *making every ride a great experience.* The mentioned company policies and practices seem to fit relatively well together, which is important according to Baron and Kreps (1999), but there are also potential challenges linked to their policies and practices, which should be considered. In addition, the flexibility they offer fits well with the broader context of the organization that is characterized by a world in constant movement. In conclusion, the examination of Uber's policies indicates that its objectives emphasize the strategic role of innovations, and that technology-based organizational innovations are considered essential for the company's success.

Values and Prospects: Technological Changes and Something More

As the Uber example shows, digital apps are not merely about creating a new business or running it more efficiently. Such technological advancements are also accompanied by a new management ethos that emphasizes new work practices such as collaboration, information, and knowledge sharing and teamwork. Workplace is rapidly changing and is seen as creating greater flexibility, efficiency, and productivity among employees in the workplace. New app-based advancements taking over the workplace and its environment are giving employees the freedom to work with design anytime and anywhere. They are increasingly changing the work processes, the way we live, and the working environment. The advancement of technology since the turn of the century has inevitably led to the increase of information and communication technology (ICT) usage within businesses. The iPad and Amazon Kindle mean that it has become incredibly easy and convenient to carry around a laptop-like device, and although initially created for the purpose of leisure, many people are now using tablets and smartphones solely for business. Subsequently, it is common for companies now not only to have websites, but also applications that can be downloaded on these devices, leading to more exposure to the public and therefore helping to streamline their business. These apps can be used at convenience and can reach millions of people through various digital platforms.

With the use of apps, it is possible to manage and control different aspects of the organization. This should in turn reduce the costs of monitoring employees' tasks and work and should increase the transparent levels across the firm. Taylorism is a process used by businesses in which activities are broken down into simpler components to make it easier for employees to complete the tasks. Taylorism and Fordism were initially applied to the manufacturing sector; however, the ideas can be used in the service sectors and how to handle the organization in general (Baron and Kreps, 1999). Currently, smartphones and tablets are important devices in the human lifestyle and using these devices in the workplace could make employees have more self-control of their day-to-day tasks in the working environment. For example, the use of smartphones in work-related tasks could promote autonomy. Autonomy is the right or condition of self-control. Autonomy and McGregor's Theory of Motivation are linked together (Buchanan and Huczynski, 2016). Theory Y of McGregor states that people want independence at work, and they are motivated by self-fulfillment. By the use of apps, employees will have more self-control, which means they have more independence and they will be more motivated to work. More motivation will lead to increased productivity and efficiency. Such app-based systems will also encourage creativity and innovation.

The technologies will inevitably simplify work processes but they will also help the business to grow and expand by creating new innovative design products and services. This is because apps could help as employees use their creative side and work as a team. This again could increase levels of motivation. Motivation is the degree to which an individual wants and chooses to engage in a certain specified behavior. If we look at Herzberg's Two Factor Theory of motivation, growth, recognition, and work itself bring motivation. Employees will feel recognized if they use their ideas to help the business grow and expand. It is in this sense that apps implementation within the workplace is more than a process of technological change; it also introduces a new value system that brings about fundamental changes in employees' behavior. Firms that can adjust to the demands of using the applications are the ones that are likely to have a competitive edge over their competitors as it changes the way jobs are performed, the work process, and other nonwork-related activities.

The development of the mobile platform has also enabled a new way of interaction between business and consumer. Successful app-based businesses are disrupting various markets as operating through a mobile app offers many benefits to a firm. First, mobile applications can facilitate the disruption of current markets and allow for new entrants where there may have previously been barriers to entry, potentially resulting in great scope for future profits. This is because the use of apps can allow for a more convenient service as consumers have instant access at their fingertips. Further, developing an app-based business model can also be beneficial because of the opportunity for cost reduction and improved efficiency. A more efficient and convenient product is likely to be highly popular with consumers as it merely saves them time and makes life easier. This is highly likely to lead to some form of disruption in certain markets as consumers decide to switch to the new, more convenient product, especially if they have little brand loyalty. Uber is an example of an app-based business which has disrupted the market in ride-hailing service. Uber allows people to request a cab via the app and track its location, as well as automatically taking payment through the app. It has become prevalent because of its convenience and has majorly disrupted the taxi industry. With conventional cabs under real threat, Uber had revenues of $11.33 billion and a profit of $2.45 billion in the first quarter of 2018 (Nytimes.com, 2019). This shows how disrupting a market can bring fantastic revenue potential.

Statistics on the taxi industry are difficult to measure because many transactions are paid in cash and many drivers are self-employed, therefore making it very difficult to record the number of trips taken. However, it is possible to track company reimbursed ground transportation, where employees are using either a taxi service or rental cars to travel. When looking at this sector, it is clear by how much ride-hailing app-based businesses dominate. Figure 1.2 shows a growing combined share of over 70% in Q1 2018 for the two biggest ride-hailing apps in the USA for the transport reimbursements sector.

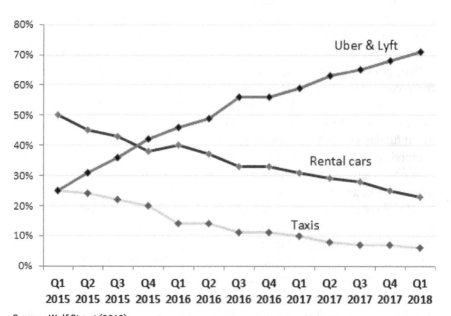

Source: Wolf Street (2019)

Figure 1.2: Percentage of ground transportation travel reimbursements

Thus, there are potentially some great benefits of using apps to create new business models because it can lead to a severe disruption of a particular industry and possibly allow for sharp gains in market share.

Second, using apps to create new business models can lead to an entirely new organizational structure. Apps can enable the population to participate in the production of goods and services. For example, take Airbnb, an app for people to list, find and rent lodging; this allows for many people to rent out owned properties as and when they wish, with Airbnb taking a percentage, without holding any properties itself. This has been a very successful new business model in the hospitality sector with over $1 billion in revenues for Q3 2018 (Bosa, 2019). The model created here leads to a very centralized organization, with head offices, but no actual properties to rent, as its product is being the medium for which others can work. This can result in very high revenues relative to the number of people employed by the organization, which may result in massive profits as the costs of the business are likely to be lower if it uses a small workforce. Thus, an app-based business has an excellent opportunity to benefit from the fact that it can reach billions of consumers with relative ease.

Furthermore, a prime example of one of these businesses would be the TV streaming service Netflix, which delivers media content directly to the consumer's devices via the app or the website. Netflix operates on a global scale, with a direct distribution channel from the business to the consumer, wherever it operates. The ability to do this has greatly benefitted Netflix's profitability as it can remain a small organization in terms of employees and offices but have a vast customer base with high profits. Figure 1.3 illustrates how Netflix had extremely high revenue per employee in 2017, compared to some of the world's largest technology companies. This is a clear benefit of using mobile applications and such technologies in a business model as it allows for a business to have global scale potential, with opportunities for giant revenues (Statista, 2019).

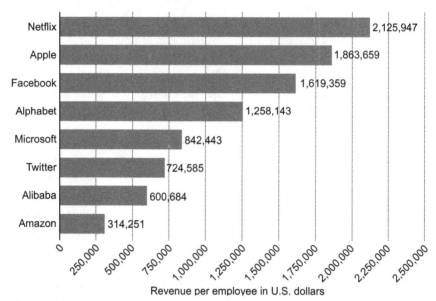

Source: Statista, 2019

Figure 1.3: Revenue per employee of selected tech companies in 2017 (in U.S. dollars)

On the other hand, using apps to develop new business models does not come without its drawbacks. Serious problems can potentially arise regarding monitoring the workforce and controlling the quality of service provided. It can be challenging to monitor the workforce for many app-based businesses because their organizational structure does not follow a classical hierarchical model. Many of these businesses run off having a labor force that is self-employed and therefore has no direct supervisor to report to or be monitored by. In addition to this, controlling the quality of service provided may also be difficult due to the same reason of using a self-employed workforce. This leads to an issue arising where the worker providing the good or service may not be fully aligned to the company's vision or carry out the service in the desired way. Furthermore, for a business of this structure, e.g., Airbnb or Uber, implementing a policy of total quality management may be nearly impossible because it requires the full cooperation of all levels within the organization, with all employees participating. This model of producing quality does not translate to some app-based business models because of how they are structured.

Overall, it is clear there are numerous benefits to creating new business models using mobile apps and other relevant technologies. The use of mobile apps gives a new business the ability to provide a product in a new way which can be far more convenient to consumers and therefore disrupt current markets.

As mentioned throughout this chapter, Uber is a perfect example of this and has quickly proved to be a massive competitor to traditional taxi services. Being a disruptor and taking a share of a market allows for immense profits to be made because of how many users can adopt a new product so quickly. In addition to this, the use of mobile applications can also allow for new businesses to have unique organizational structures. Many app-based companies benefit from the sharing economy by acting as a platform for people to buy and sell goods and services. This can result in firms with small workforces having extremely great revenues and profits. Thus showing another benefit of using apps to create new business models as it allows for outreach to billions of people worldwide.

However, creating new app-based business can potentially lead to severe issues for management, especially regarding the workforce. There is a possibility with these sharing economy type businesses that the reputation of the company rests partly upon those who carry out the service, e.g. Uber drivers or Airbnb hosts, who may be self-employed and not directly linked to the business and thus also not trained by the company. This could lead to problems with the quality of service provided. Therefore, there is a risk that instances of poor service or quality of the product will negatively affect the whole company's reputation in the public eye, and this may adversely affect the profitability of the business if consumers pay attention to this.

Chapter 2
Mobile Communications and Big Data

In a global business, communication between employees is always a vital factor for a company to run efficiently and keep productivity at its highest. For this reason, everyone in the workplace and employees that may be located abroad must be able to communicate and have access to the company's database, as well as always be able to contact other employees with ease during the day. This is vital for a company, which with the help of globalization has spread and is not just reaching its own country but also others around the world. Employees must have access to real time information at the touch of a button immediately when they need it and be able to contact and even organize online meetings through their mobile devices. This is all done with the help of mobile devices. For example, mobile applications are used by schools and universities to keep students up to date with news and events of the day or in the future, access electronic books in the library, class assignments, recording professor lectures, course support materials, and testing. This chapter analyzes the use of technological tools in the workplace and points out the benefits attached to it for both employees and employers. We first provide context to this phenomenon by discussing the evolving nature of smartphone markets and then explore their implications for big data functionalities and related technologies.

Smartphone Markets

Undoubtedly, smartphones have become an integral part of people's daily life. Individuals use their smartphones for a wide range of purposes; to call and text other people, send e-mails, browse the internet, take photos, play games, shop online, and so on. The global smartphone market increased massively over the years just after Apple introduced its first iPhone in 2007. After the iPhone, android phones were introduced in 2008 and the market received a significant boost. For example, mobile users universally consume more digital minutes per person (when looking at each region's desktop users and mobile users separately)—more than double in most countries surveyed (see Figure 2.1).

DOI 10.1515/9781547400546-002

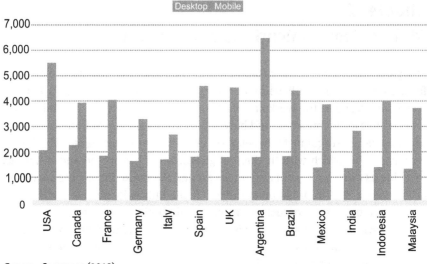

Source: Comscore (2018)

Figure 2.1: Average minutes per user by platform

There are various factors that affect smartphone buying decisions. Some of the most important ones namely brand, price, product features, and social influence are briefly explained below.

Brand

A brand, according to American Marketing Association (2016), is a symbol, name, design, or other characteristic that makes the product/service of an organization identifiable in the market and can give it a substantial, differentiated advantage among the products/service of the competitors. As in all products and services, brand name plays a significant role in consumers' smartphone buying behavior. Samsung, Huawei (capitalizing on the enormous China market), Apple (iPhone), and LG are some of the brands that can be counted as recognized brands in the global smartphone market.

Price

The price is an indicator of the value of a product/service determined by the company and should be set very carefully in order for the product/service to be successful in the market. Higher prices are mostly associated with high quality; however, overpriced products may not be purchased by the consumers if the value provided by the product/service does not meet customers' expectations. Similarly, low price is mostly associated with low quality; therefore, decreasing the price to gain a competitive advantage over competitors may not work as the customers may consider that the product/service offered by the company may be a low-quality product/service.

Product features

Smartphones have a number of features from cameras to note pads and these features may significantly affect the consumers' decisions. Accordingly, companies should be able to update their products continuously and should be very innovative in order to compete successfully in the market.

Social Influence

Consumers are sometimes affected by their friends' and families' experiences about products/services. In general friends and families play a significant role in their decisions, however, in the social environment there are also other factors to be considered such as opinion leaders, social media, culture, etc.

Social Media

Social media utilizes "internet-based applications that build on the ideological and technological foundations of Web 2.0, and that allow the creation and exchange of user generated content" (Kaplan and Haenlein, 2010). Expressed differently, social media can be described as the tailored user-created media in which the users possess higher control over the creation and use of the content compared to the various producers of consumer products and services. Keenan and Shiri (2009) stated that the social networking platforms that exist on the web are either activity oriented or people oriented, depending on how they facilitate and enhance social interaction among its users. Digital platforms that are people oriented are characterized by maintaining the user's profile in the center of communications among individuals with user profiles encompassing a great deal of personal information. In social networking platforms that are people oriented, the personal information of the users and others' accessibility to this information is controlled by the users.

On the other hand, in activity oriented social platforms, the focus is on the social interaction through content that contributes to the platform's community (Casas and Delmelle, 2017; Keenan and Shiri, 2009). In this respect, the videos that are created and uploaded to the social media platforms are one of the best examples that can be given in this category. Among many other platforms, YouTube is the most popular in this category. On YouTube two types of content are created, namely brand-generated content (BGC) and user-generated content (UGC).

User-Generated Content

Companies can use social media to collaborate and build relationships with consumers. For example, two-way communication can provide businesses with increased transparency. Using social media, consumers can also remain connected with brands after purchase (Algesheimer et al., 2005; Mellon and Prosser, 2017). This connection allows consumers to provide feedback, which can be used by the brand to increase appeal, satisfaction, and brand loyalty (Dellarocas, 2003; Aral and Walker, 2011). Drawing on these specific features of interactive engagement, research shows that the quantitative aspects of online reviews (e.g., review volume and/or rating [valance]) positively influence aggregate performance measures such as product sales. Several other types of consumer-generated content (CGC) have also been investigated in terms of their influence on consumer purchase behavior. For example, Tumarkin and Whitelaw (2001) studied internet postings in financial discussion forums; Godes and Mayzlin (2004) examined Usenet newsgroup conversations; Dhar and Chang (2009) investigated blog postings; and Albuquerque et al. (2012) evaluated user created magazines in an online platform. Their findings are in many ways very similar to the earlier work on CGC showing that aggregate level economic outcomes can be attributed to quantitative aspects of CGC (e.g., volume, dispersion).

Online consumer purchase decisions are also likely to be influenced by marketer-generated content (MGC) because of their role in providing instant information on different product attributes. MGC can also be useful in other areas such as when consumers need information about after sale support services. In these situations, conflict and disagreement may also occur in the process of marketer–consumer engagement stemming from the occasional tendency of consumers to show skepticism toward MGC (Mellon and Prosser, 2017).

Dhar and Chang (2009) conducted research on the effect of UGC on music sales, using blog data as well as data from social networking platforms. The academics observed the variations in online chatter (UGC) taking 108 albums as the research population for one month prior to and following their dates of release. They utilized linear and nonlinear regression in determining the importance of the variables in the prediction of prospective album sales figures. According to their research results: (a) the quantity of blog posts concerning an album and the prospective sales figures are positively correlated, (b) an increase in the number of an artist's friends on Myspace on a weekly basis is not significantly correlated with better prospective sales figures, (c) albums that are released by popular labels as well as albums that are reviewed by popular sources are more likely to achieve higher sales figures. In another study, Flanagin and Metzger (2013) examined user-generated movie ratings and they indicated among other things that when the volume of the user-generated ratings increases, the users' reliance on the ratings, their perceived credibility of the ratings, confidence in the ratings, and behavioral intention increases.

In their research, Grahl et al. (2014) used a social network (owned by an online store) similar to well-known social networks such as Facebook and they treated the number of "Likes" given to the store's products as a form of UGC. To identify the relationship between the "Likes" of the products in the social network and the buying behavior of the consumers they conducted an experiment for twenty-three days. Their results indicate that popularity information such as "Likes" plays a very important role on consumer decision making and sales, and especially when the consumers have not obtained a lot of information about the products that they want to purchase.

In the context of Instagram, Bahtar and Muda (2016) carried out a study to find out the effect of the product related user generated content on Instagram on the purchasing intentions of Instagram users. They (2016) claim that perceived usefulness, perceived risk and perceived credibility of UGC on Instagram affect the users' attitudes toward that content positively. They also claim that positive attitudes toward user generated content on Instagram will influence purchase intentions. Schivinski and Dabrowski (2016) on the other hand studied the influence of both UGC and BGC on Facebook users' brand perceptions and purchase intentions. In this context, they found that brand attitude and brand equity are significantly affected by the UGC on social media. On the contrary, the brand generated content influences only the brand attitude. Schivinski and Dabrowski (2016) also indicated that brand attitude and equity affect the consumers' purchasing intentions. Like Schivinski and Dabrowski (2016), Scholz et al. (2013) investigated both the UGC and BGC in online social networks. Scholz et al. (2013) conducted a study to identify whether the BGC and UGC affect brand awareness and consumers' buying decisions and they found that user generated content heavily influences the consumers' purchasing decision making leading to higher sales figures, whereas brand generated content mainly increases the brand awareness.

In the context of YouTube, Wang (2015) examined the relationship between the perceived credibility of UGC related to beauty products, the user attitudes toward that content, and other factors that can influence purchase intentions. Her results indicated a positive correlation between attitudes and perceived credibility as well as positive correlations between purchase intention and the other variables of the study. In addition, her results showed that active users on YouTube have more positive attitudes toward user generated content and as a result they are more likely to buy the beauty products that are shown on YouTube compared to passive users. Another study on YouTube by Liu-Thompkins and Rogerson (2012) looked into the dissemination of user-generated YouTube videos. Among their findings, the ratings of the users enhance the diffusion of the videos in a more effective way than the videos' innate quality.

Finally, concerning the utilization of user generated content from marketers, Forrester Research (2014) presents three main results: (a) UGC is mainly employed from marketers when they want to introduce a new product. The majority of marketers that utilize UGC in their marketing efforts aim at achieving comments and ratings from users in order to influence the consumers' decision making; actually, user generated content has turned out to be an essential instrument for these marketers to achieve this goal; (b) UGC provides a potential for establishing a brand as it gives marketers the chance to build strong brand stories and communicate those stories; in that way marketers can establish a reliable connection with their target customers. Consumers tend to have more confidence in the reviews of their peers when compared to the content that is created by professional marketers; using the UGC for storytelling can be useful in establishing brand trust; and (c) the way that marketers utilize UGC needs to be well-organized so that they can achieve brand establishing; in fact, marketers need content that is original and is created by the consumers as a result of their real fondness for the brand.

Big Data

In the knowledge economy of today, data is one of the most valuable assets an organization has, but it is also an important commodity, which can be bought, traded for, otherwise acquired, sold, and even freely released, all to assist in the organization's innovation efforts. Big data is geared toward enhancing the decision-making process within the business. While marketing may be the single greatest "beneficiary" of the data, it is equally a tool for financial and investment decisions to be undertaken. It is evident that the use of the big data provides an effectual way of progressing business entities. It is continually being used to "endorse" the decisions that business installations are making. The generation of these data, according to Lindgren (2011) is because of the extensive use of technological provisions in the business. Technology enables businesses to store, retrieve, and analyze the behavioral tendencies of consumers. Depending on how we define big data, from a pure technology benefit, the impact on the financial markets of, for instance, option trading, would probably show the most change over the past decade.

There are several other markets where big data has had an enormous influence such as the stock exchanges, medical recording, medical advances in big data, sensor technologies, and the internet of things, supply chain advances, marketing, and so on. "The autonomous vehicle, driven about 90 minutes a day, generates about 4 terabytes of data per day. Some vehicle trials are generating over a PB a month of data. By 2020, a single autonomous vehicle might produce 4TB of data during 1 to 2 hours of driving. For comparison, a single drone flight captures up to 50GB of data and a fleet of 500 drones creating maps records about 150 TB of data" (Mueck and Karls, 2018). It should be pointed out that this data has to be ALL mobile. To implement this on a large scale still requires further advancements in many technologies.

According to Gupta and Chaudhari (2015), big data is the processing of information. Hence, big data, when it is mentioned as a technology, is a part of information technology (IT), corporate application, and research and development. Comparing it with other aspects in IT, big data has the following characteristics (Zikopoulos and Eaton, 2011):

First, big data is linked with big volume. As the growing quantity of data occurs, efficiency of storage and processing information becomes the main problem. In the car example, the issues are many, including network protocols that enable the technology, ability to keep a 100% live connection, even decision making. On the other hand, as with the growing volume of the data size, data becomes more valuable for research and development. Kaisler et al. (2013) point out that big data can be defined as the amount of data that information technologies can process with. As we discuss later, a smartphone will not be performing the big data calculations but acting as the interface.

Second, big data also means the variety of data. Data can be collected in different types and from different resources (Jacobs, 2009). Data can also be collected from some new media, such as the social network media or the click numbers of videos in an online video platform. The variety of such data enables a clearer picture of their final answer, so that they can solve a problem using big data with more certainty. However, the variety of big data adds difficulty for the data analyst to process and analyze the data.

Third, big data requires velocity. This means the speed of processing, storage, and transfer of those data is important. Today, information is processed and transferred all over the world. Therefore, delay during data transfer and processing becomes a rising problem. For instance, with today's technology, the speed at which stock market transactions are carried out is important. Velocity requires big data to be processed fast enough to meet the demand of using those data (Zikopoulos and Eaton, 2011). Moreover, Gupta and Chaudhari (2015) add another three characteristics of big data: one is the variability of big data during its processing and analysis, in order to handle the large volume data efficiently. Another characteristic of big data is veracity; mainly because only the true data provides the actual research results and makes the right decision.

Finally, complexity is always combined with big data. Complexity of processing and analysis of big data always comes from the large volume, variety, and speed requirements of big data. And this makes big data technology different from other aspects of IT.

Briefly, big data can be defined as a complex information technology, for collection, storage, processing, transfer, analysis, and representation of a large volume of data, that may come from a variety of resources. Kaisler et al. (2013) also support a similar definition of big data. Moreover, Jacobs (2009) points out that, existing big data often comes from observation or testing a large volume of people, for their behavior or response, in a large volume of situations and in different times and locations. Initially, noted Simon and Shaffer (2008), tools such as customer communication and feedback, demand-price analysis, competitor analysis, location strategy, and brand strategy had been used as the main component of big data analysis. The emergence of big data, however, has revolutionized the manner in which commercial domains strategize their businesses for growth. Marketing data gives an in-depth evaluation of the consumer behavior that applies to make accurate forecasts on their purchase decisions. Big data is essential in the drafting of practical marketing and/or advertising strategies for the businesses. As Simon and Shaffer (2008) mention, the relevance of this data is witnessed in its ability to form a concrete spine of any decision-making platform.

Open Data and Open Innovation

The concept of "open data" is very new and scientific knowledge with regard to the subject is lacking, since research surrounding it is still nascent and has only now started gathering momentum. Additionally, the emergence of an abundance of terms that include the word "open," such as open innovation, open data, open source software, open government and others, has resulted in some confusion regarding the way these terms relate to one another, especially since all the mentioned terms are new and, some more than others, underdeveloped. Open innovation, as Chesbrough (2003) suggests, constitutes a new paradigm in the ways companies innovate; and open data seems to fit within this theoretical framework, at least if the descriptions forwarded by the different proponents of open data on its impact on innovation, are to be considered. Innovation ultimately is about converting new knowledge into new products, processes, and services; and putting them to use. Especially in the case of private organizations, innovation is about putting new inventions into the market and gaining some kind of financial benefit. Crucial in gaining financial benefit is implementing a business model that will allow the creation and appropriation of value by an organization.

Open innovation, from its inception, was conceived as a fundamentally different way in which new ideas are innovated and brought to the market (Chesbrough, 2003). Chesbrough (2003) went as far as to suggest that open innovation was so substantially different from previous methods of innovation so as to constitute a "paradigm shift" (Kuhn, 1968) in the ways companies bring new knowledge to the market. At this point it would be useful to clarify that in Chesbrough's work, the term "innovation" is defined as a process that involves the transformation of new knowledge into new products, processes, and products and the successful introduction of those into the market (Trott, 2008; Teece, 1986).

Open innovation combines internal and external ideas into architectures and systems whose requirements are defined by a business model. The business model utilizes both external and internal ideas to create value, while defining internal mechanisms to claim some portion of that value. It assumes that the internal ideas can also be taken to market through external channels, outside the current businesses of the firm, to generate additional value (Chesbrough, 2003). The following have been identified as sources for external ideas: suppliers, customers, universities, governments, private laboratories, competitors, and other nations (von Hippel, 1988). In order to make the definition more explicit, it is essential to take a brief look at the older paradigm of closed innovation. The paradigm of closed innovation is based on the following set of implicit rules: Companies should employ the smartest people in the industry, innovation should take place within the company, first mover advantage is paramount for company success, leading the industry in R&D investment will translate in market leadership, and finally, intellectual property (IP) should be strictly controlled so competitors do not profit from it (Chesbrough, 2003).

On the other hand, open innovation is based on the following premises: The number of smart people that do not work for the company is far larger than the number of those who do; therefore, the company needs to work with both groups. Both external and internal R&D is needed to create value and capture a part of the value, respectively. Innovation need not originate from the company in order to profit from it. Putting together a good business model is better than first mover advantage. The best use of external and internal ideas will mean success for the company. Finally, the company should benefit from both importing and exporting IP.

Big Data, Digital Apps, and Organizations

The smartphones are making everyone's lives a lot easier with access to the internet, e-mail, and video conferencing on the move; people no longer need to wait until they get home to check their e-mail or make a Skype call, they can simply do it while shopping or having a coffee at Starbucks. The main benefit of such technologies of mobile applications are the fact that they are portable, wherever you take your phone, your apps are with you at all times giving you access to whatever the application supports on the move. This allows the user to communicate with and have access to all employee's data, leading to engagement from one employee to another seamlessly without any effort; the employees no longer have to send e-mails or call one another, they can communicate through a simple app designed to suit the situation. Mobile apps are available whenever the user is available; you can use the app whenever the user likes. There is no opening or closing time. This allows all users to access contents of the application on the move and be able to receive updates to their mobile devices without even opening the app. For example, the user may be asleep, but as colleagues update information they may receive a push notification to a mobile device and view this change or updated information in the morning. This feature allows the user to be always connected and receive news and updates about the company at all times without missing out on anything.

Furthermore, availability always means sharing at all times. Users will be sharing information as they work and update the app's information/database, this will generate more creativity and ideas for other users as two brains are always better than one. Other employees will be able to access critical knowledge and generate other ideas from there on. Because the application is being run on a mobile device, which is either a smartphone or a tablet, this allows you to share your screen with others and show what you have done and how you have progressed electronically in the cloud. This is a very efficient way of running tasks and sharing because you do not have to carry a massive amount of papers and documents with you and spend time searching for a certain piece of document, you can just carry your tablet or smartphone and everything will be with you on a single device.

The biggest advantage of using mobile applications as mentioned before is the ability of the user to access data easily, but why? What is the need and uses for this? The user can, for example, use the mobile device and show products from the company to the customer and without the use of complicated documents, which the customer may not find easy to understand, but this can be done through the application of the business with little hassle. This has many advantages through the customer's eyes, it shows the customer that this is a well-organized and well-run business and that they value their customers to the utmost and aim to deliver maximum customer service. What is more, as well as being able to access information on the move, it is just as important to be able to upload information to the application, too. The user must be able to upload new documents and even media such as photos and videos with ease for other colleagues to see. In addition to uploading information manually, company machinery such as website servers can upload information such as website hits, advertising reactions and data so that the employees and supervisors can see and examine website traffic without going to the office and looking manually. This information can be pushed to the mobile devices saving time and money thus increasing productivity in other more important tasks.

A mobile application is generally a simpler and more user-friendly version of a desktop application with a more streamlined and simpler user interface, although the user interface of an application on a computer has an advantage. The space is not limited which requires the programmer to get more creative and also to provide compatibility with the computer. Because the overwhelming majority of the people in the business world use smartphones, the applications of their companies are compatible with their own smartphones and the company does not need to provide the employees with extra phones and devices. This has many advantages for both the company and the employees of the firm. It makes the employee feel safer and more secure, more at home, and more relaxed while working and dealing with everyday tasks that need to be accomplished. Feeling relaxed and at home in a more comfortable environment increases the creativity and efficiency of the employees as well as the employees trust toward the company, thus favoring for the good of the company, in return increasing profits, and reducing loss as the firm does not have to provide its workers with extra devices.

As the use of mobile apps becomes more prevalent in organizations, these applications could be expanded to provide reporting data in real time. While apps would need to be specialized to specific firms they would allow for a move to a technologically driven, Open Book Management (OBM) type leadership style where financial data are relentlessly shared with employees (Baron and Kreps, 1999). This leadership style has been shown in a number of cases to lead to higher employee commitment and increased work productivity due to the employee's goals and actions being more closely related to the owner's; this can also help reduce the traditional principal-agent problem (Baiman et al., 1990). It must be noted, however, that full company involvement in OBM, including offering appropriate employee incentive schemes, must be made in order for it to be effective. Furthermore, technology has led to organizations gathering data, with greater efficiency, hence, at a lower cost. Bloom et al. (2010, 2014) suggest that: "Cheaper information access has an empowering effect, allowing agents to handle more problems they face without relying on others."

This results in an increase in employee productivity. With the help of mobile apps, information is made more regularly available and shared among colleagues. Bloom et al. (2014) further suggest that improvements in technology should push decisions down the corporate ladder, leading to decentralization. If an organization has a decentralized structure, there is a risk of control loss—the agent's activities may not contribute to the objectives of the organization. If an organization has a greater access to information, in particular agent inputs, it gives agents motive to act in the interest of the organization, hence, reducing risk of control loss. Rasel (2016) has shown that a combination of IT and decentralization can lead to a significant contribution to productivity. Additionally, with increased information flow through mobile apps, firms can further increase productivity— through greater information—leading to less dependency of centralized managers. Greater information on workers' inputs does not just benefit organizations; additionally, it can have an effect on the job market. As there is greater information on effort of workers, from a theoretical economic point of view this could increase competition between workers, thereby, reducing costs to organizations.

As discussed, mobile apps reduce cost for the company and provide a more efficient business, but what are these costs and how does it increase efficiency? First, the biggest factor is that, as its name suggests, mobile apps are mobile and this eliminates the need for the employees to travel to an office or a certain area to gather information (mobile apps are also generally laptop compatible). This means that any area of business that needs streaming can benefit from a mobile app eliminating the need to travel. Another problem before mobile apps were introduced to businesses were the complicated papers that employees and customers were to deal with, which at times could lead to larger errors as customers' handwriting could not be read and employees had to ring the customer back for a confirmation, thus reducing productivity and stealing from precious time of the employee. Mobile apps have made orders more organized and user-friendly, reducing paper work and human error, as computers and servers are doing the work for you as programmed (Herrera, 2010). As the firm's servers are handling all the processes electronically, this reduces overhead costs such as ink, paper, photocopiers, and staff to operate and maintain this equipment. As said before travel costs will also be reduced, which is a firm's major cost factor.

Companies generally absorb the cost of an employee's use of a cell phone if used for company purposes. The change in technology to auto updates on a PC and cell phone were huge wins for corporations, which allowed for company-issued smartphones to be used and updated as a PC would be updated. Finally, the prevalence of the cloud has vastly improved usage of apps for business. The cloud makes it far easier than before for businesses to share information across departments, offices, and even countries. An excellent example of this is G Suite: Google's apps for business allows employees to share a variety of information effortlessly across the cloud including: calendars, word documents, spreadsheets, and slides. Google Apps is available across a variety of smartphones and tablets and is not the only app of its type, competing with the widely used for-pay offering from Microsoft, Office 365. This further emphasizes the sheer range of services available to businesses on the app market to save time and to cut costs.

Overall, the advent of mobile applications for smartphones and tablets has opened an entire range of opportunities for commercial firms. Numerous benefits are available to businesses using applications, which would not be possible otherwise. The use of apps in workplace environments and for work activities has revealed many opportunities for businesses to save both human and physical resources. The major use of apps in the workplace is in situations that cut the length of time something takes to do. Whether it is to send a colleague files or to present new health and safety training update apps can shorten the time frames needed by the business. In the modern world this is extremely valuable and important. With the shortening of processes comes cost savings in many cases. With ever increasing globalization, meaning that communication needs to be constant, apps offer perfect solutions as information can be shared across the world with minimal effort.

Chapter 3
Management of Enterprise Resource Systems

Mobile apps have made a sudden and massive appearance in most aspects of our everyday life in the past ten years. The iTunes app store has seen the release of more than 2.45 million apps that amount to 180 billion downloads overall, and the Google Play store that has 1.6 million applications amounting to over 50 billion downloads (Statista, 2016, 2018). These apps have impacted almost every aspect of our everyday life, from messaging apps to food delivery and fitness apps, it can be said that the invention of the smartphone has created a real "mobile revolution." This chapter examines how firms are coping with these revolutionary trends, principally the use of excess capacity and sharing-based models, the streamlining and democratizing technology, the reduction of capital spending on hardware, and the improvement in communication at a low cost.

App Types

The term app extends to non-mobile sources such as web apps, but the word is most commonly associated with applications for mobile devices. Today, apps are generally thought to be programs that perform a limited number of functions, while applications may provide for a wide range of functions. Apps can be informative, such as the *Times* newspaper app, or social, such as the Facebook app. Apps became popular in large part because they could be used in offline mode without an internet connection and synced later when the internet became available. With mobile data (4G/3G), it is easy to use them on the train, plane, or when walking. Apps rose to prominence alongside the emergence of Apple's iPhone, as well as the competing Android devices. With the introduction of Windows 10, Microsoft jumped into the app market, introducing app development for computers tablets and Windows 10 compatible cell phones. In January 2011, the American Dialect Society named "app" the word of the year for 2010 (Small Business Trends, 2011), highlighting how popular the term became at that time.

While the growth of apps has slowed in more recent times, there is still a huge market for developers and programmers to attempt to create the next big thing to take the app store by storm—the best example of this being the app "Flappy Bird," which was downloaded over 50 million times and earned its creator as much as $50,000 a day in advertising revenue in the nine months of its availability, having been removed from the market by its creator (Stamford, 2013; BBC, 2014). Mobile apps can help business managers provide customer service,

DOI 10.1515/9781547400546-003

add value, make money, or perform business tasks. A mobile app should solve a problem for a business or a customer, and do so while on the move rather than at a distance, or in person (Queensland Government, 2016). *Companies are becoming much more dependent on apps in the daily running of the business, because they make work a lot easier.* In fact, 91% of organizations planned to have a mobile workstyle strategy, and "many organizations give their employees the right to use their own devices" (ClickSoftware, 2017). Figure 3.1 shows how even in mature markets such as the United States, smartphones continue to squeeze share away from desktops and tablets.

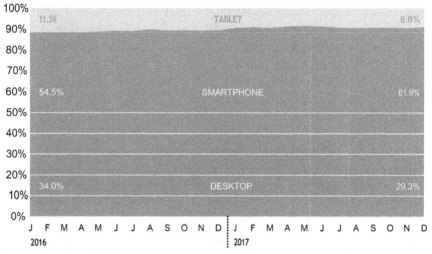

Source: Comscore (2018)

Figure 3.1: Share of total digital minutes by platform (US)

Of course applications on handhelds have been around since the 1980s, with the Psion EPOC being one of the early handheld computers that had basic applications (e.g., a diary) and used the Open Programming Language (OPL). Now, apps can be used for virtually anything, from checking stock quotes and booking flights to helping individuals complete daily tasks such as scanning and sending documents, tracking expenses and income, and navigating from A to B. These programs can help individuals save time, stay organized, keep up to date with information on the go, and connect with people quickly and easily from anywhere. Consequently, apps can benefit firms of any size, in both the short term and long term, as they promise a more productive workforce and smoother running of operations across all departments, for a very low price—for example, the communications app, Skype, offers businesses deals from $1.50 user/month. Today, the distinction between app and application is less clear cut with applications and apps being available on all types of phone or computing devices. Therefore, the distinction now is more that an app is generally considered a program that accomplishes a limited number of functions, whereas an application generally is considered to have a wide array of functions.

Companies are making the switch from manual processes to mobile apps for a number of reasons. First, according to a survey, of those tracking their cost savings, 81% of respondents claimed annual savings of between $1,000 and $25,000, while 17% saved over $25,000 from going digital with their work processes (Go Canvas, 2015). The companies featured in the survey used image capture (56%) and signature capture (52%) features the most, removing the need for cameras, as well as the manual signing of forms and documents. On the other extreme, today you can use SAP Business One to access SAP on a smartphone and there are mobile apps for Android and iPhone, although with limited functionality. The fact that all these features are available on any employee's mobile device increases the efficiency of the workflow and saves money in the long run.

Second, online banking apps such as Santander and Natwest, as well as general payment apps like PayPal are readily available to be used instead of taking a trip to the physical branch. Security is at an all-time high with multistep activation and features such as fingerprint login on iPhone, iPad, and Android phones (Natwest, 2016), meaning you can safely and securely check balances, withdraw cash without using a debit card and make payments to contacts. These features allow businesses to save time by having all their information at their fingertips; thus, freeing up resources to be allocated elsewhere, increasing productivity and efficiency. It is common for businesses to produce their own mobile apps for use by their customers. Statistics show that the average American spends more than two hours a day on a mobile device, with 86% of that time spent on apps (GeekWire, 2014). Although most of this time will be spent on games or large applications such as Facebook and Twitter, it still pays to have your company's app accessible to customers—being "in the way" can be an advantage, as our mind unconsciously records every image and text it comes across (Forbes, 2014).

In conclusion, although it was once an unknown world, the now overwhelming presence of social media has led to the rapid development of apps to achieve greater connectivity and online presence in a mainstream setting. The popularity of apps provides an incentive for developers to keep progressing the technology, meaning they are now used in many different contexts and industries such as manufacturing and tourism. It is this fact, along with the accessibility to wider populations (especially in emerging markets), which allows them to begin to be used effectively within individual organizations.

Apps are currently categorized into three broad types: Native apps, mobile web apps and hybrid apps.

Native Apps

The first type of mobile applications are native apps; they are directly downloaded and installed via app store on the mobile device. Native apps are developed for a single operating system such as iOS, Android, Blackberry or Windows phone and are sold or available for free at the app store. Objective-C, Swift or Java are the most used codes for writing native apps. They are characterized by their full access to the functions of a mobile device, for instance, GPS, camera or fingerprint, and the possibility to run offline without internet connection (Raluca, 2013). Furthermore, native apps can access the notification system and initiate push messages to the user. They have high costs for development because they have to be developed for multiple operating systems and they share profit with the app store in the form of commission per sale.

Mobile Web Apps

Second, mobile web apps are another common app type. Contrary to native apps, they need a browser to run, do not require installation, need constant internet connectivity and are based on HTML5, CSS or JavaScript. A slow internet connection can cause noticeable delays in interactivity and usage. Mobile web apps can not access operating systems core functions, for instance, graphic processing and the notification system. They have low costs for development and maintenance as they are based on servers and updates do not have to be done on every client's device.

Hybrid Apps

Finally, the third category of apps is the hybrid app. Hybrid apps are part native app and part mobile web app. They combine several features of both app types, for instance, they are developed platform-independent and thus can be implemented for any operating system. The cost of developing hybrid apps is lower, because not two, but only one app is developed. Similar to native apps, they are able to access functions of the mobile device (Rouse, 2018). However, good native apps are rated better on average and rank better in the app store than hybrid apps.

How Can Companies Benefit from Using Apps?

Mobile applications offer many advantages to companies. First, using apps, no matter which type, increases brand awareness and visibility for a brand. According to a study conducted by the company Comscore Inc. (2018), for example, American adults spend an average of 2 hours and 51 minutes on their phone every day. Therefore having an app for a mobile device offers the chance to be visible for the user every time they unlock their phone and use it. In the same way, a location-sensitive push notification when customers are in the area of a company's shop increases visibility and awareness. Having the app right there on the screen increases brand consciousness and reminds the user constantly about the company.

Second, customer loyalty can be increased through mobile applications. To add more value to customers, a loyalty or rewards program can be created within the app. A loyalty program where customers exclusively as app users can collect points in order to receive special rewards increases the likelihood of them buying more. Customers want to come back because they want to collect more points and thus, favor the company over competitors without such a program. The customer feels valued receiving rewards, and the company can boost their sales (Blair, 2018). Third, the company receives more user data. In addition to data available through websites and store research, the app collects analytics on how people use the app. Blair (2018) states that the company can gather information on how long the customers use the app, which products are clicked on the most and how much money is made from each in-app purchase. Furthermore, location-specific data can be used to release target-oriented marketing offers. Customer-targeted and personalized marketing based on data can increase revenue and win back churned users.

Overall, the additional analytics help the company to understand the customer's needs to create the best possible customer experience. Finally, apps reduce marketing costs. Having the possibility to approach customers via mobile push notifications is more unobtrusive, instant and cost-effective in comparison to traditional media, which are far more expensive. Furthermore, apps reduce the workload of help requests by providing all information within the app. Less marketing costs lead to more profit or more budget for other tasks.

Successful App Examples

We now analyze two successful mobile applications and why they are so appealing to customers and what makes customers come back to use them. The first example is the *Starbucks* app, famous for coffee and other beverages, founded in 1971 in Seattle, now operating almost 30,000 locations worldwide. Starbucks launched its app for Android and iOS in 2011. The unique feature of the app is the in-app payment. According to a study conducted by eMarketer (2017), the Starbucks app is the most popular payment app with approximately 23.4 million users in 2018, more popular than Apple Pay and Google Pay.

It allows customers to store their bank or card details and pay directly through the app whenever they buy drinks of food in the store. This is not only convenient and user-friendly but also practical because in case somebody forgets their money or card, they only need their phone and can still get their drink. The layout is well thought through, and the navigation is simple with high ease of use, and it takes hardly any time for a user to understand the functions of the app. Furthermore, the app adds value to customers by giving them loyalty points, savings and specials for ordering through the app. Moreover, Starbucks benefits from the data collected. The analytics allow Starbucks to optimize and adapt their strategy to fulfil customer needs. Once customers take advantage of the loyalty program, they want to earn more points and repurchase from Starbucks for free drinks and special offers, which results in more profit for Starbucks.

The second mobile application example is the *Domino's* app, an American pizza chain, founded in 1960, with 13,811 locations worldwide. One special feature of the app is their system to track pizzas on their way to the customer, and this adds value to customers because they do not have to call the stores to ask when their pizza is going to arrive as they can track it right on their phone. The layout of the app is very straightforward and user-friendly; users can order a pizza with only a few clicks. An unnecessary number of steps in the order process is avoided as this could lead to the customer not wanting to order any more. Domino's pizza published that 52% of their online orders are made through their mobile application.

Enterprise Resource Planning

Initially, in the 1950s and 1960s, computers were used to process large volumes of data, and fast, to support a specific business operation. In the 1970s, specific systems were created to address the need that most large, complex organizations faced: the need to control the production of parts and products to fit their production schedules. As a result, material planning systems were created. Moving on to the 1980s, these systems grew, and became more focused on efficiency benefits and sought to optimize manufacturing processes. Their scope increased to cover related business processes, such as shop floor, distribution, project management, human resources (HR), and finance. Thus, *manufacturing resource planning began*. Then the big breakthrough in the late 1980s was the enterprise resource planning (ERP) systems, which sought to integrate systems with business processes across both front office and back office processes. These are traditionally very expensive systems to implement and maintain, but the key benefits that these systems offer include; reliable information based on well-defined *database management systems*, avoidance of data redundancy, cost reduction via time saving, improved scalability to allow the system to grow as the size and complexity of the organization grows, and improved support and maintenance.

Prior to 2000, growth and acquisitions led to Oracle, SAP, and Microsoft dominating the market, which is still largely the case today. The explosion of the internet and the dominance of e-mail in the workplace and the advances of technology led to further major benefits for ERP systems. Increasing speed of infrastructure, databases, and applications meant that global companies could run their organization from one single ERP system. E-commerce and e-business led to fast, secure, automated business transactions to be conducted between separate organizations via their systems. This also led to the subsequent implementation of *business intelligence* and *workflow technology* across ERP systems, changing the focus of these systems from simply gathering, processing and reporting data to routing both transactional and reporting data to the appropriate person, at the right time, for either further processing, such as approval, or for information purposes. Vendors now offer their technologies as services: Software as a Service (SaaS) and Platform as a Service (PaaS). They have taken responsibility to host those elements of the technology stack via secured servers in their own data centers with access controlled through secured private networks accessed via the internet.

This move toward cloud-based computing, combined with the proliferation of smartphones, tablets, and other mobile devices in the work place, has led to ERP business applications offering functionality via mobile applications. It is interesting to note that Salesforce was founded as a SaaS provider in 1999. SaaS the business practice was used in the 1960s but lost favor to LANS and eventually to application service providers. As technology changed, application service providers could not keep up with the changes in technology, therefore, software as a service provider sprang up offering more automated features such as security as the technology improved.

Developing apps is largely dependent on customer feedback and demand. A degree of flexibility is available, with enterprise apps and applications being largely custom made for firms, to suit their specific preferences and needs. Apps, by embodying the culture and values of an organization, are able to increase employee engagement leading to greater participation in the technology.

Consequently, apps have an advantage over other technologies because of the way they can be developed, leading to a high degree of employee and customer satisfaction.

Enterprise Applications

Quite often, businesses will find that the software they are looking for does not currently exist, or is not specialized enough to meet their own needs. In these cases, they may decide to build their own applications, allowing them to integrate the application into any existing information technology (IT) infrastructure used by the business, as well as ensuring they have access to a tool that does exactly what is required. By creating a first-party application, the business will also always have full control over all its features, and future changes. Third-party apps always have the possibility of being updated, removing or changing parts of the app outside of the businesses control, which could be disruptive. Apps designed specifically with the needs of the organization in mind, rather than an end client or customer, are often referred to as *enterprise apps*. One such instance of an enterprise app being used to improve the work process can be found in the waste management firm, The Green House. Claiming "each morning, our drivers check their vehicles before they start their shift. How much fuel is in the tank? Is the tire pressure OK? What's the mileage? Any cracks in the mirrors? Previously our drivers used pen and paper to file their reports so the whole process took a lot of time" (*The Guardian*, 2018).

To streamline the work process drivers were facing, a custom-made app was developed, allowing drivers to quickly record the data, which is then saved into the firm's IT system. The benefits of this approach mean that less time is wasted, and the information is never lost. Other firms might identify problems unique to their own business. Enterprise apps are being increasingly used to simplify unnecessarily complicated tasks, such as signing in and out for the day (mobile apps can replace paper registers) but can also improve many other aspects of work. Personalized "hub" or "portal" apps allow users to connect to a homepage specifically designed for employees, keeping them up-to-date with the latest news within the firm and allowing them to quickly access any digital tools that might be useful for their work (such as company e-mail accounts). Effectively, this means it is easier for employees to stay connected with the business they work for, but it can also provide a useful tool for higher ups to pass information down the chain of command, increasing motivation and saving time. Firms looking to improve more generalized work processes might seek to make use of a third-party app already on the market. Firms wishing to improve areas of work unique to their business might seek to develop an app with their own specifications. In both cases, the benefits are often a more efficient way of completing a task than has been previously possible before. With smartphones having become integrated with our everyday livelihoods, employers can benefit by allowing employees to make use of a tool they already know how to use.

Cloud Computing

Within the current external economic environment, wide ongoing developments are being made, making it essential for organizations to constantly update aspects of their company, for example, the technology used within their work processes. However, the evolution of apps has enabled companies to find an easier way to streamline such work processes and enhance their competitive advantage through increased efficiency of tasks that are essential to the running of the firm internally. The benefits and implications of such applications will now be discussed in further detail starting with cloud computing.

Filing paper documents about client information is an inefficient way of storing documents, as locating these documents can often be time consuming. On average it takes 18 minutes to find a paper document (Peck, 2014), and on a wider scale, a substantial amount of time can be lost in locating paper documents. Having them on a desktop computer can also cause inefficiencies as employees are still required to be at their office to access client information. Such obstacles can be prevented by using cloud storage applications. Cloud storage applications such as Google Drive and Dropbox enable users to store documents online, and allow them to view the documents anywhere through the mobile application (Tatley, 2017). However, managing Dropbox files and Google Drive applications can sometimes be problematic, especially if you have a large number of files on Google Drive. Besides, new versions require training. These applications can be integrated with other applications such as Adobe Acrobat or Microsoft Word Mobile, to allow the user to view and edit documents on their device, without having to be at their office desk. In instances of hardware failure, traditional methods of storing documents are at risk of data loss, with the cost of data recovery being extremely high. Cloud storage, however, provides users the option to back up files online (NT, 2014), reducing the potential for losing files. Companies who send large files on a daily basis such as media companies can greatly benefit from cloud storage applications as it eliminates time spent in sending large files. Traditionally, files would be uploaded and attached to an e-mail and depending on the size of the file (NT, 2014), it could take several hours, which is not ideal if sending large files daily. As cloud storage applications use the internet to store files, users can access the files, provided the owner of the account shares the web link (NT, 2014). Hence, uploading is no longer necessary, and simply forwarding the link will direct the recipient to the user's shared documents.

Branded Apps

In the United States and the U.K., 98% of those ages 18–24 own a smartphone, spending 61% of their digital minutes engaged on the device (Nielsen.com, 2016; Comscore Inc., 2017). This is a level of penetration, which has transformed the digital landscape for marketers. Figure 3.2 shows apps account for over 80% of mobile time: when considering mobile (smartphone and tablet) minutes in isolation, they are overwhelmingly dominated by app consumption.

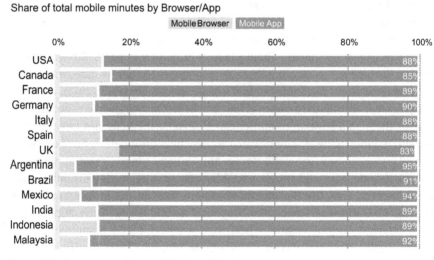

Figure 3.2: Apps account for over 80% of mobile time

Mobile marketing is defined as "a set of practices that enables organizations to communicate and engage with their audience in an interactive and relevant manner through any mobile device or network" (Mobile Marketing Association, 2009). Mobile display advertising once presented itself as the epitome of mobile marketing. However intrusive to the small screen, raising concerns over unnecessary data usage (Mintel, 2016a) and disliked by four out of five consumers (Gupta, 2013), companies such as EE and O2 introduced ad-blocking tools in late 2015 to eliminate the disruptive ad format (Mintel, 2016b). To compensate, brands have instead adopted branded mobile applications (BMA) as a platform to communicate (Kim et al., 2015).

BMA are conceptualized as "software that is downloadable to a mobile device and prominently displays a brand identity" (Bellman et al., 2011). Applications have become a dominant tool for marketers and subsequently a vital marketing strategy adopted by organizations across all sectors. Apps popularity as a marketing tool originates from the accelerating trend toward app dominance (Taivalsaari and Mikkonen, 2015). Gupta (2013) explains that consumers value apps for their functionality or entertainment value and so they are not perceived as interruptive. This nondisruptive experience is also aided through the voluntary downloadable nature of apps (Kim and Ah Yu, 2016). Marketing through a BMA puts the consumer in control of their advertising exposure allowing consumers to begin the communication with the brand while also exposing them to self-selected marketing content.

Moreover, the uninhibited design aspect of applications offers flexibility to organizations and opportunity to adapt and develop apps with the goals of achieving different marketing objectives (Zhao and Balagué, 2015). Bellman et al. (2011) investigate the relationship between BMA, brand attitude, and brand purchase intention. Key findings state that consumer engagement in apps has a positive impact on increasing interest and attitude toward the brand and brand product category, but only informative apps effect purchase intention. Several researchers also determine relationships between branded application use and users' purchase intention (Seitz and Aldebasi, 2016; Kim et al., 2015) while Kim and Ah Yu's (2016) findings ascertain that holistic brand experiences have significant effects on brand loyalty.

Despite the successes academic research ties to the implementation of BMA, merely designing and launching an application does not assure brand related benefits. Dredge (2011) explains that most apps fail to achieve any success, for reasons including poor quality, un-functional "pure" marketing design and poor application promotion. McKinsey (2014) extends this argument, highlighting that while apps are effective in targeting current loyal customers, targeting and encouraging downloads and thus building brand awareness from prospective consumers is difficult.

Large and Small Firms and Applications

Large enterprises do have a cost advantage when it comes to developing and maintaining an application, as there are large set-up costs involved as well as a requirement for continuous development. Bank of America and Citibank make their app free to use and download because they can cross subsidize the cost of the app using their other streams of income. In general, smaller firms have less access to such large amounts of capital and therefore may be unable to fund the initial development of an app even if it were likely to improve their business prospects. The question lies with whether small businesses would benefit as much from an app as a larger one. Streamlining small companies could have detrimental effects on business if they tend to thrive on a committed group of loyal customers that enjoy the service, even when purchasing a tangible item. Although a small firm may benefit from the creation of an application as business can grow without the need for human interaction, this could reduce staff numbers to a minimal and jobs could be lost. Using an agile, minimum viable product approach, for a small company or start-up can be a way of avoiding this problem.

Small companies have also started using applications to increase satisfaction of customers, revenue, and brand reputation. Small firms' use of applications may also enhance employee participation, make their operating processes easier and improve the relationships with customers. Currently applications such as PayPal, Dropbox, and Salesforce are used by approximately 60% of the companies (Smith, 2014). Additionally, small companies may use cloud systems, which is another type of application. Cloud computing has different categories as SaaS, PaaS, and Infrastructure as a Service (IaaS). The use of on-the-go technology aids to ease the workload on the employees by providing several benefits. First, the main idea behind using apps on tablets and smartphones is that it is an efficient and cleaner means of communication to which employees are almost already accustomed. This could be an advantage for companies because each newly hired employee can come with the basic knowledge of how to operate a smartphone, and is crucial for the running of business, if the workplace communications is run by mobile app software. Even employees working in a field distant from the use of technology are accustomed to the use of mobile apps, and improvements in app technology making them user-friendly, thus providing a more efficient work stream and increasing the usage rate as well. The widespread use of app technology in the workplace can be highly beneficial, mainly because it is crucial for the operations and communications to run smoothly within the business, while also having its upsides for a better means of instant communication and a tool for more efficient organizational arrangements.

Along with the tasks being handled more efficiently, the availability of instant communication also provides advantage where employees would have faster information exchange with their colleagues. Therefore, this would boost up the work processes in organizations. Additionally, not being able to send reports of an incident within the company is becoming a thing of the past with the spreading of apps and can also allow workers to share photos on the spot.

This would assure that everyone within the company, from the manager to IT, can have insight on what is going on around the workplace, so the job can be handled more thoroughly and provide coherent information for the entire hierarchy. Moreover, it is considered that one of their crucial upsides is the apps' way of sending push notifications in case of a major notification. This can secure the employees and managers be kept in light of the most recent updates. It could mean that the growing use of apps can bring a faster and clearer communication among the colleagues, without the delays and misinterpretations caused by traditional ways of communication, such as cellular voice services.

Those points show how having mobile and tablet apps in the work place help firms to achieve a more efficient way of getting work done by having faster and clearer communication. Eventually, instant and better communication way, and high efficiency with the help of a new app would enhance the work processes and accordingly reduce the workload of the employees. Hills et al. (2013) suggested how today's workforce is not just diverse in respect to culture, gender and ethnicity, but also in regard to age. Consequently, younger generations are more fluent in technology than the previous ones. Maitland (2009) talked about generation Y and how one of the factors that set the generation apart is the "unprecedented pace of technological change." With the greater presence of technology in the workplace, managers are now able to give feedback quicker. It is suggested that generation Y has a characteristic of craving feedback. As Martin (2005) argued, generation Y had developed high expectations for instant feedback due to the immediacy of technology.

Consequently, technology being able to compile performance data, and further extract valuable information only taking a few moments, has led the younger generation to feel the benefits of the speed that technology such as apps provide. However, more recently, the Global Leadership Forecast 2018[1] pointed out that generation X (1965 to 1981) now account for 51% of business leadership roles globally and that 54% of generation X and 56% of millennials (millennials being 1982 to 2000) reported that they are digitally savvy. Generation X showed more time spent on smartphones than millennials.

---

[1] Global Leadership Forecast 2018, DDI, The Conference Board, EY and CNBC, https://www.cnbc.com/2018/04/11/generation-x--not-millennials--is-changing-the-nature-of-work.html

Chapter 4
Technology and a Firm's Capabilities

In the words of Adam Smith in his book *An Inquiry into the Nature and Causes of the Wealth of Nations*, "The greatest improvement in the productive powers of labor, and the greater part of the skill, dexterity, and judgment with which it is anywhere directed, or applied, seem to have been the effects of the division of labor." Smith wrote those words in 1776. He was right to attribute such importance to this idea of splitting large tasks into their component processes so they can be performed separately by specialized workers; it is a practice that is ubiquitous in modern society. The division of labor creates problems of its own though. An individual worker was at one time the sole determinant of output, but this is no longer the case. As such, the labor force must be coordinated, and for this to be done it must also be controlled. Coordination is the process by which two parties needing to engage in an economic transaction are brought together, whether that is within an organization or through markets. Control is the concept of imposing a predictable pattern on the previously haphazard behavior of workers, resources and interactions between the two. Attaining coordination and control over the workforce is critical to the modern organization—otherwise, the division of labor simply could not exist.

Current academic approaches provide managers with three very different ways of thinking about how to coordinate and control their organizations (Henry Mintzberg's typology of organization configurations, Max Weber's bureaucratic structure, and economists' Principal-Agent Theory), but can they actually be of use in real world scenarios? Mintzberg's typology, while largely accepted as a fair summation of the mechanisms used for coordination in different types of organization, is a positive explanation. It does not prescribe how an organization *should* be coordinated, rather it describes how they *are* coordinated. In this sense, it is of little use to a manager. Weber's bureaucracy is a normative argument, proposing an ideal type of organization. While this may be more helpful to a manager, it is also implausible in reality, where it is difficult to design a set of rules to govern each and every decision. Even if it were, the bureaucracy would need to be supported by an explanation of exactly how to ensure that the rules are obeyed, which simply does not always happen in real life, even where there is legitimate authority.

Bureaucracy also suffers from being too inflexible in its use of personnel, and promotes employees until they reach their level of incompetence. Most important, the rules that govern the organization can only define minimum acceptable performance levels, making this type of organization far from ideal. There are

DOI 10.1515/9781547400546-004

also strong criticisms of Principal-Agent Theory, notably from sociologists and psychologists who assert that employees are individuals for whom strictly financial incentives can not be used as effective mechanisms for control. These groups opine that values such as self-esteem, culture and working norms are also worthy of attention. Kohn (1993) points out that workers rarely see money as the most important factor in job satisfaction. Critically, the idea of the rational actor is also fundamentally flawed. Human actors display bounded rationality, something which Principal-Agent Theory fails to account for. The theory also struggles to solve problems with multiple interdependent agents.

On the other hand, the constant development of technology is affecting the work processes of many companies. *The use of technology within the workplace is increasing in order to make the lives of the employees and employers easier.* The rapid change in technology within the past decade to help employees communicate, store, and manage data within the work place has become cheaper and more accessible. Workers are now able to have access to work material and communicate with their fellow colleagues 24 hours a day with just a smartphone and the internet. As a result, digital transformation occurs that not only frees employees from the shackles of daily administrative routines, but also encourages a highly collaborative environment. Contributing to employee's accessibility of data, cloud computing has helped revolutionize how workers can take their work "on the go"—cloud computing is the delivery of data storage as a service. Cloud computing allows employees to access their files, store, process, and backup data via the internet, rather than using a local server on any smartphone, tablet, or PC (laptop), which is connected to the internet.

Mobile apps mostly come with the support of—or even solely function through cloud computing. Accordingly, this can allow businesses to cut significant overhead in their operation. For example, in an expanding business there are needs for additional computing and processing power, hence, investment in new infrastructure is required. High initial costs of equipment are coupled with additional overhead relating to hiring information technology (IT) staff, planning and future cost projections that ensure high performance and reliability of new apparatus. Not to mention related higher energy bills as well as costly software maintenance. On the other hand, mobile applications that use cloud computing can mitigate the aforementioned cost disadvantages efficiently. Upkeep of software and maintenance issues are done remotely at the server center for a relatively small fee. Furthermore, demanding computation tasks are done on low-priced terminals that draw processing output from the internet. Consequently, cost of initial set up as well as maintenance and especially the addition of services is low.

As a result, growing companies can cut expenses and at the same time provide staff with exceptionally powerful tools in the workplace. For rapid expansion of an organization, it offers a fast solution and one where large errors in estimating future growth and service needs are minimized. Nonetheless, it is important to note that access to high speed internet is required for the company to operate in this efficient way. Thus, operational advantages of mobile applications are pronounced, but conditional on good network infrastructures being present. In this context, this chapter explores how apps affect a firm's capabilities and enhance its managerial resources and effectiveness in particular areas of operations.

Web-Conferencing

Cameras are on the majority of devices that are used for communication, which makes video calls and web-conferencing easier than ever before. Web-conferencing consists of live video or audio meetings between two or more people from different geographic locations via the internet. Employees that use web-conferencing are able to exchange information and receive prompt feedback. Web-conferencing provides benefits for employees who often have to travel for work by providing them with the chance to access and provide a contribution to meetings. Furthermore, the use of web-conferencing allows employees who work remotely to find the correct amount of work-life balance by providing employees the chance to collaborate with fellow colleagues from a remote area. It is important to continue to provide the opportunity for employees who work from home to still be able to contribute to all aspects of the business.

Business conferencing calls also play a major role in the daily functioning of multinational corporations. On a regular basis, senior members within the hierarchy are in contact with their cross-border counterparts; conducting this face-to-face would be costly and time consuming for the firm. The introduction of apps such as Skype for Business (www.skype.com) has meant that corporations such as General Motors can conduct video conferencing calls from their own offices to any part of the world. The immediate benefit of this in the short term is significant cost savings; money that would have been spent on travel and accommodation as well as working time lost during this period. The saved opportunity cost here means the firm can invest money and time saved into innovation; developing new products that will keep the firm ahead of its competitors. Thus, this clearly represents one significant benefit of using apps within the business to streamline the processes.

E-Learning

E-learning is a form of multimedia learning that uses electronic educational technology. E-learning within the workplace is beginning to increase and is most commonly used for business inductions, and information and communication technology (ICT) training. E-learning allows the company to customize their training packages. Allowing the employers to customize their online training helps them supply exactly what they need their employees to learn, without spending a lot of time on aspects of the training, which may not apply or is less significant to the particular firm. Moreover, e-learning allows the employees to revisit aspects of the course they may find challenging. According to David et al. (2012), e-learning is not only about training and instructions but also about learning, which is tailored to the individual; it is important to take into account that each individual learns differently and some may find certain aspects of the training more difficult than others. By giving employees the opportunity to revisit chapters of the training the firm can guarantee their employees have thoroughly learned what is intended.

Employee Relationship Management

An important benefit of using a smartphone in the work place is that relationships within the company could strengthen. Although many people argue that smartphones disconnect workers from real life, it can be argued that a relationship can be built through the internet and apps. Apps such as Microsoft Outlook can help the employees set up meetings easily, have online chats, and have message boards, which in turn can increase efficiency within the work place. Real time collaboration is the use of software that includes instant messaging, videoconferencing, editing documents online, etc. These collaborative software applications increase transparency levels within the working environment and more trust can be built up as everyone can see what each other is doing. The top level of management and superiors of the company can use the smartphone apps to engage with employees further down the hierarchy. Many companies are using apps such as Microsoft SharePoint, which can connect the entire company together.

The fact that so many people are using these apps in the workplace already proves the point that communications can increase and levels of transparency are increasing. However, a drawback of building relationships via the internet platform is that the workers will not be able to distinguish the difference between work life and home life and between real work and made up work (*Economist*, 2012). Workers usually have two aspects of a workday, which consists of attending meetings, producing reports, and conducting business, as well as the admin side of the days such as keeping up with the e-mails. This can take a toll on the personal lives of employees as they bring the stress from work home, for example, replying to e-mails. Vice versa, employees can bring their personal stress to work as well. Furthermore, using apps on tablets will streamline the work process but if other apps such as Facebook and WhatsApp are downloaded, employees could become less efficient. These programs can be used via tablets, mobile phones, and computers. There is evidence that smartphones and tablets can distract workers. Second, the use of smartphones and tablets can make it easier for the company to control and monitor their employees. Traditionally, many companies use the hierarchy to control and manage activities of its employees; however, for this to work, each constituent member must follow orders from its superior in order for the system to work.

With the use of apps, it could be possible to manage and control different aspects of the company. For example, there are many apps that control the finances of a company. Employees can see how much money comes out of each department, etc. However, technology is always changing and being improved, which would require expensive updates and require training for the employees, which in turn will reduce production levels for a while. The short-term productivity loss and the increased cost of the upgrades could result in a decrease in profit. Furthermore, employee morale could fall as they keep having to learn the new software to meet the demanded standards. One may argue that the costs of monitoring would not decrease or that they never existed in the first place. For example, economists believe that in perfectly competitive markets where they are at equilibrium prices, there is no need for monitoring, whereas organization theorists have suggested that monitoring is universal and there is no such idea of "costless observation" (Buchanan and Huczynski, 2016; Douma and Schreuder, 2008).

Research indicates that employees have individual differences and that if companies cater to these individual differences, employee's level of motivation could increase (Buchanan and Huczynski, 2016). The use of apps could promote performance-based management. Many companies have implemented the Bring Your Own Device Policy (BYOD). This scheme has increased productivity levels by increasing the number of working hours because employees could work from home or on the go and improve the employee's efficiency. However, we also have to look at the politics of technology. Braverman (1974) argues that advances in the technology sector could give managers chances to reduce skill and discretion. He suggests that technology is used as a political tool that managers use to manipulate employees; "this is the only way to do this work because of the technology." The argument is used in the context such that the manager will be safe-guarded from unpopular decisions. In addition, with BYOD, generally employees are not getting overtime for their work at home, so the company is not paying for the extra hours delivered.

The benefits of using such technologies in the working environment will depend on the type of business organization or sector. For example, the use of such technologies in a hospital will benefit the company, but banking companies or recruitment agencies could gain greater benefits from using such technologies. The use of smartphones/tablets within the working environment effectively increases the economies of scale within the organization. The app could increase efficiency and productivity levels, which will increase output, and cause costs could fall. Likewise, autonomy can bring self-satisfaction to the employees. Relationships will become stronger, which means there will be a wide spread of knowledge, which in turn will increase levels of self-development and teamwork. This is why companies should continue to use smartphone apps to streamline their work processes. Hence, businesses that do not use apps in their work environment can use basic applications such as Outlook because it will make communications much easier, which will simplify the work processes.

Workplace Technologies

Apps have many functions, including news feeds and general information, but vitally, they normally always include contact information for the mobile owner to use should they have any issues, queries, or complaints. The information provided by the app will also be available immediately with the app typically running 24 hours a day, 7 days a week, rather than the customer having to wait for business hours to commence or even for a store to open. Despite the constant availability, it will not provide answers to all questions and services, particularly very specific queries from meticulous customers and therefore is not always better than calling the company's customer service helpline. However, it will be in connection with the customer, at their beck and call, without the moodiness and sullenness that sometimes accompanies physical staff. The "direct marketing channel" created between the company and customer via the app further improves customer service as much of what they want to or need to know is at their fingertips. This can have the domino effect of advertising the brand or company, as people will recommend their products or services when they are very satisfied with what they were provided and certainly if they felt the customer service was of high quality.

This is also accomplished through providing more value to the customers, such as by offering a loyalty scheme through the app whereby customers can accumulate points from purchases, which can contribute to future purchases for a discount. Companies can then manipulate the app to their advantage by personalizing each consumer's app based on their preferential choices, sending pop-up notifications whenever new additions are added, which are similar to their order history. Urban Outfitters are an example one of the many companies which participate in this scheme, as through using the app, they allow customers to "get special offers, earn exclusive rewards and enter to win one-of-a-kind prizes as an Urban Outfitters rewards member" (Apple, 2017). Offering these deals exclusively to app members is a great way to increase the number of downloads and is even more beneficial for the company—increase in sales, as customers will look to take advantage of any possible discounts.

Companies must be careful though, as despite all the positives discussed thus far, a mobile app is not guaranteed to be successful, with a large cost at stake if it is not a big hit. Creating an app is not a cheap endeavor, with apps for smaller businesses, built by "2–3 people, likely to cost anywhere between $50,000–$100,000" (Yarmosh, 2015). Even for larger, more powerful businesses, creating an app can still cost as much as $1,000,000, showing the extent of the investment that needs to be made. Of course, the app might increase sales and brand recognition, but it can just as easily lead to a large loss if not enough time or effort is invested in creating a beneficent and worthwhile app, so companies will have to stay committed to it should they decide to go down that route.

Furthermore, this may only be the cost to create the app on one platform, for example, the App Store, which will exclude Windows and Android phone users and alienate many customers. Several different versions of the app will need to be created, meaning even more time and money will need to be invested in producing the app, although these resources might not be available to all businesses. It is also worth mentioning that two different types of phones are rarely identical in screen size and proportion, so form factor is another important consideration. These changes may only be relatively minor in the context of application creation, but it will only increase the overall cost of it—to the point that it is now a burden on the company rather than an investment opportunity. Smaller businesses are far more likely to be affected by the cost and difficulty of producing the app and as a result may struggle to penetrate the technological industry in terms of advertising and marketing, which could see them fall into administration and maybe even liquidation.

It is unequivocal that, should a likeable and easy-to-use app be produced, the company will almost certainly reap the benefits, be that from an increase in sales due to customers buying the product directly or from having the brand's reputation amplified due to an increase in people discovering and learning more about the company. However, the success of the app is largely down to its design and its professionalism, an issue that normally arises from the extent of the resources of the company. Consequently, the company will not experience the benefits of an app if not enough time and money was devoted to improving their business. Despite that, more companies of all different statures and sizes, than not have developed an app that has been successful in benefitting the company, proving that creating an app is not an impossible feat and companies should be able to take advantage of the benefits they offer.

Supply-Chain

It is possible to argue that the first step to seize total alignment between employees and the company's vision and strategy is to construct a well-functioning and efficient supply-chain where internal processes for procurement are clear and easy to perform. In order to exemplify how apps may benefit the optimization of the supply-chain from an economic and time-efficiency perspective. Microsoft is an example of an organization that has implemented an "app scheme" to improve its supply-chain internal processes. Microsoft, being a global enterprise, found itself having a significant percentage of its workforce working remotely. Such situations highlighted the need to improve the company's bureaucratic approval system as it translated into both a money/time loss for the company due to a fundamental lack of uniformity of the firm's lines of business (LOB) within their corporate network. When an employee needed to approve a purchase order, the approval process could only be accessed from within the corporate network. Hence, all these bureaucratic cavils negatively affected users' productivity within the Microsoft supply-chain. In order to solve this situation, Microsoft IT managers decided to craft a new approval service centered on cloud services (Azure) and on modern application technologies renamed MSApprovals, downloadable on any internet device for approvals across all Microsoft lines of business.

This strategy would ideally standardize and streamline the approval process across LOBs as well as promote the BYOD strategy among its workforce to render MSApprovals feasible (Microsoft, 2018). As a matter of fact, regardless to their location, operators gained access to a common Microsoft portal where they could administer all their approval requests on a regular basis, regardless of the LOB. Therefore, through this cloud-based app scenario, Microsoft workers are now able to use any device to receive email alerts and manage work-related material at any time on any mobile device if there is an internet connection. The MSApprovals did not only solve the company's approval issue but also created a more standardized and intuitive work experience for its personnel that led to greater productivity levels and lowered costs of IT maintenance (Microsoft, 2014). Additionally, the main benefits experienced by Microsoft through the MSApprovals scheme within its workforce can be portrayed as a greater alignment with the company's vision and strategy and greater workers' satisfaction levels attributed to a more solid synergy between employees and company needs.

Personalization and Unison

The next set of organizational benefits coming from mobile applications relates to personalization and unison. Personalization combines user identification and geographical localization while unison allows for consistent views of information across multiple mobile devices. For example, workers can use a calendar application to customize their schedules according to where they are at the moment. Moreover, this timetable can be reliably shared with other workers who can choose to join the planned timetable on any device. As a result, multiple versions of personalized data can be securely created and shared to increase collaboration as well as flexibility. Moreover, organizations can utilize this solution to instantly review, update, and consult core organizational systems like enterprise resource planning or customer relationship management (CRM).

The result is that businesses can become more agile and able to withstand fast pace changes in the enterprise environment. What is more, several more opportunities like improvement of business partner coordination and enhancing customer service are available. Overall, mobile apps can improve businesses structure this way. Nonetheless, it is worth mentioning that some causes of concern come from enterprise users themselves, where they raise privacy issues as a problem of personalization. The feeling of being tracked and spied on is the result of sharing confidential schedules and other sources of data. Therefore, companies should take those issues into account; thus opting for clear power of choice and transparency that maintain a healthy balance between sharing, tracking, and privacy in their mobile environment.

Accessibility

An important aspect of business functions that benefits from the mobile apps is accessibility. For example, in order to seize potential opportunities, managers need to combine a variety of critical information from different sources. This means easy access to rich content is crucial. Furthermore, any obtained information needs to be compared and cross referenced in order to achieve accurate outcomes in a timely manner. A real world example of technology that helps scientists/managers to do that is ChemDraw, that gives access to 30 million chemicals from multiple databases. This app allows for search of virtual information that is equivalent to the holdings of a major research library. As a result, scientists can easily access creative content and quickly integrate and merge different sources of data. This not only benefits the time keeping but also significantly cuts cost during the research process. Furthermore, it also improves collaboration between scientists since new findings are readily available on the common sharing platform. On the other hand, limited memory of the devices used can be overflown due to sheer amount of data. Thus, work conduct should rely heavily on the internet and the cloud computing implementation to mitigate those limits. It is vital for organizations to test enterprise applications that access large data sources to make sure that remote employees or employees in the field are not sitting waiting for a response from the application. This remains a common problem today both in front of customers or with frustrated end users. Altogether, ubiquity and unison of data provided by mobile applications greatly improve the availability of rich content at work. At the same time, need for its storage is easily met by using internet cloud solutions leaving most benefits to be easily maintained.

Internationalization

Another common issue with international organizations with the use of apps is language. Companies often make the mistake of excluding users from translated versions of their most vital applications, including enterprise level applications. It is important that the organization understands its own users and also its customers. Having employees use online translation tools to interpret an application in a foreign language to do their daily work is not acceptable. Seeking apps and applications that accommodate multilanguage application development using the Unicode standard is common. It is vitally important that customer facing applications are available in a language the customer can understand and speed is a key factor, especially if a sales representative is presenting to a client on a device.

Transparency

Mobile applications facilitate human life in many ways. An example of the advantages provided by mobile applications is transparency in the work place. Dropbox, a great success presented by cloud computing is one of the most downloaded applications in the mobile application market. With over 400 million users around the world, Dropbox is a storage service based on cloud systems.

It allows businesses, students, and everyone connected to the internet to easily store and share their files, photos, and anything on their computer. Businesses can use Dropbox as a common server where employees can upload and edit files. Furthermore, storing the organization's documents such as financial reports in a shared medium promotes transparency within the firm. This can strengthen the bonds between employees and employers, and build a mutually trusted working environment across the hierarchy; in an organization where there are high levels of mutual trust, improved service quality can be maintained at lower costs, since the firm can recruit and retain motivated employees. Dropbox is an application that even today can cause confusion to untrained users. Like many apps, an assumption is made of the user's ability. The danger of accidentally deleting important data, or purposely losing it is real. Since anyone can open a Dropbox account, it is an app that the organization often does not monitor and sharing often is conducted with non-employees. So, it is an app that can go under the radar in an organization and one that the employee should make IT aware of.

In summary, using an app can be hugely beneficial to a company as it allows the business to be conducted more efficiently. Increasing speed of service and branching out to customers 24 hours a day may not have been available prior to the creation of an app. Although for small firms the start-up costs are large, which could result in repercussions; for larger corporations this is a risk they are generally willing to take. It is possible to argue that there is a positive link between mobile/tablet application and the optimization of work processes as demonstrated throughout the chapter. Particularly, the main areas in which mobile applications deliver significant benefits to both customers and the firm's workplace environment can be depicted in the supply-chain, sales area, and in the relationship with the customer sector who are substantially rendered more immediate and multifunctional by app technologies. Additionally, such technologies do not only increase business-to-customer (B2C) connectivity but on a general basis also increase workers' potential by augmenting their average productivity through virtual tools such as MSAapprovals and Salesforce that businesses did not possess in previous times. Furthermore, apps also aid companies in the process of cutting costs by often eliminating certain roles that can be completely substituted by technology as in the case of the MyVodafone app.

Project Management

Project management applications such as TaskRay for Salesforce (https://taskray.com/) are used to track, manage, and communicate the companies' work goals. Apps like these have gained traction as they have reduced the time-consuming practice of conducting meetings to ensure everyone within your team is on track to meet their deadlines and instead provide a platform that allows the team leader to manage their employees efficiently, by giving them a clear action plan for them to follow. This form of management is likely to increase productivity, which is due to the Hawthorne Effect (Buchanan and Huczynski, 2016), as there is a tendency for people to work harder and perform better if they are being observed. By using these apps, managers can observe the performance of their employees and provide feedback as and when it is needed, resulting in a likely increase of productivity. Although observing your employees has been proven to increase productivity, the manager must still consider individual needs and ensure their employees have a sense of importance and independence so they can remain motivated without the need for constant observation, through achieving self-actualization. These applications also allow managers to build effective teams by matching people that have performed well with each other in past projects as they have good working relationships that are easily identified by the communication network that is provided. The communication channels can also be used to identify employees that may feel an absence of relationship between themselves and managers or coworkers. This will allow the manager to take steps to integrate that employee further, improving Frederick Hertzberg's hygiene factors, by ensuring the employee receives the correct levels of attention to form supportive relationships (Buchanan and Huczynski, 2016).

Accounting Apps

Accounting within businesses can be complicated and time consuming, especially for new companies. This has spurred an increase in available accounting apps such as Zoho Books (https://www.zoho.com/books/) and Xero Accounting Software (www.xero.com), these allow businesses to track the money going in and out, by quickly invoicing and billing, completing expense reports and providing the infrastructure for easy bookkeeping for a monthly fee of up to $50. This is important for small businesses as it allows someone without the knowledge of accounting and money management to easily perform the tasks, that otherwise would be performed by a professional worker. Mobilizing this work process enables employees to complete tasks from any location; an example is the ability to have the estimated inventory levels on your device and have employees update the information on the fly, reducing the possibility of discrepancies in reports of current inventory levels. Companies may choose to use this software instead of hiring a dedicated employee or spending their own time on estimating inventory levels. This is a process of Taylorism as it reduces the complexity of accounting to the simpler task of data entry, therefore, lowering the difficulty and the necessity to monitor transactions constantly—the act of data entry on a platform is visible to every party that is given access to the software increasing the overall transparency of the performed tasks (Mee, 2016).

Marketing

The use of smartphone technology has given marketing great advantages as well as with many new short message services (SMSs) there is now a faster way for the business to reach their consumers. Many studies have shown the superiority of text messages in marketing when they are compared to e-mails; on average people respond to texts 15 minutes after receiving them and marketing has a 12% response rate compared to 3% with direct e-mails. Less than 10% of texts are spam whereas 65% of e-mails are (Lacais, 2016). With texting and other communication mediums a business can reach the consumer quicker and put the information right in front of them. This is shown by the higher response rate. SMSs are also more relevant to the time. There are also other ways in which smartphones could be useful in a marketing sense. Due to how dynamic they are and how widely carried around they are, smartphones can be useful in any marketing situation where timely delivery to an interested customer is involved. Smartphones make the consumer readily more accessible. On average an American will spend two hours or more on their smartphones per day (Statista, 2018). Sending push notifications can allow the consumer to be readily accessible. A smartphone has many functions of a computer yet it has the advantage of mobility where the business can have easy access to the consumer.

In particular, access to information on a sales call and being able to deliver materials immediately, in a form agreeable to the customer, or on screen, is a significant advantage. Smartphone apps can be accessed all day whereas desktops only have limited access time that in a sales situation can be problematic and without immediate texting capabilities are not nearly as flexible a solution. Furthermore, the increasing number on Wi-Fi spots available throughout the country means smartphone users practically have unlimited access to the products these, and many more companies, are trying to sell. The convenience of portability acts as a catalyst for reminding phone and tablet users of the business, as it is visible on the screen at all times. As a result, even if the app is not used regularly to begin with, the user's mind will subconsciously notice it, and may eventually start using it, helping to build loyalty with customers. It also provides a much quicker alternative to web browsing, as it involves a solo click, as opposed to loading the computer, typing the URL and waiting for the site to load. This could lead to more sales, even if only marginally, as some people will be put off by the time needed to make a purchase, especially if their computer needs to be turned on. However, it is important to note that the proliferation of company apps is staggering. At this point most phone users are at the point of making decisions about what to keep and what to add.

Whether a business is new and recently up and running or having already been in operation for a decade, a mobile app can enhance its brand recognition. Creating an app that has both likeable and helpful features encourages consumers to use it regularly. While engaging with a company more regularly, such as through the medium of a mobile app, a trusting bond between consumer and supplier can result. The stronger this bond grows, the more likely the consumer will be to pay attention to any future advertisements the company will release, and thus, more likely to make a purchase. Furthermore, with just the app appearing on programs such as Apple's App Store or Android's Google Play, there is a high chance that it will be noticed or viewed by hundreds of thousands of people every day. Therefore, even if those people are not downloading the app, they are still slightly familiarizing themselves with the brand and helping to enhance its reputation.

The clear advantage of developing digital apps is that they are an effective platform for business advertising. Simply by downloading an app, a company's logo will appear on a smartphone or tablet home screen even when the app is not in use. Apps therefore use subliminal advertising daily as soon as users download them; a technique that can not be competed with, especially considering how often smartphones and tablets are used. This is a clever way to enforce an advertising technique known as *effective frequency*, the number of times a consumer must be exposed to an advertising message before the marketer gets the desired response. The value of this number is widely disputed, but if smartphone users are exposed to a brand logo every time they use their phone, it is likely the brand will be seen enough to enforce it in their mind.

Loyalty programs, are also being digitalized. Costa Coffee and Starbucks are just two examples of retailers who offer mobile phone applications that allow customers to collect reward points with their purchase. This method is convenient for customers, who are much more likely to be carrying their mobile phones than loyalty cards; and will also allow them to look at their account and see how many points they have accumulated at the touch of a button. This provides added value to their purchase, and encourages customers to return to the business and purchase goods again. Another excellent aspect of apps is mobile geotargeting. By integrating geolocation technology into a mobile application, businesses can send special offers to customers who are near stores (CIO, 2016). This means that businesses can reduce the amount they spend on general advertising, and narrow their focus to deliver targeted advertisements to consumers at the right time and place (CIO, 2016). Finally, consumers can seek help and/or information about a company through their app. Many businesses will supply general information, which may be useful to the customer, but also will have a section that consumers can access if they seek to find specific help through speaking directly to a member of the staff at the company help desk through the app—again removing the need to phone the company or visit them at a physical location to find the answers they desire.

Consumer Intelligence

With advancements in consumer technology, companies have implemented different methods to meet the demands for convenience in both the service and retail industries. *One of these methods that has greatly increased since the introduction of smartphones and tablets is the use of apps to allow their customers to more easily access their online platforms and streamline company processes.* The enterprise mobility market is predicted to reach a value of $500 billion by 2020, showing that it is a rapidly growing market and is being adopted by many businesses around the world. Companies can use these apps for project-management, business-to-business payments, accounting, communication, etc. with the goal of improving external customer engagement and greatly increasing productivity within the workplace.

With the increase of technology and the feeling of always being connected to the internet the information industry has gained huge traction. By tracking customers spending habits and online presence, apps have allowed companies to market their products to specific individuals. Business intelligence apps such as InsightSquared (www.insightsquared.com) deliver powerful business analytics, allowing companies to gain data in the form of easy to comprehend statistics. This has made the decision-making process a lot quicker, as they can use their own data and reports from other companies within the sector to identify problems and quickly find solutions. By giving employees the appropriate tools these applications can boost individual employee knowledge and skill and give them a sense of empowerment, increasing levels of job satisfaction, this in turn should increase their output (Miller, 2015). Due to the importance salespeople still have within a business, making their job quicker and easier allows them to spend more time interacting with other customers and driving up sales.

In recent years, as discussed above, there has been a surge in the adoption of sales and marketing apps. It is important for salespeople to continue face-to-face relationships with other businesses as it greatly improves their chances of securing repeat purchases for their company. These apps have improved the convenience experienced by these employees, as they automate their day-to-day activities such as quoting contracts and improving CRM. Apps such as Salesforce (a leading CRM application) provide a platform that is used to drive up the sales of a company; they achieve this by integrating apps that focus on customer analytics, improved customer service, marketing, and commercial access (Lacais, 2016). Salesforce is a set of online tools marketing can customize and scale for their entire company. It tracks customer progress with a single customer view helping companies to close deals faster. It spends less time on administration and more time selling with customized integration with the marketing department's business tools and on-demand reporting (Salesforce, 2018). Some companies even drive their sales through apps that utilize gamification, the type of applications that use characteristics of a computer game to engage the customer, salesperson, or both.

These apps can be used to motivate their employees using an incentive and then show their progress toward that incentive in the form of points, etc., sometimes even pitching employees against each other with the person that achieves the most sales getting the reward. Gamification has proven to be extremely effective in the training of employees, using apps that show the employee their progress in the form of a game increases their drive to perform. Often their scores will be presented on a leader board, encouraging healthy competition and usually expediting the process, as trainees can visualize their end goal (Pandey, 2017).

Sales Force Automation

Another corporate area in which app technologies significantly affected the way business operations are carried out is the sales process. With the influence of modern technologies, sales have become more immediate and according to Motorola (White, 2015) "with mobility in hand, the productivity of the sales force increases by an average of 15% to 20%." Sales force automation (SFA) software automates business tasks such as inventory control, sales processing, and tracking of customer interactions. Traditionally, managers seek to reach a situation where they can reduce expenses and enlarge their market coverage. Through mobile devices and applications, there is significant room for further progress in productivity and sales force management. SFA can be divided into two categories: data regarding the product and data regarding established or potential clients.

Regarding SFA concerning the product, in the current market scenario, companies remain highly dependent upon their sales forces to increase revenues. Hence, it is crucial for corporations to make their sales forces as efficient and productive as possible. One strategy to increase productivity in their sales force is to create a direct connection between staff and the firm's back-end business in order to expose all the data and information required to close deals on the spot (White, 2015). To exemplify this, there is the example of IBM who uses an application called Sterling Order Management for its sales force to manage transactions and product information. On one side, salespeople through specific apps such as IBM's, can check product availability and price, get the signature, submit the order real time, and with a mobile payment and card reader, process payments instantly. On the other side, the firm can calculate the time spent on average with each customer and also look at information on specific customers for future offers. These applications, accessible from mobile devices, do not only streamline work processes, but in turn also guarantee greater productivity, thus allowing the employees to conclude more sales per day. Such interaction between the firm and the salesperson via smart-devices benefit both parties by creating a paperless transaction process that eliminates significant bureaucratic practices for the company and the customer.

As previously mentioned, SFA can also serve as a tool to manage clients as a whole. More specifically, through smartphone or tablet applications like Salesforce, a company's sales teams can efficiently divide possible client prospects among the different salespersons by simply accessing the app. Other features of the application include the possibility of constructing a personalized path of different clients to visit in a day or week by each staff member. All of these features simplify and rationalize the operation processes of a company by creating more company to staff feedback as well as fostering greater customer satisfaction by offering better interactions and guaranteeing better participation to customers.

CRM

Salesforce (www.salesforce.com) is an example of an application in a crucial area in which app technologies are involved. CRM software enables companies to guarantee real-time service via application technologies to their customers—to manage their interaction with current and potential future customers. Today, customers expect a continuous interaction with each brand on different virtual or physical platforms such as social media, mobile through application technologies, call centers, and websites.

This trend is backed by the increasing interaction between companies and clients via the CRM application as in the case of Vodafone who took this opportunity to respond to customers' needs and to operationalize interactions with its customers. Specifically, 89% of these interactions are maintained virtually and up until 2017, 13 million customers used the mobile app My Vodafone regularly to manage their Vodafone accounts. The My Vodafone app revolutionized the way Vodafone approached its CRM; the app is aimed at increasing the connectivity of the firm with its clients by offering a real-time and self-service scheme to the customers who facilitate their experience. Such strategy adopted by Vodafone benefits the clients and the firm by eliminating significant bureaucratic barriers for all members involved; while eliminating the step of speaking to a sales representative to manage the company's offerings, hence, reducing time and money-related costs for each transaction. Additionally, the sales team, through a customized version for the company's personnel, can access on the spot the clients' history to obtain a clearer overview of possible future offers to be made to each specific client, saving time to both parties.

Internal versus External Relationships

Although app technology is growing at an amazing rate, most apps are not used for work processes and business streamlining but instead to socialize, inform, and entertain. However, as discussed above, apps are increasingly being leveraged by businesses in a range of areas, from capturing customer information, publishing journals and the like, recruitment, and appointment reservations to corporate communications, for example. Apps play a key role in communication, in modern internal and external corporate environments, allowing for faster and better interactions between peers and candidates. Internally, employees can communicate with one another regarding tasks in order to share information and assist in answering queries. Likewise, managers can interact with subordinates (and vice versa) so as to voice concerns or clarify worrisome areas in an immediate task or on a wider HR-related scale, on a real-time basis. This can take place on a streamlined app that allows for direct communication, rather than the standard e-mail model. This "live chat" type service provides a faster and less formal communication stream, meaning that decisions can be made at a quicker rate and with greater ease.

Similarly, there may also be an element of physical streamlining in the time and resources saved by using the app and not traveling around the office, meaning staff can spend more time working. For example, a service such as WhatsApp integrated into a specific app could mean that a query could be resolved in a matter of minutes with an employee from a different department or area, rather than the face-to-face alternative, thus increasing productivity. Likewise, an organization may be more able to conduct external communication through an app. This could range from gaining customer satisfaction, to the possibility of recruitment, or even further afield. Many apps request a rating from the user on a regular basis and this is something that could be very useful for the organization in question: this feedback service is very quick and takes virtually no time for the customer, who also has the option to leave qualitative feedback. These critiques of the business could be instrumental in illustrating what improvements can be made, as well as highlighting successes and points of interest for the firm.

It is a simple way to gather vast data about consumer insights, which can then be used to develop and grow, alter and improve. This route is far more effective than the alternatives for gathering data as the communication that happens through this app vehicle is likely to be more honest than what would occur in a face-to-face interaction, due to people being wary of offending those asking the questions. This communication stream may also improve advertising and make consumers aware of current deals and offers, meaning that the organization may indeed drum up more business in the process of also gaining insight as to the opinion of their consumers. The external communication that will occur between consumer and organization will be hugely helpful for making improvements, while also having a positive impact on output. Not only would this external communication allow for interactions with consumers, but also up the supply chain to those individuals supplying goods and services to the organization in question. More frequent interactions with a supplier may mean that coordination is improved and that specific management styles can be adapted to improve efficiency. For example, "Just in Time" production would be more affable if a team were to know exactly when the goods were being delivered through a tracking system, rather than a rough estimate.

This is more than achievable as it can be seen in practice: the likes of ParcelForce (www.parcelforce.com) and DPD (www.dpd.co.uk) communicate in real-time with their users regarding delivery timings, etc. In a production setting, this may mean that the lead time and other important aspects such as the reorder point can be improved, reducing waste and improving customer satisfaction. Both benefits can be linked to enhancements for the wider organization, improving reputation and revenue for a marginal cost to the business. On a managerial front, apps can really streamline the workload by allowing for remote control at a higher frequency than what has traditionally been achievable. By having an interface that allows for greater monitoring, planning, and control, managers will have more time to make better decisions and follow through with superior actions. They will simply have more time and greater resources to be able to then push toward meeting organizational goals and targets, rather than struggling through the daily routine of checking up on individuals and their tasks. All the information managers need would simply be at their fingertips at any time of the day or night, ready to be scrutinized and coordinated in the appropriate way. App technology may also enable workers to be able to complete tasks remotely, away from the office. This is because the streamlining nature of an app means everything that employees will need is at their fingertips and all in one place. Any place a Wi-Fi connection is available, tasks can be completed.

As we have noted in a previous chapter, studies have shown that there is a link between the ability to work from home and productivity: workers are happier, feel more valued, and are more productive. This app may not be an app in the traditional sense of the word, but indeed a portal that allows workers to access the tools and programs that would be on their work computers. There should, as such, be no limit to the ability to work from home apart from for meetings and conferences where physical attendance is necessary. An added benefit of this streamlined way of working is that, apart from the benefit to individual workers, the organization as a whole should benefit from the decreased running costs that arise from not needing such extensive floor space (often very expensive, especially in business hubs).

To conclude, apps can have a significant impact on individuals and the organization as a whole regarding efficiency, productivity, and costs. On an individual scale, improving the ease of working for subordinates will translate to the wider scale of improvements in output and thus revenue. Uncertain, however, is the ability of the app technology to translate between service-based industries and the goods-production trades. There will never be an app that solves all the problems each and every business may face because of the uniqueness that occurs in each business model. For this reason, also, the cost of developing such a versatile app to a point where it is actually useful and holds the above benefits may outweigh the benefits themselves. It is likely that businesses on a smaller scale will not find benefits of the same scale while still facing the monumental costs, so as such it may not be that an app streamlines their business but indeed slows it down. It could be that in some cases, apps do not streamline but indeed delay work processes, especially where such technology is not intuitive or integrated in the process itself. Teaching some workers how to operate the technology may also be a problem and a hindrance, rather than a beneficial use of time. This is especially true if the task is only repeated occasionally with enough time between so that a process may be forgotten. These potential obstacles must be analyzed for every business that is seeking to incorporate such advanced technology.

Retailing

Retail is an industry that has been significantly influenced by technological applications due to changes in the way consumers are shopping. As previously stated, statistics suggest that approximately 51% of electronic sales are now made through mobiles and tablets (Statista, 2018). First, it is a method of communication with customers. In the case of John Lewis, a large chain store retailer, staff are equipped with tablets loaded with the John Lewis app (www.johnlewis.com), any queries that are received regarding products can be located immediately. The benefit of this in the short term is that it increases efficiency; queries can be processed at a faster speed, meaning exceptional customer service can be maintained. In the long run, this is likely to lead to repeat customers as an efficient and effective service is likely to lead to customers wanting to come back to shop again. Consequently, this will affect the future business revenue positively, leading to higher profit margins through increased sales. Second, given that around two-thirds of the population now own a smartphone, it has become a common and convenient method of shopping. If customers can be shown how the apps are operated, they are more likely to use the method as a means of purchasing in the future. This can be applied to specific segments of the market, for example, the *elderly*. If they are aware of how to use the technology from the comfort of their own home, they are more likely to want to shop using the app rather than going to the store. Widespread use is likely to result in greater levels of market share, which in turn means that the firm can achieve greater levels of economies of scale; higher volume is vital in developing a cost advantage.

The incorporation of "apps" into the selling process can also increase value for customers. Starbucks is an example of such a company, through offering a loyalty program to customers. Within their mobile app (www.starbucks.com), rewards are offered exclusively to customers who have signed up for the app and customers can order and pay directly through the app. This in turn creates a greater incentive for the customer; through offering an efficient service and making customers feel valued, the company is more likely to sell a greater number of products. Given that the market for coffee shops is highly competitive, it will also help to ensure that Starbucks continues to maintain its large market share of approximately 25% and increase this figure further in the long term through product differentiation.

Retailer Apps: An Example

There are a few ways in which McDonald's uses apps to help streamline their business. They have apps for the customers, the day-to-day workers, and the managers. The app for customers is a great way to socialize with the customers when they are not at the store; they are able to send them notifications of new promotions and even give them a reward-based system for repeat purchases. This is a common feature with food-based businesses. With these sorts of apps, you are able to order from your phone before you are even at the restaurant so it will be ready when you arrive, saving on the time you wait and, therefore, making you happier with the business and more likely wanting to come back. This works really well as McDonald's is a fast food company, the customers want fast food and this will give them an even faster experience.

The app for the workers is great to have on their phones. This app shows your schedule, as it changes from week to week. It also tells you when someone wants to change a shift. A notification pops up and tells you that a shift is available, and you can take it if you want. This helps businesses, as they will never be short on workers. You are also able to see when you clocked out for your break and when you must return; you can also see your live pay for that week and any expected pay in the weeks to come. This will enable the staff to plan their spending in the coming weeks to fit with how much they are going to work. This will keep the staff happy and make them work harder to see live what they are earning. It also helps by telling you the new promotions; to know the up and coming promotions in a place like McDonald's is important as they change on a regular basis. Promotions let the customers know if their favorite meal is coming back anytime soon, for example.

The manager's app is one they use for staffing costs and when they should allow breaks to take place. As they can see live expected sales on their phone they are able to see if it is going to be busy in the coming hour and can therefore figure out if it is suitable to send workers on breaks. It also sends workers notifications to say they are over spending on labor for that hour and that a break should be sent out. This means the managers are ideally never going to over spend on labor if the sales predictions are spot on, which they normally are. In conclusion, the apps McDonald's uses makes the business run very smooth. Everyone knows when they are working; what their pay is will help increase productivity within the business. The app helps the managers in the running of the business, with live and up-to-date predictions of sales; it allows staff to do their job easier and better as they will know whether to send them on a break or keep them on for the estimated rush that they might not have known about.

Mobile Context

More people are now spending time on their mobile devices as compared to other traditional media such as television or computers. A high mobile penetration means that companies have to adapt their communication channels and deliver branded content and advertisements straight to the mobile screens. Furthermore, mobile adoption growth has gone in parallel to many tech advances, especially sensors, geotagging, and spatial location, enabling companies to alter and reimagine their services and to collect, process, and circulate information about their users. Sensors in particular have broader uses that can also connect with mobile data. For instance, tiny ubiquitous sensors can be grafted into shopping centers' lifts, vendors, and settees. They gather context data and adapt systems behavior accordingly. This way information on how customers navigate their surroundings can be used later with mobile apps to target customers with special needs, and offer adapted services and products. Such sensor embedded technologies and service processes are classified as context-aware systems. Context-aware systems increase the usefulness, usability and value of mobile services, as they provide new opportunities to extend mobile commerce and to create services with immediate and accurate response to customers' needs in their current physical environments.

As the context-aware system increasingly matures and the market of mobile advertising is growing, mobile advertising based on context awareness is gradually emphasized by service providers and advertisers. Meanwhile, some emerging applications and services have appeared. For instance, location-based mobile advertisements; according to the geographical location of the mobile device's users, advertising messages about surrounding businesses are pushed to users' screens. Inevitably and gradually, the transition of marketing from passive users triggers initiative recommendation. By this token, the combination of the context-aware system and advertising service has broad prospects. However, such personalized service has also brought some problems. For example, what is the consumers' perception of this innovative service? How many consumers are willing to accept and use such services? And how can trust between service providers and users be built to promote this service and develop in a healthy manner? Moreover, compared with traditional mobile advertisements, the content of context-aware-based mobile advertisements is becoming more complicated, which will result in higher privacy concerns among users. These privacy concerns may cause consumers to resist context-aware-based mobile advertisements. Thus, it is crucial to understand the influencing factors that affect customers' acceptance of context-aware-based mobile advertisements.

Context Awareness

Humans can convey ideas and interact with each other successfully since they are context-aware and have a rich understanding of everyday situations on which they ground decisions and communication. Today, efforts to make computers also context-aware in order to improve service quality and the levels of human–

machine engagement have spanned across many markets (Athey and Gans, 2010). In order to use context effectively, an increasing number of researchers have discussed the challenges in determining context awareness and developing underlying apps and services. Previous studies have pointed to the fact that context refers to "where you are, who you are with and what resources are nearby" (Schilit et al., 1994) which is too specific. Hence, Dey (2001) supplemented and redefined context as "any information that can be used to characterize the situation of an entity, where an entity can be a person, place, or physical element that is considered relevant to the interaction between a user and an application, including the user and applications themselves." Consequently, marketers consider context as an important attribute and take advantage of context to offer task-relevant information or services to users, which are called context-awareness or context-aware computing.

There are different forms of context awareness. The most popular one is location awareness, which "is used to adapt services to the current location of a user" (Raper et al. 2007). The FCC's E-911 legislation requires that mobile phones' emergency calls must involve location-based services (LBS), which promote the development of LBS in the United States (Totaltelecom, 2007). Giaglis et al. (2002) divide LBS into six categories, including emergency services (e.g., automotive assistance), information services (e.g., mobile yellow pages), marketing services (e.g., mobile advertising), navigation services (e.g., personal navigation), tracking services (e.g., vehicle tracking), and billing services (e.g., location-sensitive billing). However, according to Kaasinen (2003), LBS "are services that are related as such or by their information contents to certain places or locations," and location-aware services (LAS) are making use of users' location to adapt the service. Hence, the LAS can be classified a special case of LBS. So far, the research on LAS mainly focuses on two aspects: technical and users. For example, Tesoriero et al. (2010) proposed a RFID-based indoor location system as GPS is not suitable for indoor location-aware applications, while Kaasinen (2003) concluded five key issues: topical and comprehensive contents, personal and user-generated contents, seamless service entities, smooth user interaction and privacy issues, that related to users' need for location-aware mobile services. Another well-known form of context-awareness is socially aware services which are mining an abundance of social information about users to offer improved services. Nowadays, socially aware services have adapted in various fields, such as security and spam protection, and emergency medical alerts. Those applications rely on social signals, which exist in internet- or phone-mediated interactions. Specifically, MSN Messenger, an example of socially aware services, collects user information, including profile, preferences or behavioral history to facilitate chat and offer accurate MSN-based services.

The intention of users to share their personal information is a challenge in this field. A considerable number of studies have explored users' acceptance of LBS and other context-aware services that are based on systematic collection of users' data. Kaikkonen et al. (2005) found that user acceptance and actual use is strongly influenced by a user's context or situation. Koolwaaij et al. (2006) conducted an experiment on ContextWatcher, a context-sharing mobile application that allowed users to share not only their whereabouts with friends, but also any other piece of context-related information they may want to share, ranging from body data to pictures, local weather information, and even subjective data like moods and experiences. They found that users are willing to share much more context-related information than expected.

Moreover, according to Hofer et al. (2003), the fundamental objective of context awareness is to "provide services not only to people at anytime, anywhere, with any media but specifically to communicate the right thing at the right time in the right way." Therefore the technical support and model's improvement of context-aware computing is an important motive for context-aware services' acceptance. Recently, studies have suggested computational models or approaches to improve the use of context-awareness in traditional computing applications. For example, Salber et al. (1999) presented and updated the Context Toolkit, an architecture that can capture and access context, storage, distribution, and independent execution from applications to make context-aware applications building easier. Also, Sørensen et al. (2004) suggest that it is important that the new generation of context-aware applications is capable of simultaneously possessing six characteristics: sentience, autonomy, time criticality, safety criticality, geographical dispersion, and mobility. Recent developments in apps technology have benefited from these insights.

For context-awareness mobile devices, Hofer et al. (2003) stated that context of the application on mobile devices is highly dynamic. Typically, mobile devices often move with their users; they are not permanently connected to a network. Aalto et al. (2004) previously introduced a novel B-MAD system, using Bluetooth positioning and Wireless Application Protocol (WAP) to perfect the use of context awareness in mobile devices. Besides being different from traditional desktop computing, computational services also need to be mobile to access and evaluate users' constantly changing context. Salber and Abowd (1998) identified some fundamental issues of traditional computing and present four different solutions to free the context-aware computing. As the computing environment is becoming refined, a variety of application areas have adapted context-aware content (Athey and Gans, 2010).

Mobile Advertising

Generally, advertising is purchasing time and space from any mass media to inform the target audience about products and services, whether through magazine outlets, TV channels, or online (American Marketing Association, 2003). For a while advertising was the prerogative of TV channels, the printed press and radio. However, online advertising is now well established and constitutes on its own a major chuck of marketing budgets. Compared with traditional channels, online advertising can be more interactive, in that it allows the audience to take part in the message more pro-actively (Macias, 2003; Bergemann and Bonatti, 2011). It can also be "closer" to viewers as it can be delivered based on users' preference and directly to their mobiles. Particularly, the American Marketing Association (2003) defines mobile advertising as "a form of advertising that transmits advertisement messages to users via mobile phones, personal digital assistants (PDAs), or other wireless communication devices."

Mobile advertising is often delivered in two ways: via SMSs (Short Message Service) and via multimedia message services (MMS). Instead of traditional synchronous voice communication, SMS has made communication more flexible and interactive. There are two basic functions of SMS. One is that it can send automatically generated messages to users, such as notification of voice mail. The other function is that it can be conceived as a way of interpersonal communication, such as sending greetings. The SMS text message is the most widely used form of mobile advertising since it is cheap and in straight text format that is readable by nearly all cell phones. However, the characters of text are limited to 160 characters to ensure the storage and speed of mobile devices, which unfortunately is less appealing visually. With the development of high-speed bandwidth and multimedia smart phones, mobile content can now break the limitations of SMS text messaging, enabling the transmission of prompt and interactive texts, images, voices, and video, which is called MMS. Nevertheless, MMS is relatively more expensive to use as compared to SMS.

Also, mobile advertising is of two sorts: push and pull advertising. Push advertising means that mobile advertisements are proactively delivered to users. For example, Celltick, a U.K. mobile advertising platform, will send advertisements to users when their cell phones go automatically on standby. Users can click this advertisement when they are interested in the content. Pull advertising links consumer to related websites, trying to collect data on their preferences and habits in the process. As a result, the advertisers can effectively send relevant advertising messages to specific audiences, such as promotions and coupons. For instance, Turkcell-Tonla Kazan, a Turkish mobile operator's subscribers can choose to receive product advertisements when they register or opt out (Jhuang,

2009). This results from three possible types of interactions with consumers: permission-based advertising, incentive-based advertising, and location-based advertising. Permission-based advertisements are only used to send messages to individuals who have indicated a clear willingness to receive advertisements. Instead of the advertisements that are directly pushed to the mass market in traditional channels, such as TV and radio, which will be ignored by most of the audience, the specific targets of permission-based advertising have a relatively higher intention to accept advertisements. Incentive-based advertisements in particular are delivered to individuals who agree to receive promotional events with specific rewards. For example, mobile operators previously awarded free wireless network connection time when users read and clicked on advertisements. Furthermore, because of mobile devices and wireless networks, the advertisements can be sent based on users' current location which enables customers to have real-time interaction with service providers and improve the effectiveness of advertising and marketing to some extent. In fact, Kaasinen (2003) showed that mobile device users do not mind being pushed information, as long as they need it. Specifically, when customers stand in a shopping center searching for something, there are various brands and information about that item that surround them in that moment. In that case, the mobile advertisements that really meet customers' needs and preferences are necessary and important. Hence, targeted advertising plays an essential role in context-aware-based mobile advertising.

Targeted Advertising

Targeted advertising is a new algorithmically managed form of online adverting that adapts the selection of an ad (content) to a given pool of data, that is, users' data, personal details, or their membership (Bergemann and Bonatti, 2011; Plummer et al., 2007). The data are often users' demographics, such as gender, age and race, or psychographic, such as customers' attitudes, value, and lifestyle (Jansen et al., 2013). A behavioral variable, such as users' purchase history, can also be viewed as a kind of trait that automatically directs ad choices and delivery, assuming this way of identifying potential interested viewers will reduce the waste of resources.

Targeted advertising can be of different types for different marketing purposes, including contextual targeting, social media targeting, and location-based targeting. Contextual targeting is often based on the theme of the medium; for instance, if a customer reads a beauty blog online, the advertisements associated will be on cosmetics. Also, advertisements will be sent based on consumer behavior, such as when they are searching for words on websites (Schlee, 2013).

However, the advertisements may fail to adequately match content at the time of the search, which may cause annoyance. Thus, social media, the second type of targeted ads, can have a higher matching level and can be more effective as it is based on general targeting attributes, for example, geotargeting and behavioral targeting. For example, Facebook collects personal information about users, including gender, age, address, and education, which is used to create categories for targeted ads. Furthermore, ads on social media are more time-sensitive (apps on mobiles) in which information is used to improve matching power. Finally, after reviewing 53 cases, Park et al. (2008) conclude that the third type of targeted advertising, i.e. location-based, can have the highest matching power with users' interest in a point of time, which involves delivering advertisements to specific customers based on their geographic location. This kind of targeted advertising means that users will be prompted with services or products around their activity area. However, Banerjee and Dholakia (2012) state that location-based targeted advertising can be intrusive since it collects users' personal data.

Advertising and Privacy

Chaffey et al. (2009) define privacy as "the moral right of individuals to avoid intrusion into their personal affairs by third parties." That is a non-neglect issue in people's lives since it helps individuals maintain their autonomy and individuality. Recently, context-based apps and services have caused major privacy concerns. Hence, the debate in media as well as in academia (Athey and Gans, 2010; Dwyer et al., 2007) is on the need to reduce customers' privacy concerns and protect their data. The main reason for that is that privacy in absolute terms is not customers' main issue, but the loss of control over information is. Burggon (1982) states that privacy has four dimensions: informational, psychological, social, and physical. From the perspective of mobile advertising developers, the informational and psychological are particularly important. Accordingly, Fried (1968) argues that privacy "is not simply an absence of information about us in the mind of others, rather it is the control we have about information about ourselves." Also, privacy involves the rights to decide "what, when and to whom to disclose personal feelings and thoughts." For instance, social media platforms, such as Instagram, allow users to decide what feelings or thoughts they have on privacy and to share them, which make them feel more in control over information.

Generally, that information refers to the personal information that "can be connected with or linked back to a certain individual" (Seigneur and Jensen, 2004). The privacy of personal information is one of the most discussed issues in this area (Mills, 2008). In fact, personal information contains public information and private information, and public information means the public fraction of personal information that individuals are willing to expose. Definitely, organizations gathering, storing, or manipulating personal information will lead to individuals' resistance and antipathy, but when the information belongs to public information or can give individuals a valuable reward, people would like to release control and their privacy concerns will be reduced. Consequently, individuals' trust toward third parties will be increased accordingly, because there is a negative relationship between privacy concerns and trust levels. Besides, Madden and Smith (2010) point out that a growing number of young people are increasingly conscious of privacy issues. However, most of them are seen to hold vigilant, but laissez-faire attitudes toward their personal information. Marketing wise, privacy concerns can be helpful for marketers to build a close relationship with customers through reinforcing willingness for openness, sincerity, and truthfulness. In order to reduce mobile phone users' privacy concerns about personalized and localized advertising, increased security is put in place.

The European Union has recently promulgated specific regulations for data protection. The General Data Protection Regulation (GDPR) is a regulation in EU law on data protection and privacy for all individuals within the European Union (EU) and the European Economic Area (EEA). The regulation aims primarily to give control to individuals over their personal data and to simplify the regulatory environment for international business. Under the right of access, citizens have the right to access their personal data and information about how this personal data is being processed. Therefore, the data controller must implement measures which meet the GDPR principles of data protection by design and by default. For example, data protection measures need to be designed into the development of business processes for products and services.

Chapter 5
Management Processes and Decision Making

The act of streamlining work processes, by definition, aims to "increase an organization's efficiency by simplifying tasks, bypassing unnecessary steps and cutting waste, all by using the most modern process modelling techniques." There are many ways in which the use of smartphone/tablet applications can benefit employee productivity. The advantage of such technology in the workplace includes improvements in communication and human resource (HR) management, encouraging innovation and creativity, creating mobility and saving time. For organizations to thrive, five fundamental points should be considered with each stage of the streamlining work process, enhancing its value in order for the final product to be recognized as something of value. The first stage of the process is known as the Value Chain Analysis, whereby tasks are analyzed by how much value they add to the process. By scrutinizing tasks, conclusions can be made as to whether tasks can be eliminated or if they should be improved. Designer perfumes are an example of this. The packaging design and the creation of the logo increase the value of the final product; therefore, this stage must be undertaken with maximum efficiency.

Nonetheless, this stage is not as important for a market-based perfume brand whose focus is on low prices. Instead of employing a team of designers specifically for creating packaging, the company can use standard packaging offered in the market, therefore eliminating or minimizing this stage in the process. It is therefore crucial for organizations to establish the value of their tasks, in order to save time and reduce costs. Based on this example, of the designer/market perfume brands, once a company has decided on their packaging and label designs, it will be more economical and efficient to use machine(s) and systematize the labeling process instead of undertaking repetitive tasks, such as filling and packaging individually. However, this process can be linked to high maintenance costs. Therefore, if a repetitive task, such as the one above adds a high cost to the chain, it may be wiser to opt out. Similarly, in looking to streamline all work processes, bottlenecks at a given stage should be a point of focus as they "block" workflows. This "blockage" may occur due to the lack of access to resources, such as materials, information, services, technical inabilities of employees, or equipment deficiencies. Streamlining business processes is a meticulous task, which requires a significant amounts of analysis and a great deal of teamwork. In order to contribute to the success of streamlining business processes, a collaborative, cloud-based tool with access across multiple mobile devices can be extremely beneficial.

DOI 10.1515/9781547400546-005

It is therefore not surprising that a vast number of businesses are progressively turning to apps to improve their business performance, generate sales leads, and promote their brand. One key benefit is the ability to store files offline. As business leaders communicate across multiple devices during the day, the cloud-based nature of many apps ensures content can be viewed at a convenient time. Saving time and creating mobility are key benefits of using apps. Apps also contribute to improvements in communication, changing the way in which employees interact and communicate in the workplace. Various communication tools are now available to use by employees to interact or exchange information at work. For instance, employees from different departments in a company can use virtual meeting applications such as Skype to share and exchange information. The same is true for customer interactions. Employees can use the internet to establish ways of promoting a business online, such as the social enterprise networks Slack, Yammer or Facebook Workplace. These applications are used for private communication within organizations, allowing employees to socialize and interact with other employees from different organizations. This interaction between employees results in the exchange of information, and the encouragement of brain storming on several work-related issues; thus, contributing to creating innovative business ideas.

Technological tools like virtual meeting applications save employees time, and the mobility makes employees stay in control of their jobs. For example, mobile workforce management software allows field workers to access real-time work information while they are on job. Examples such as these indicate how technology can be used to automate various tasks in the workplace, thus guaranteeing efficiency and increasing productivity. Furthermore, using databases to capture and store information can facilitate quick decision making, whereby business information is easily accessible to employees via one single database. By using applications like Dropbox, Google Drive, and Microsoft OneDrive, information can be edited and saved for later use, hence, saving time and creating mobility. Many organizations are looking for advanced ways to use the internet to help digitize the value chain. In these cases, they have already implemented technologies to help them collect more data, and to learn about their overall process proficiencies and inconsistencies. Additionally, many more organizations are starting to enforce such technologies that are best suited for their businesses, such as sensors, mobile technologies, and cloud-based technologies. Nevertheless, attributed disadvantages are linked to such technologies in the workplace. The occurrence of potential risks, such as cyber-attacks to interconnected systems and counterfeiting of parts in mobile technologies, therefore, should be considered throughout the process.

Nevertheless, all technological devices hold the risk of cyber-attacks. However, when properly configured, the use of smartphones/tablets can avoid the need for locally stored data, thus reducing the exposure of sensitive company information due to theft, loss, hacking, or other intrusion attempts. Therefore, it is essential to test a smartphone/tablet application before implementing the devices for your entire company, to ensure all procedures are implemented. Despite the attributed disadvantages, inclusive of distractions at work, idleness, and cyber-attacks, when such applications are established with a robust cloud-based platform, the use of smartphone apps is a powerful tool in the workplace environment. In this chapter, we discuss how the implementation of many different apps is changing the architecture of managerial decision making and work-related processes.

Apps and Workplace Efficiency

The invention of a wide array of technologies has improved the efficiency levels in the workplace. It is worth citing that this enhancement can be regarded as the primary driver of globalization. The argument is based on the fact that innovations allow enterprises to create stable communication with other individuals or businesses in different regions. In most cases, many organizations are seen as moving toward the adoption of online business platforms. The move is prompted by the need to secure a vast client base (Patterson et al., 2017). Moreover, the use of different applications can be regarded as forming the basis of the communication features in many organizations. For example, virtual meeting software is utilized in most firms. It is critical to note that the applications allow managers and other learners to conduct frequent meetings with other stakeholders who are in different geographical regions. Numerous benefits are linked with a virtual meeting software. One such benefit is that it helps improve the decision-making processes (Chen, 2015). The argument is centered around the fact that it allows for consultation with different individuals. When compared to the traditional meetings, it is apparent that the virtual ones are less expensive and time-consuming. The resources that are saved from such a process can, thus, be used to improve the efficiency of other services.

In other settings, it would be challenging to conduct meetings with individuals who are in different regions. This issue is most prevalent in scenarios where an organization has operations in other countries. However, the use of the virtual meeting applications ensures that executives can create centralized management, thus improving the implementation processes (Kavanagh et al., 2017). It also serves as an ideal tool where managers can instruct junior workers, as well as monitor their activities. Having a regular follow-up of all activities plays a vital role in minimizing the chances of risks or losses.

Another area can be seen in accounting where there has been the adoption of different accounting and enterprise software. The examples of such applications include the Microsoft Dynamics GP, QuickBooks, SAP ERP, and others. Accounting activities can be regarded as a part of the aspects that require a high level of efficiency. It is through such processes that an organization can determine its financial positions. Accounting further forms the basis for making business forecasts. While accounting activities in small firms can be relatively easy to manage, they pose a lot of difficulties in large organizations (Andreadis et al., 2015). In such firms, it is essential to integrate various technological innovations into the accounting operations. Contrary to the conventional mode of accounting, it is critical to note that integrated computerized accounting comes with huge benefits. Some of them include improving the speed and accuracy levels, as well as flexibility. Additionally, there has been the emergence of new technologies in accounting. An example of this is evident in cloud computing, which allows for web hosting off-site. Using this technology makes it possible to coordinate accounting activities in a department (Avram et al., 2014). There is also the impression that the use of the applications can help in enhancing the security and the scalability of an organization's operations.

That notwithstanding, there is also the view that the integration of different software programs allows for high levels of efficiency in scheduling. The applications, thus, play an important role in the coordination of field activities that require accuracy. A look at many of the fieldwork projects indicates they tend to be linked with numerous challenges. Such difficulties include high costs, obstacles in the analysis of information, time wastage, and other logistic problems (Andrade et al., 2015). The failure to address the listed challenges may be a major setback in attaining the desired objectives. However, there have now been big changes in the robustness of corporate applications and gathering data, data analysis and connections to customers, sensor, BI reporting, and the like. The technology has changed and with that comes more and easier control over data in the organization. The use of apps can get out of control and it is the control (connectedness of the apps) that makes them such valuable tools. However, the use of the applications such as these ensures that business is in a position to continuously monitor its activities.

Building a Best of Class Solutions for Your Organization

In creating the right platform for your company, the traditional method was to develop from scratch or to use an off the shelf application and customize them to fit your needs. Both solutions have benefits and issues. One important area of integration in the development process that has become increasingly popular in the creation of best of class applications or web platforms using third-party APIs (application programming interfaces) to perform specific tasks rather than building all the bells and whistles into the system yourself. When you are considering creation of a large system or improving/updating it, rather than building everything from scratch, your developers should be looking for available best of class solutions to meet the particular needs of your project. These apps are often open source or cut the third party in as part of the transaction. They are often directed at a specific problem such as using PayPal for transactions. They are generally thoroughly tested, fast and easily integrated into your application. By partnering, you can gain best of class solutions, speed development time, and best utilize the abilities of your development team. Third party APIs should be considered as an option in your planning of any development project.

Using Visuals and Other Innovations in Your Platform to Improve Decision Making

Over the years, there has been the adoption of real-time reporting in charts and graphs. They ensure that managers, dispatchers, sales representatives, and so on, can have stable communication, as well as equally enhanced collaboration. In any large organization, there is a need to ensure that all individuals have a centralized command center (Wilson et al., 2014). While in the past goal setting and maintenance was achieved through the holding of frequent meetings, it is now possible to employ different communication applications to carry it out. Not only does the move serve to address conflicts among the stakeholders, but it also seeks to ensure that the opinions of individuals are incorporated into the decision-making processes. There is also the benefit of increasing both creativity and innovation. Technological innovations are often credited for being highly effective as compared to human beings. There are different platforms that can be used by the workers to come up with innovative features that would help lower the operating costs while equally raising the production levels. Applications also form the basis of where workers can interact with their peers or consumers. In the case of the customers, having stable communication means that an organization would be in an improved position to determine the changes in consumer behaviors (Mansuri et al., 2014).

Using Apps to Measure Employee Productivity

The other benefit that is linked to the use of the application in workplace settings relates to enhancement in HR management. Large organizations are noted for having the problem of ensuring there is improved management of the workforce. Difficulties may increase the levels of laxity and poor performances among the workers. However, the integration of the applications enables the managers to conduct screening and recruiting of employees with enhanced efficiency. Such programs are also used to evaluate the reporting time of the workers. In addition, recent developments have made it possible to monitor the contribution of each employee with ease. While the excelling workers are given rewards, the underperforming ones can be summoned by the management.

Unlike human beings, the use of various applications can be explained as having the benefit of improving the mobility levels. In this regard, it is vital to note that internet features often have important characteristics such as the elimination of space limitations. It holds that the applications may be used for storing data in an organization. For example, virtual meeting software can be used in different locations (Mansuri et al., 2014). On the other hand, mobile workforce management software also allows the managers to monitor and manage activities of the workers on a regular basis. The change is remarkably important in ensuring that they are in a position to detect possible losses. Mobile technologies also provide an ideal platform where an enterprise can create stable communication with clients. A look at the behavior of many individuals indicates that they tend to conduct most of their communication via online platforms. The examples of such platforms include Facebook, LinkedIn, Twitter, and many more. It is significantly possible to integrate these major media platforms with different software. Using social media allows an enterprise to create awareness of its products and services. When compared to other modes of marketing, it is apparent that the use of different internet platforms is crucial in yielding better results. The cost of utilizing them is also lower when equated to the traditional methods.

Additionally, the use of the application has the benefit of improving the connection of an enterprise with other businesses (Nwankpa et al., 2015, p. 342). An example of this aspect can be seen in a setting where an enterprise opts to utilize the services of logistics and distribution firms. The interaction ensures that the concerned organizations can harmonize their operations, as well as closely monitor the costs that are linked to the process. A similar case applies to the sharing and storing of information. Information stored on online platforms or computer devices can be shared easily, enabling the organization to adapt to growth or shrinkage in a flexible manner. The process, thus, allows a business to expand its operations to different regions, as well as partner with other individuals. Some tasks can also be regarded as challenging and would require high levels of HR capacity. However, contemplating a move would mean a short-term significant increase in the cost of doing business. An increment in the operational expenses would translate to a reduction of the profit margins. The benefit of using computer programs is that they tend to lessen the number of individuals that are needed to execute a specific task. The saved money can be used in carrying out other operations. In short, the utilization of the applications helps improve the efficiency, speed, accuracy, and the overall production levels.

Organization Use of Smartphone Apps

As more employees use mobile devices to streamline their work processes, more organizations are embracing the use of smartphone and tablet applications. In the previous two decades, PC hardware and software replaced paper-based systems of organizing and processing work. This past decade has witnessed the development of smartphones and tablets with their software of "apps" replacing less portable hardware, for instance, desktop computers. Technology enables all parts of an organization to communicate at more convenience; for example, using intranet e-mail systems, forums and discussions for sharing and providing feedback on work. The use of apps to streamline work processes is relatively new for companies and not many companies may actually have an internal app for their workers, but may encourage the use and download of external apps to assist them with their work processes.

Fred Fiedler's Contingency Theory of Management states that success often depends on a variety of situational factors, the amount of information the manager has available to make an informed decision being one those factors (Buchanan and Huczynski, 2016). With the availability of apps and such technologies in their workplace environment, managers have more information at their disposal than ever before. An internal app for a company is extremely useful and becomes even more so when it is personalized based on the user of the app's current location or operation. Advanced apps have the ability to utilize geolocation technology to identify a worker's location. This could help the manager to monitor the performance of their subordinates effectively, observing if they are doing what they are meant to and if they are where they are supposed to be. Similarly, communication, like organization, is fundamental within a business and should be considered when managing any company. Within the business, quick, easy communication methods can lead to increased efficiency, drastically improve team work and overall streamlines almost every operational process. Without effective communication several problems can arise such as lack of work, workplace conflicts, and general misunderstandings. Due to apps primarily existing on communication devices (phones/tablets) there are a wide multitude of various effective apps that have specific uses to help improve communication within the workplace.

Work Processes

A work process is an activity, or a set of activities carried out by an organization with an end goal in mind. Organizations will often have many work processes, and work processes vary from organization to organization, often tailored around the type of business the organization is dealing with. A call center might have specific work processes in place describing how operators should communicate with clients efficiently; a fast food restaurant might have work processes describing how each task in the kitchen should be carried out; in both organizations managers might follow specific processes detailing how they ought to control and monitor staff effectively. Work processes already allow for jobs to be carried out faster and more efficiently, especially when steps are repeated. However, as technology continues to grow, there is always room for improvement.

In today's world, many businesses have realized the potential of smart devices and their impact within the workplace. A wide range of third-party software "apps" are readily available, offering many quality of life improvements to the worker, including time-management and scheduling apps, digital notepads, online document sharing, and the ability to access a wide range of information on the go through internet browsers. The utility and skillsets of workers can be improved vastly by simply having access to a phone or tablet. In some cases, businesses may opt to have their own custom apps developed, allowing them to be more personalized with specific tasks in mind. These apps may be designed for customers, workers, or both, and can significantly simplify, alter, or even automate areas of work, shortening and removing unnecessary steps in the work process, effectively streamlining it. There may be some disadvantages to allowing smart devices in the workplace. Employees may not use them for the purposes intended by the employer, leading to a potential reduction in productivity, however, there is much more to be gained from their usage, especially as technology continues to grow each year.

Third-party apps are apps developed outside the organization, usually with the intention of having a wide range of users and with a general-purpose task in mind. In some cases, third-party apps can be customized for a specific organization or user, however, in these cases, changes are usually nothing more than a layout change of a premade template app. Two of the more popular third-party apps adopted by businesses are Evernote and OneNote. Essentially digital notebooks are available online and on mobile devices, both apps have potential (and even features specifically designed) to improve organization within the workplace. These apps aim to reduce the amount of physical handwritten notes required in the workplace, which clutter offices, need physical storage space, and can easily become lost, damaged, or forgotten about. Notes and pages can be a mass of disorganized and nonuseful information, wasting people's time and affecting their ability to record actions taken. In many workplaces, shared notes are not allowed any more as they were found to be a time waster. "Notes" or "Pages," the terms used, describe online entries by the respective apps, can be shared between other users of the apps, co-workers or clients, saving time which might otherwise be spent sending e-mails and searching through inboxes, as described by one app user "Mateo put frequently used reference materials in Evernote notebooks and invited others to join. Keeping it all in one place—and out of inboxes—gave everyone instant access to the info they needed" (Evernote, 2018). Outside of their core functionality (as a notepad), both apps also contain additional features such as the ability to use tags to organize and search notes quickly (instead of looking through physical pages or sheets of paper), the ability to scan physical or online documents and turn them into notes, and the ability to set reminders of upcoming events and deadlines.

Enabling groups within organizations to easily communicate with each other can lead to vast improvements within the workplace. A concept design department could share sketches among each other, even if they were separated by long distances, and collaborate on a set of final designs, which could then be shared with a client or manufacturer who would then be able to instantly provide feedback in the same digital notepad. These apps consequently can be used to streamline work processes through their sheer flexibility, and by reducing the need to constantly hold meetings or stay in touch via e-mail to know how work is progressing. Some jobs, especially those where workers might be expected to be more independent (but still need to report their progress), such as some office work, or any sort of design and development roles, can especially benefit from implementing these types of apps.

By using applications companies have greatly increased the accessibility of company files and information. Applications such as Ebsta (www.ebsta.com) (provide tools for businesses to drive customer engagement) and Cirrus Files (connect folders and files in Google Drive to standard and custom objects in Sales Force) integrate the channels that contain business information so that employees can access them in one place from wherever they are. Although by increasing the amount of computing technology within a company it would seem counter-intuitive to forgo the need of an information technology department, these apps are easy to use and do not require specific coding skills to set up, as all the infra-structure has been completed already. It is also common for the companies that created the apps, to offer continuous support, therefore the need for an IT depart-ment is outsourced to these companies.

Management

The gradual gaining popularity of apps has called into question and led to criticism of the traditional tools/processes used in organizations, eventually stripping them of their purpose (Athey and Ellison, 2014; Moore and Rugullies, 2005). First, traditional tools became disjointed and fragmented. Employees began to use separate tools for processes such as e-mail, creating and editing documents, and participating in business processes. This leads to a lack of coordination within an agent's own tasks, culminating in a lack of coordination throughout the organization. Second, agents have been continually required to step outside of their business processes (such as solving a customer service issue) to find the required information and help to resolve the issue. This is, in the simplest words, an inefficient use of time. Finally, traditional technology has (until recent times) only been fully available to office workers. Now, there is an increasing need for those who work remotely such as engineers on call to also have access to the same volume of detailed information, to make amend-ments, share information quickly to those who require it, and enhance/stream-line various functions of organizations.

Apps for the workplace can be categorized into three segments, depending upon who they are aimed at. These sections are customers, employees of orga-nizations (including managers), and external business partners (such as suppli-ers) (Gröger et al., 2013). Although three categories are recognized, the following examples focus largely on managers as this was seen to be the most appropriate. One app aimed at managers is 15Five (www.15five.com), which focuses on agent engagement and performance, specifically looking to streamline the process of feedback; the software claims to make continuous employee feedback simple to drive high performing cultures. This is done through requiring employees to give regular, concise feedback through the app, as well as providing weekly details regarding progress on set goals; managers can then answer directly via the app, set a meeting to discuss issues further and pass responses directly to senior man-agement (Torrevillas, 2016). The feedback process (specifically regarding agent performance) is key to control within organizations, with it being shown to contribute to organizational effectiveness, innovation, and competitiveness (Ruck et al., 2017). However, despite the advantages feedback provides it is often very difficult to time and present it in a manner that is not destructive (Besieux, 2017). 15Five begins to tackle feedback efficiency through removing unnecessary layers of formal hierarchies; the way feedback is provided means the app has the potential to bypass several overheads between subordinates and upper management, especially in large organizations.

Greater efficiency will help to ensure feedback given by agents is as current as possible, which in turn will work toward ensuring managerial decisions and organizational policies address current desires/issues expressed. This efficient communication is also beneficial to working toward organizational goals (Widhiastuti, 2012). Moreover, streamlining the feedback process using apps means that middle managers are being given greater responsibility, which (if handled correctly) has the potential to result in increasing recognition from senior management and their self-esteem. These phenomena are tied to motivation theories, which will be discussed at greater length in a later section.

The actual feedback being given can also be improved. For example, managers are able to provide high quality feedback in a remote setting rather than one-to-one, freeing up their time while reaching a greater number of employees than perhaps previously possible. The barriers between managers and employees are also addressed; often both parties can be reluctant in giving feedback due to factors such as fear of reaction or fear of the superiors (Anderson, 2012). However, the use of an app to give and receive feedback allows the option of anonymity, as well as removing the resistance a superior's presence can unknowingly give. This should give the opportunity for more honest (and ultimately more constructive) feedback to be given. However, it should be noted that an app such as this is best suited to organizations with a flatter structure, otherwise a "bottleneck" may be created for middle-lower line managers if they have large spans of control. Bottlenecks can cause inefficiency and increase the project life cycle time and project costs (Intense School, 2014), therefore, undermining the fundamental purpose of using the app.

Likewise, it is not wholly suited to organizations with a matrix structure as subordinates are often under dual management (Writing, 2018), confusing the pathways for sending feedback. Relatedly, Power BI (https://powerbi.microsoft.com/en-us/) is Microsoft's business analytics tool that connects to several data sources on premises and in the cloud. It simplifies data ingestion, transformation, integration, and enrichment and can create reports using built-in visuals (Microsoft, 2018). Microsoft (2018) itself describes Power BI as "... a suite of business analytics tools that deliver insights throughout your organization. Connect to hundreds of data sources, simplify data prep, and drive ad hoc analysis. Produce beautiful reports, then publish them for your organization to consume on the web and across mobile devices. Everyone can create personalized dashboards with a unique, 360-degree view of their business. And scale across the enterprise, with governance and security built-in."

Apps for Communication and Management

Apps are also being used throughout different industries to improve communication and coordination between different functions of organizations. Communication is essential to achieving organizational goals and occurs vertically (through hierarchies), laterally (such as manager-to-manager) and externally (with suppliers); however, it is often hampered through factors such as a dishonest culture and unclear channels leading to resolution (Fielding, 2006). Essentially, coordination aligns organizational activities, so efforts put toward achieving organizational goals are more effective. One category of app which works to improve communication and coordination are engineering apps or "eApps" (www.eapps. com). eApps aim to integrate the activities of product design, process development, factory/production planning, and factory operations, breaking down communication walls caused by segregated applications previously used for each function (Volkmann et al., 2016). The development of these apps has been largely driven by the evolution of factors such as shorter product life cycles and greater variety of products, which have led to greater complexity in the activities previously described (Volkmann et al., 2016).

The benefits of eApps are largely focused around time saving, cost reduction, increased flexibility, and increased quality. First, communication is improved through reaction time being lowered, due to the relevant departments being more aware of each other's progress when the project lead asks for updates (Volkmann et al., 2016). Positive knock-on effects of this are mostly seen in situations where the next stage of the process requires confirmation of the previous stage being complete (Hoos et al., 2015). Similarly, activity execution time is decreased while flexibility is increased as apps allow tasks to be set remotely at any time (Hoos et al., 2015). Second, costs are reduced through these time-saving measures as process development and factory operations will be optimized to remove unnecessary delays, which can prolong the processes. Waste can also be reduced between the four activities as they are better coordinated and aligned, saving resources, time, and money. Last, the quality of organizational processes can be increased as digitalization of information prevents media breaks or disruptions, as well as allowing easy access to previous information logged, which may be required later (Hoos et al., 2015).

These two examples show the great potential apps have in aiding many elements of organizations, making them more efficient and streamlining functions. This will culminate in savings, which can be widely grouped under the headings of time and money, for both agents and principles. Given the rate of technological development it can be assumed that apps will become commonplace in the work environment, suggesting that organizations and sectors who show willingness to adopt new technologies have the potential to gain a great advantage over those who are not. This is an idea that could accelerate technological development and result in apps, which can alter business structures entirely. Needless to say, the overwhelming number of apps and the integration of apps into systems require further work as this can pose problems for the integration of data.

Management is an important key area of business that encompasses many other areas such as communication and organization. Good management ultimately decides whether or not the business makes profit. It is important for employees with managerial responsibility to delegate roles appropriately, consider constraints such as time or money and manage employees effectively. Although a lot of the apps we have already discussed can be used to increase management there are others designed specifically for managers. Expensify (www.expensify.com) uses cloud technology (like Google Drive) and is used for paying, monitoring, and submitting expenses reports. It can link to credit cards and the pictures on phones (so one can take pictures of receipts and transactions). Expensify displays the date, person, and amount of a transaction allowing an employee to easily see important financial data. This app is useful for management primarily because it allows employees to monitor and plan important transactions. Managers can easily see where money is going in and out making Expensify an excellent app for understanding the cash flow of the business. Tripit (www.tripit.com) is an app used for people to plan trips and for traveling. You can sync the travel plans with your calendar, create an itinerary, and share everything among groups of people. This app is useful for managers as they can utilize it to arrange business trips and conferences and ensuring that they are carried out successfully.

Buffer is an app used to promote businesses on social media. Buffer is used for businesses that already exist on social media sites like Facebook and schedules their posts on these sites so they appear at the most popular times of the day, increasing fan engagement. It also gives the business the opportunity to look into the analytics of the company's presence online by displaying information such as "followers" into graphs. This app is particularly useful for marketing managers as it provides them with rich information and insight into how their business is performing in the virtual world. Keeping employees connected and well-informed is especially important for successful completion of activities such as total quality management (TQM) programs, which require strategic commitment and employee involvement.

Apps can also significantly enhance managerial performance, especially in small organizations where managers have a wide span of control, and they can also make it easier to pass information up and down the organizational hierarchy. By improving communication between management and employees, apps make it much easier for management to plan, control, organize, and lead. It also simplifies processes for those following Open Book Management practices, which focus on relentlessly sharing financial and operating data with all employees (Baron and Kreps, 1999). Furthermore, instant and constant feedback from different departments regarding the running of operations and issues encountered can help the manager select more realistic objectives, and with up-to-date information it is much quicker and easier to adjust human, financial, material, or technological resources whenever necessary. Plus, apps could make organizing the workforce less time consuming; it is possible to personalize apps based on the employee's role or location, so they can be kept up-to-date with the exact information they need for their particular job. This may, therefore, help to attain objectives efficiently and effectively. However, having notifications constantly pop up on the screen could become distracting, making it harder for employees to focus on the task at hand, therefore, individuals should restrict notifications only for very important news and updates.

Another benefit of using apps in workplace environments is improved performance evaluation and employee recognition. Managers may use survey/poll applications, such as Survey Analytics (www.surveyanalytics.com), to gain a better understanding of how well individual departments are functioning and the level of employee satisfaction with regard to the organization and their roles. The HR department could use an "emotion monitoring" app, where employees must select an icon that best represents their current emotion; if done regularly, issues could be resolved before they get worse. If a large portion of employees are constantly unhappy, this signals managers that there is an underlying problem that requires immediate attention. Applications could also be used to show recognition and appreciation for employees' achievements, especially in large organizations, where there tends to be a divide between top management and employees, making individuals feel invisible and unappreciated. The importance of recognition is emphasized by Abraham Maslow's hierarchy of needs. Assuming deficiency needs are met (physiological and safety), growth needs (belonging, esteem, self-actualization) will need to be met in order to enhance the individual's development and well-being. Globoforce Mobile (www.globoforce.com) is an application that allows managers to announce an individual's achievements to the rest of the company, praising them for the efforts and reminding them that they are an important asset for the company. With this app, employees can also claim "eRewards," which could be used to purchase items from any retailer, thus overall providing both monetary and nonmonetary incentives. Being recognized and appreciated by the management team for their contribution toward the company's success inspires a high level of motivation for employees, which could lead to an increase in productivity, higher retention rates, and reduce costs relating to inattentiveness (e.g., poor customer service).

Applications are proving to be an excellent, cost-effective asset to businesses of all sizes, as they improve communication within the firm, enhance team and individual performance, and are also useful in motivating employees by acting as a medium for the management team to show their recognition and appreciation for employees' efforts. However, individuals should also take into consideration the disadvantages of using apps, such as the possibility of them becoming a distraction, and take the necessary precautions to minimize the impact. Sensible and efficient use of applications in workplace environments could significantly increase employee well-being, managerial performance and, ultimately, overall productivity.

Knowledge Management

Organization is crucial for businesses as it directly impacts how structured a business operates. As well as organization, knowledge management focuses more so on information and both are integral parts of everyday business activities. If departments are badly organized, then it could lead to lower work efficiency. This is like personal employee organization, if employees are unaware of their current tasks, have cluttered work spaces, and have no structure to their job then it means they can not be doing their role to the best standard. Thankfully there are many apps that can aid an employee's organization and knowledge management. Google Drive and Dropbox are two similar apps that allow people to upload and share files with other people across the internet. Using cloud storage technology, users can even look at files on the go. This can streamline work processes as employees will be able to access work files at home and have the ability to edit them and send them back to their bosses. This helps improve knowledge management as employees can keep track of files on their devices and it allows them to share them among colleagues.

Wunderlist (www.wunderlist.com) and Evernote (https://evernote.com/) are two apps that both revolve around users organizing work tasks and creating lists.

These lists can be shared among groups and some users can delegate tasks to others. This is great as it allows employees to have more organization of their daily work activities. Tasks and lists can be sent online, which is really effective for employees working at home. Wunderlist and Evernote are also like another app called iJobber (www.ijobber.at). iJobber is more focused on time management on specific projects and allows the users to keep hold of statistics that they can export to a work calendar. Overall, these three apps can greatly increase knowledge management practices of an organization; they allow employees and managers to clearly see what tasks need to be done and who is doing them. When used appropriately these apps could also streamline other important areas of the business such as communication.

Information Management

Since the industrial revolution technology has been used to streamline and improve the efficiency of work processes using specific tools. With the invention of the internet, access to these tools has been elevated tenfold. As previously discussed, an example of such tools is apps; in this section, we will discuss how these apps can benefit the workplace in two specific areas, on work-related processes and increasing worker efficiency, as well as discussing why they can be superior to computer programs (their close substitute). Apps are useful for accessing information. There have been many apps developed for notes management, such as Google Drive. Not only can you scan important paper documents onto these apps, but they also sync up with other devices meaning if you have notes on your computer that you want to have access to on your phone you can instantly transfer them. Coupled with the internet, such apps allow anyone to access all the relevant work-related information with ease, which is much more manageable than having to sift through paper notes. In the discourse: "your mind is for having ideas, not holding them," Stephens and Allen (2013) talk about how trying to keep track of tasks while doing work hinders your productivity. As such, he argues, one way to maximize productivity is to not keep tabs on tasks in your head, instead of jotting them down to benefit from increased efficiency. This highlights the importance of task management to an individual's potency.

Again, apps are the most effective tool for this, programs like Google Calendar and to-do list help you keep track of activities on a daily, monthly and yearly level. Having this on your phone again makes it more accessible than jotting down such activities on paper. For example, let us say I am a manager in a production firm that wants to find out what combination of inputs gives the maximum amount of outputs given specific constraints. This work process can be done by hand, but this method is arduous and complicated. Instead, this process can be streamlined quicker with apps; in this instance, Edexcel solver is perfect for this as it has functions where one can input such constraints and find the maximum output. This can be done in several fields, the photoshop apps for designers, Mathtech for engineers, Epocrates for medicine, etc.

There are also the intangible effects of apps. Apps can help increase job satisfaction, in turn improving the individual's effort levels leading to better job performance. Literature has concluded that the following three factors lead to higher job satisfaction: relationships, knowledge sharing, and autonomy (Miller-Merrell, 2012). The proven principle that drives autonomy is the Bring Your Own Devices policy (BYOD). This allows each worker to bring their own customized device (specifically smartphones) to work. This gives the workers a choice, such as allowing them to choose the model of phone, which combination of apps to use, etc.—which can lead to higher motivations. If each person felt their own devices were supported by the company, they would likely want the company to succeed even more. What a BYOD policy does is allow people to tackle work-related problems with any number of combinations of apps at their disposal. This allows them to take their own initiative and, as such prove more effective as a worker. However, this assumes that the worker has some idea of the best apps or setting them up properly to do their job functions correctly. Furthermore, if effectively utilized, apps can transform phones into an engagement tool with the organization around them.

This can be done by setting up an internal social network within the company, to connect everyone from CEOs to lower level employees. Microsoft uses such a strategy with their internal blog "Microsoft SharePoint." After beta-testing the application the company CEO had this to say: "Employee feedback from the beta testing was extremely positive, as employees developed deeper relationships with their fellow employees, increasing their satisfaction with the company culture and work environments" (Miller-Merrell, 2012, p. 4). As seen by this, not only will relationships with peers be strengthened, but also those with superiors. This, in turn, can increase motivations of the individual to work harder and become more productive.

Apps on smartphones will expand knowledge sharing to a significant degree. Using aforementioned internal networks as apps can boost the amount of total information available to the entire company, allowing employees from all levels to distribute knowledge among themselves with ease. An example of this can be seen with General Electric's internal network that contains a massive amount of field experts answering all questions placed on the network about work. Such knowledge sharing means every worker is equipped with the same amount of "human capital" (knowledge) at any given time, increasing the total company's productive capacity. An important note to think about is how accessing apps using your phones is more advantageous than using similar programs on company computers. Add to the fact that people tend to carry their phones with them; using apps on mobile devices provides an enhanced level of convenience compared to computers.

Also, consider that more and more companies are implementing Bring Your Own Device (BYOD) policies, depending on the nature of jobs. The definition is in the name; companies allow workers to bring their own devices into work. Not only does this provide reduced expenses (the firm does not need to provide any technology) but people were more pleased with the situation. (In the United States, if the company has a BYOD policy, they have strict rules and can have liability and compensation issues as well as HR issues.) This is shown in the case of Ford Motor Ltd., who has implemented this policy in twenty different countries. Randy Nunez, senior network engineer had this to say about why their policy was met with appreciation: "people want to be able to use it in the way they want to use it. They have certain preferences around either virtual keyboard versus a hard keyboard, for example" (Torode, 2011). It seems that people have preferences in software and hardware that they have, in purchasing and customizing their phones, have inadvertently integrated with their devices. This makes them better for individuals compared to company computers, which tend to have less opportunity for personalization.

The last point to think about regarding phone use versus computers in the workplace is the design and affordability of apps. The most successful apps have been designed for ease of use, having a simpler interface than what is typically seen in equivalent computer programs. This makes using the apps have a lower barrier to entry than aforementioned computer programs, which means the managers can spend less time trying to get newer employees up to speed on how to use some of the broadly used programs the firm uses. Also, apps tend to be more affordable than their substitute on the computer; for example, look no further than the Microsoft Office programs, whereas similar in function apps can be found online for free or much cheaper. This, in turn, means fewer expenses on the company's behalf.

Task Management

The use of applications has increased over the years and platforms, such as Google Play Store and Apple App Store, have allowed consumers to conveniently discover new applications for different purposes and download them to their devices. This convenience has been transferred to the workplace environment, where day-to-day business tasks can be completed more efficiently, by replacing traditional methods with the use of applications. Companies that require monitoring the progress of tasks and duties may find that observing the progress of individual activities is difficult, when exposed to several tasks occurring at the same time. The adoption of a task management application can simplify tasks into segments and eliminate the need to go through several e-mails to find individual tasks. Consequently, many companies have a group of required applications and a selection of others recommended.

Managers and employees can benefit from a task management application such as Trello (www.trello.com) (Tatley, 2017), which allows users to see on-going tasks on a single dashboard, rather than traditionally having to go through each e-mail to locate each task. Launched at the end of 2011 the app now has just over 10 million regular users. The application mimics a Kanban board, where each task is organized into new, pending, and finished, helping employees to easily identify the progress of tasks. Like a Kanban system, employees can leave notes and create checklists, and unlike a traditional Kanban board, the application enables employees to upload files to the card. Essentially, an application can take the basic frameworks of a familiar management tool and enhance its capabilities further. The Trello application is a perfect example; having the Kanban like system at close proximity on a device, enables managers and employees to view tasks anytime and anywhere. Whenever tasks are complete, employees can sign them off through the application, which will also notify employees joined to the group, keeping everyone updated with the progress of tasks. Likewise, notifications on employees' devices can be enabled to alert when new tasks are added or tasks are approaching their deadline. All these additions are only capable through an application and could not be done through a traditional Kanban board.

The benefit of this app is that it keeps everyone within the project group informed on developments with the project while allowing a medium to comment on proposed changes. The ability for everyone to communicate complex and subjective opinions on different areas of a task in a medium where body language cues are less important can lead to a more open and democratic communication process than could be achieved in an office-based environment. For employers, the use of an application such as Trello can provide a solution to the Control-Commitment Dilemma, as employees can be easily monitored and evaluated based on their input within the project group. As all the information is stored in one location, monitoring and evaluating costs will be low and will not be seen as obtrusive which could lower employee trust. Finally, the end-to-end encryption that is provided with the application will ensure that the company's sensitive data is secured. Employees working remotely will reduce office overcrowding, which can allow companies to save considerable fixed costs on expensive office space. There is a danger, however, that employees can become disconnected from the company's organizational culture when working remotely, so using applications such as Trello to communicate the firm's ongoing goals and values is an invaluable tool to maintain company alignment.

Scheduling

Scheduling within a business is a key factor, and the use of mobile applications can help ease the process. A common issue faced by managers is the ability to arrange a meeting with a group of employees. Traditional methods require managers to e-mail employees regarding their availability, to formulate a suitable time for all. This back-and-forth task of e-mailing can be considered as a time-consuming process. By integrating a scheduling application such as Office, managers can request employees to submit their available times through their devices (Wagner, 2013), to automatically narrow down results and generate an optimal time. This benefits managers because of major time reductions.

Easy Access to Real-Time Data

Companies are developing their own applications, to incorporate real-time inventory data into a mobile application (Kosir, 2016). This is integrated with the device's camera to allow the employee to search for an item's details through scanning its QR code, eliminating time spent on searching. These applications allow access to information regarding the product's inventory level, location, and delivery dates. Such key information can be accessed by any employee and enables improved customer focus, since customer queries can be dealt with by lower level staff, who have the application installed. This results in faster response times to customer queries which concern product information and locations. The use of financial data can assist managers in making better, informed decisions. However, in most cases such financial data are stored on computer databases and can be a time-consuming process to access, hence may discourage the use of financial information in decisions. The benefit of having data on a mobile application, will encourage managers to use financial information in all aspects of decision making. For example, an app like Power BI can be used by a manager to regularly check the company's cash flow, enabling them to highlight potential problems arising before they occur.

Work Flexibility

The advancements in technology have allowed the capabilities of mobile phones and tablets to carry out similar tasks that computers can do. More specifically, applications such as Citrix (www.citrix.com) (Bianco, 2016) allow mobile and tablet holders to mirror their computer desktop to their phone or tablet anywhere, if internet access is available. This combined with communicational applications such as Skype—a video conferencing application (www.skype.com), can introduce flexibility in work processes to allow employees to work from home, which can pose benefits for both employers and employees. The flexibility will enable employees to better balance their work life with their home life, and gives them more autonomy to decide their own hours when working toward company deadlines. The increased level of responsibility will result in greater intrinsic motivation; hence productivity is likely to increase, benefiting the employer. This can be explained by research carried out by Staples, which revealed that employees who work from home, tend to be "happier, healthier and do better work" and also discovered that 80% of employees' satisfaction is improved as they obtained a better balance between work life and home life (Conosco, 2015).

Furthermore, a mobile workforce working from home can eliminate the number of absences. It can also help a business reduce operating costs associated with running offices, as less space may be required (Conosco, 2015). Costs of electricity, heating and rent can be greatly reduced if employees are working from home and consequently employees can reduce their commuting costs (mostly when using computer-based applications). *Mobile and tablet applications have completely changed the way in which businesses carry out their day-to-day tasks. They have provided an efficient way to help cut down complex tasks which were before time consuming to complete. With millions of applications available, there is bound to be an existing application to assist any business, either small or large.*

Teams

Team coordination depends upon a manager coordinating the team rather than controlling the team. This is because the output of a group of individual workers does not depend solely upon the sum of their individual inputs such as effort. The inputs are complementary rather than separate (Alchian and Demsetz, 1972; Pugh, 1988; Roberts, 2004; Williamson, 1985). Hence, apps that can help coordinate teams are extremely useful within the workplace. A new application called Slack (https://slack.com/) excels in this region; it allows teams to chat in channels, which are further divided into subjects. Hence, coordination is much easier, as projects can be broken down into sections. For example, one chat subject could focus on new ideas where a resource investigator would excel, whereas another channel could focus on the strategy needed to complete parts of the project where an implementer would excel. This division of chats allows individuals to give their full potential to overall output and allows easier coordination through breaking down stages of work within the team and can show what stage in the Team Formation theory by Tuckman the group is in.

Further, we see that these apps aid in moving from stage to stage, apps mentioned before such as WhatsApp and Facebook messenger allow new teammates to communicate more frequently, which can reveal key traits about each member, for example, a dominant speaker who likes to take control and a potential shirker who does not contribute much and is absent in most early discussions. This increased cohesion can speed up the forming stage and give clarity to roles for each member. Through more communication, members become more comfortable and open with one another, which is key for making it past the storming stage where potential conflict can occur.

Living in an era of globalization, with businesses shifting from centralized organizations to decentralized ones with departments sometimes in separate countries, coordination is more important than ever. It is essential that departments align their efforts in order to achieve a common goal. A lack of coordination and the difficulties that follow this, arise from a lack of shared knowledge. Therefore, apps that allow individuals to share information should help to eliminate this problem. One such app is PingPong, which allows users to share reference material and create questions that team members can respond to during a team discussion, to ensure that everyone is on the right track. Team performance could also be significantly improved and individuals encouraged to work as a cohesive unit toward their common goal. Applications such as Evernote allow individuals to connect their work with their team members, so that everyone in the group can submit, view, and edit documents in real-time, on the same platform. This means team members can always stay connected, contribute, discuss the work, and suggest improvements. Such applications also encourage innovation and creativity as they provide a good environment for brainstorming and very often with groups, one person's idea may trigger comments and new ideas from the rest of the team, which yields the best results. Furthermore, it is important to appoint a monitor (a superior) when work is done in teams, to ensure every team member contributes to the tasks. Applications can simply perform the monitor's job as it is much easier to observe individual contribution when all the work is submitted on the same platform, thus helping to prevent social loafing.

Teamweek (https://app.teamweek.com/) is a project management app that allows employees to create and schedule projects and tasks. At Kleurvision

Inc (graphic design and web specialist company), employees use Teamweek as a simple way to track events and long-term progression as well as for planning strategy and collecting team feedback. Employee work-life balance may be improved through using Teamweek in a number of ways; it allows for better organization and time management, which means employees can manage their schedules more effectively to ensure that tasks are being completed, but also so that time outside of work is clearly identifiable so they can schedule personal time for themselves. Teamweek also highlights who is responsible for certain aspects of a task, identifying responsibility, increasing clarity and therefore reducing stress for the employees. Furthermore, the increase in globalization in the past few decades has led to large firms, to have groups of employees working together across multiple continents, forming virtual teams. Mikkola et al. (2005) discuss the greatest impediment to the effectiveness of virtual teams being the implementation of technology. Furst et al. (2004) suggest that consequently, virtual teams should choose appropriate technology based on the type of interaction. Subsequently, with new era of mobile apps, firms have a greater choice over which technologies can increase the effectiveness of teams. For instance, with the range of file sharing apps available, members of teams have more accessibility to files and can work on files from any location they choose.

However, a main drawback to a large degree of information sharing could be security risks. Enterprises may find it hard to monitor apps and protect devices from malicious downloads (Thomas-Aguilar, 2015). The risk is made even greater with many mobile apps using cloud-backed services. As a consequence, firms may restrict the amount of information available to mobile devices; less information having a corresponding decrease on productivity.

Work Design

There are two meanings to the term technology; "material technology," which are the physical components, that is, tools and machinery. In addition, there is "social technology," which are the methods that order the behavior and relationships of people in systematic, purposive ways through structures of coordination, control, motivation, and reward. With regard to smartphone and tablet technologies, many apps can be related to both meanings of technologies as many people can interact with the app in a physical manner, but also it can play a role in communicating information to users. The first benefit associated with app technologies can be identified in affiliation with "material technology." The physical components of technology can greatly improve work design for employees. For example, 63% of people who use apps at work are much happier due to the time-saving qualities associated with such technologies (Statista, 2016). Furthermore, some of these benefits include effective task management, and the ability for employees to work on-the-go. A real-life example of how companies can use app technologies can be identified within Apple's buying process. Employees are actively on-the-move with hand-held devices throughout the store, which allows the execution of payment for products. This has the benefit of not only increasing employee performance but also, economically generating more sales at busier times.

LA Law Ltd. is a personal injury firm situated in Brighton, which is in the process of creating an app specifically designed to streamline work processes. The app will allow clients to access up-to-date case updates as well as allowing paperwork to be e-signed from a smartphone or tablet rather than sending it via post. This should dramatically decrease the volume of calls the First Response Team receive as clients can access the information they require on the phone at the touch of a button. For LA Law Ltd. this will be very useful for the workplace environment as case handlers can focus on running cases rather than updating clients. The creation of the app for small businesses is just as significant as for larger corporations, as is demonstrated by the small firm example just described. Apps are also being used by firms to help with project management tasks; *Asana* is an example of such an app, used by corporations such as Intel and Samsung. The purpose of this app is to delegate tasks, reduce internal e-mails and monitor the progress of projects from a central dashboard. Traditionally, these tasks would be completed manually by potentially multiple members of staff, requiring vast amounts of time. One of the benefits of adopting an app to complete such tasks is that it increases accessibility; a central dashboard means anybody can view information regarding the project. Employees can also be assigned tasks and communication can be completed through the app. Overall, this is likely to increase productivity within the firm and is likely to result in projects being completed successfully, due to the scope of human error occurring being reduced, while simultaneously having a greater degree of organization within the firm.

Business Process Reengineering

The "McDonaldization" thesis proclaims to affect social and organizational lives. Originally the argument was a reflection upon the fast-food restaurant giant McDonald's, however, the same principles can be translated to other organizations, for example, Apple, adopting similar aims. Considering this thesis, there are four key elements: efficiency, calculability, predictability, and control, which all apps deliver. All of these features act as secondary benefits to a system that is standardized and routinely carried out. With developments in smartphones and tablets, come new possibilities of efficiency for areas of the workplace. By focusing on a process, a specific horizontal or vertical organizational system that incorporates similar activities, business processes reengineering (BPR) can bring improvement in terms of quality, cost, and satisfaction (Baron and Kreps, 1999; Prahalad and Hamel, 1990; Mintzberg, 1989; Chandler, 1962). BPR has numerous techniques; we will discuss the ways applications can streamline how a firm functions and how using these apps can enhance firm capabilities.

Whether the process is a formal, documented procedure or one more colloquial and unofficial, improvements can be made to ensure maximum efficiency for a company (Blau and Schoenherr, 1971; Penrose, 1959). Various stages of a workplace process can be targeted for development. Initially, mapping the process with the use of flowcharts and diagrams can help. Be it an app for creating flowcharts like Lucidchart (www.lucidchart.com) or more general apps for project management like KeyedIn Projects (www.keyedin.com), important jobs like scheduling or arranging priorities are made easier. The eventual familiarity that project teams will have by using apps to plan tasks can ensure consistency in their execution. Having a clear plan to refer back to means it is easy to identify and implement improvement solutions. Along with this, an easily accessible diagram or flowchart the whole team can view is likely to help the smooth operation of the rest of the process. Whereas hand producing and distributing a hard copy of the plan to all members of a team can be time consuming, having one on an app to revisit and edit prevents significant additional effort. However, it is important to note that the discipline of project management is one of the most published areas in business (in fact, the Project Management Institute's [PMI's] project management certification is one of the most successful book areas). Therefore, the project management process is quite uniform.

Following this, analyzing and redesigning the process is useful for firms. With emerging markets and turbulent business environments, firms must adapt to stay competitive. Making changes in response to customer feedback can provide companies with the ability to stay prominent in the market. A survey has shown 41% of retail firms who took part use apps for customer surveys (Statista, 2016). The convenience of answering feedback questions by your mobile phone results in a higher volume of responses and, therefore, more constructive criticism. The benefits of this can be seen in firms who adapt accordingly to these surveys, guaranteeing them customer satisfaction and loyal customers. The future revenue of a company can be secured if high levels of customer satisfaction are maintained. However, this is assuming the public do in fact use mobile apps to complete customer feedback questionnaires. Just because a large number of firms offer the service does not necessarily mean many customers provide them with responses.

Firms may have to seek feedback in other ways so they can adapt and improve what they offer.

Aside from the need for work tasks to be perfectly organized, the different types of systems in organizations can be separated and addressed (Prahalad and Hamel, 1990). An aspect of businesses that requires attention of managers is communication. Whether between departments or employee to manager, sharing knowledge effectively is another way of confirming competitive advantage. The interactions of workers within a company occur more frequently than those between companies, so inside a firm divisions and departments can grow and learn from the experience of others. One way of assuring the communication of employees is a work e-mail account. Having the mail app on smartphones and tablets lets employees quickly access work e-mails. Different speeds of communication in a business inhibits the development of mutual knowledge, therefore, providing employees with a common method of e-mailing is a way of prevention and increases horizontal and cross functional knowledge sharing. Apps for e-mails can be downloaded onto home devices such as iPads, meaning important mail can be reached at home. However, the efficiency of communication may not necessarily improve because many factors, including home schedules, part-time work at a second job, laziness of employees, and so on, may still affect the speed of contact. Also, having an app accessible by home devices for e-mail can disrupt the work-life balance, a topic we will discuss further, limiting any benefits to the company.

The evolution of computers has made once handwritten accounting possible on automated machines. Now, with apps that contain various calculators, tax tables, and currency converters, accountants can achieve optimal results. Popular apps QuickBooks (https://quickbooks.intuit.com) and Sage (www.sage.com) assist in dealing with operations in numerous currencies and market types. All size firms rely heavily on a finance department, therefore, if the quality of work performed here is maximized, the rest of the firm is more likely to thrive. At the top of many businesses' aims is putting clients first and satisfying their needs, incorporating apps into the process can have positive effects to their experience as client to advisor relationships will be reinforced.

The rise of apps extends further than the general market, as many companies now use applications in their day-to-day running of the business. A prime example of this is U.K. Shoe retailer, Clarks. In 2015 Clarks started using their new method of measuring children's feet, which involved a mechanical device that holds the iPad, loaded with their new Clarks app. The app features cartoon characters, which aim to guide the children through the process, and distract them from the usually trivial task of staying still and patient when having their feet measured. The iPad foot measuring system has won several industry awards. These have cited the device's success at holding a child's attention (BBC, 2015).

Not only does the app succeed in this respect, the addition of the technology has streamlined their work process in several ways.

Consequently, the use of the app means that the foot data can be collected and analyzed, building a more accurate sizing system for the future (Pocket-Lint, 2014). This data will allow Clarks to generate a precise range of sizes, as the app records the measured sizes so that surveys and samples no longer have to be taken in order to gain an understanding of the range of shoe sizes in a particular country or region. Clarks now operate in over thirty-five countries around the world (Clarks, 2018), with varying size trends across the globe, so this information will save Clarks valuable time and money in this sense. In addition to this the Clarks app, complete with iPad and gauge, gives a much more accurate measurement of the size of the foot, as it does not rely on the naked eye. The benefits of using this technology are clear to see, as Clarks have been able to increase the efficiency of their service, while constantly collecting information for their database of foot sizes and typing. Other than Clarks, many companies are using mobile applications in the workplace, and the most popular use cases of mobile business apps are inspections, work orders, checklists, and surveys—all of which can be applied to several different industries including construction, retail, and health care.

HR Management

Apps have also been adopted by HR departments by firms to streamline the recruitment process. One example can be seen with Royal Bank of Scotland (RBS) who have developed a game in the form of an app to gauge the skills of potential graduate hires. One distinct benefit of this is the potential to attract a diverse range of high caliber applicants; graduates are accustomed to one process that follows traditional testing and interviews. This unique approach may attract a greater variety of applicants due to the distinct process; one which may seem less intense in comparison to others, thus, meaning the firm gains competitive advantage over competitors. Also, the incorporation of apps represents a saved opportunity cost; the time that would have been invested in personally interviewing candidates has been significantly reduced through viewing the results of a game. Thus, the time saved can be used by staff elsewhere within the business, bringing potential benefits in both the short term and long term.

The use of an app such as ShiftPlanning (www.shifo.global) can allow a company to manage employee shift scheduling, time clock, and attendance and specific HR documents. The ability for management to place this information in a singular piece of software, which can be remotely accessed by all employees greatly reduces instances of control loss or coordination loss within a company. Sharing information such as shift scheduling in an open space such as in Shift-Planning also allows employees the capacity to request extra work shifts or transfer work shifts between different employee's thereby encouraging autonomous work groups; this can benefit the company as it can increase employee satisfaction and reduce administration costs.

Controlling and Coordinating Employee Activities

We can categorize control into a limited range of tasks performed by standardized and uniformed employees. Firms have used apps in the twenty-first century more frequently to monitor and coordinate activities carried out by employees on a day-to-day basis, acting as a "control and coordinate mechanism." An example of a company that is participating in such technology is the plumbing and heating merchants—"Brennan and Son." They use an app called Commusoft that not only manages jobs in the diary, but also assists with customer relations. This form of data monitoring brings many positives to managers including; allowing the effective processing of real-time data quickly and at a low cost. Although, in today's world, we identify this form of technology to be in use throughout many firms' business processes, back in the mid-twentieth century, Braverman published a work, which proclaimed that managers would use scientific management as a key method to directly control their employees. This is more commonly known as the "Braverman thesis." He had identified that the introduction of new technologies in the workplace would have profound effects such as "reducing workers' autonomy" and "decreasing laborer's discretion in performing jobs." Much like the example outlined earlier with regard to "Brennan and Son," organizational deskilling involves workers not being required to plan journeys, but instead an automated computerized application preempts the route beforehand.

Apps are greatly diversified and many are suitable for helping to improve work processes. Skype, for example, enables team members to have group video meetings online on their tablet or phone as well as the PC and this enables a huge amount of flexibility in the work place. If team members are assigned a project to complete, Skype can immediately remove the cost to teams of "coordination costs." If colleagues are limited geographically, Skype removes the need to coordinate on where meetings must take place, which can save monetary costs with regard to the cost of travelling, but also the more significant opportunity cost. The opportunity cost is far more difficult to measure, as data, which is not quantifiable such as time and motivation, must be measured. Therefore, these benefits of increased ease of communication and coordination affect nearly all workers in a national or international organization.

Furthermore, applications such as Google Drive also enhance processes within the workplace environment. If a group needs to deliver a presentation to a potential client, then the presentation could be worked on by uploading it to Google Drive. This would enable colleagues to work together on the presentation, simultaneously and or sequentially. Progress is displayed by member's work being highlighted in a color relating to a different teammate meaning the rest of the team can see each other's progress. This may also have another advantage as the "Hawthorne Theory" is utilized in this case (Baron and Kreps, 1999). This is the theory that workers may perform better or worse due to being observed. Thus, the fact that workers are being monitored by their colleagues while using app brings this theory into play causing either positive or negatives effects. However, this app may actually also tackle the other issue of "shirking." This is where members may relax and their output decreases, as they believe that other team members are making sufficient progress so that they need not contribute as much. However, shirking can be tackled if all team members agree to not shirk and so no output would be lost. The Google Drive app would aid this because as mentioned above, all progress of members will be monitored and thus anyone who does break this promise could be identified and removed from the team. This app is, therefore, promoting symmetrical information between colleagues. In addition to this effect, there is the apparent purpose of the app which is to enable workers to be able to be flexible with their work and adapt what they are writing based upon what others have already written. This can save time, as no one would write the same thing twice as they would know what is necessary for their section.

The biggest problem with Google Drive is with regard to Hawthorne theory. Hawthorne says that if individuals are subject to observation, then they will change their behavior. However, this depends on the individual whether it will be a positive or negative change. So, there is a significant risk that individuals working on the app may change their behavior for the worse. For example, an individual may begin to type rapidly or just stop entirely as they may become nervous if a teammate is just watching them work. Thus, it is a gamble whether this will be a good or bad change. The process of selection is one of the challenges, which teams have to deal with whenever they need to hire new people. LinkedIn is known for being a pool where professionals can display their credentials in the hope that employers will identify them and shortlist them for potential employees. If teams who are hiring individuals can effectively manage this app and process, then the cost of hiring is reduced. This app thus decreases the costs of working in teams, as selection is a team process. This can then lead to reductions of other costs if used correctly. Conflict in teams and risk seeking can also be selected via the careful use of this app. Assuming a potential employee is very transparent on their page, then a manager will be able to make the most informed decision about a new worker as they will know more about what they are likely to be like. For example, if an investment bank was hiring a new broker, shortlisting those who are slightly more risk averse might be an effective idea for them, and the use of this app can help tailor the HR team to understand exactly what their candidate requires to succeed.

Furthermore, when a team is being created, an ideal team would cover a range of skill sets so that there are no real weaknesses leading to a balanced team. LinkedIn would also be helpful as individuals would be potentially hired due to their listed skill set. For instance, if one of Belbin's team roles was required (Belbin, 2012), then a manager might actively be looking for a "specialist" with lots of prior experience in the area where a project might be aimed at, hence, this would streamline the work. Despite this app making work processes seemingly easier, it would be a large risk for a manager to hire someone based purely on LinkedIn and this would still not save the time that a real face to face interview would take up. Therefore, this app only streamlines the work process to a certain extent and it can not be used for the whole system, which is a limitation of this app in the working environment. Furthermore, this app is very expensive and would only be suitable in large corporations due to their need to hire more individuals.

Control and coordination aspects are also improved by the use of messaging apps such as texting and Facebook. Facebook can to a certain extent also remove monitoring costs because employers are able to have their employees on Facebook, their progress can thus be tracked more effectively. This can be used to ensure that employees align with the company's values. For example, it could be necessary for a company to check that its employees were not displaying racist behavior on their profiles. If they wrote inappropriate posts then the individual would be associated with the company they work for, which would lead to bad publicity. Furthermore, any rational company would not want this type of behavior in their company so would be able to dismiss any employee whose views were extreme or deemed inappropriate. In addition, texting and Facebook Messenger can be used by managers to communicate with the team more effectively and this adds flexibility to work processes. Furthermore, this promotes clarity in the work place, as this functions as a faster e-mail and managers can get more updated information.

There are drawbacks to monitoring on Facebook, however, namely the controversial argument of privacy. This assumes that trust within the organization's culture itself is insufficient to be able to ensure everyone is behaving appropriately. Therefore, employees may feel alienated and anxious if their activities are also measured on social media, which could lead to dissatisfied workers and tension in the work place; both of which would be detrimental to output and welfare. However, in some companies, culture is built with respected boundaries and trust. It would then be difficult to uniformly measure workers' activities as companies vary in the trust they place in their employees. In conclusion, apps are greatly diversified and generally significantly bolster productivity throughout various workplaces. There are some drawbacks that can be related to them, though these are insignificantly compared to the added output potential they can provide. Technological progress is one of the fundamental ways that economies increase their output, and thus apps help to boost the principal ideas of management of control and coordination and, therefore, they are incredibly beneficial. The biggest constraint on apps is on social media regarding the ever-controversial debate of privacy. Despite this and the temptations distracting social media, apps have a huge positive effect on work and will continue to make work easier for workers worldwide.

Communication

Communication is a big problem in many organizations; but new technology is also radically changing the patterns of communication (Fliplet, 2016). There are many examples in the modern workplace of how technology is being used to facilitate the communication process, for example, e-mails and intranets. However, with the adoption of "apps" companies can streamline workplace communications even more easily. One illustration of how a firm is able to increase efficiency even more, can be seen from many organizations' personalized apps. Unlike most generic apps that are targeted at consumers, these apps deliver differing functions comprised of e-mails, company magazines, and bulletin boards (wikis) along with many other useful links. The overall aim of this type of communication process is to allow members to gain relevant information quickly and effectively without having to establish an internet connection each time. Additionally, linking back to our discussion of work design it also allows access no matter where, both day and night. On the other hand, organizations may have invested in technological applications but if the "app" is not easy to use or many employees are not interested in the operation, then ultimately it would be a waste of resources and time. Therefore, to ensure that smartphone and tablet technologies are well received, organizations need to recognize some possible factors for consideration; by building alliances across the organization to support initiatives and by recognizing that no one method will be entirely effective.

One of the first communication apps used, after e-mail, was instant messaging (IM)—the real-time communication between users sharing the same network. Since then, however, there has been much more development and improvement. One such development, is Slack, an application used for not only messaging, but also group chats, and document-sharing. One of Slack's many users is the online fashion retailer, Zappos, where approximately two-thirds of its employees have chosen to install it. In a manner similar to many communication apps, Slack syncs all information across the multiple devices that may be attached to the network. The use of technology within communication can streamline the process, making it more efficient and allowing employers to be more productive. For instance, it can reduce filtering because communication is more direct, with fewer intermediaries and vertical levels, leading to less manipulation of information. The group chat element allows for virtual teams to be set up, increasing efficiency with the digital delegating of tasks and sharing of information.

Embracing the digital workplace and using apps is an effective way to enhance the three key factors of productivity, customer satisfaction and sales, while cutting costs to improve the efficiency of an organization. There are numerous apps on the market, which allow companies to make group discussion boards and polls for collaborative decision making for improved communication, which are utilized by many organizations. Apps that integrate message boards or e-mail accounts are also a better way to share business concerns and any arising issues with other employees with instant messages for individuals or selective groups. Companies are additionally using apps to communicate with their customers, with mobile versions of their website with optimized interfaces and faster loading times to effectively address customer satisfaction.

WebEx (www.webex.com) is a video conferencing app that allows users to deliver presentations online. The app has a very large focus on businesses and has many other uses such as an online training center and event center. This app can drastically improve the company's communication, allowing employees to carry out meetings and conferences at any location. Skype is another useful app for communication, which is like WebEx as both allow users to talk and see one another. Although the focus is not necessarily corporate which means there are less features geared toward businesses, Skype is one of the biggest apps with total users spending more than 2 billion minutes a day using it. WebEx is slow and lines are as likely to be bad as they are on Skype. But you can also phone someone on Skype at fraction of the cost of an international call. These apps can streamline other work processes besides communication as it can also aid teamwork within the business.

Monitoring

In the digital age, we are becoming more and more reliant on technology and our workplace is no exception. Each day several applications are created in order to improve the effectiveness or the comfort in our workplace environment. Big companies like Apple, General Electric, and Deloitte are implementing the use of the apps and encourage their employees to make use of them to streamline their work processes. Companies are now big and spread out and have numerous offices all around the world and coordination can sometimes be difficult, but modern applications help employees keep track of everything around them from their smartphones.

Organizations lack information on the true effort of workers, hence, a degree of asymmetric information persists. As a consequence, to encourage more optimal behavior from employees, an organization must provide motives for workers to act in the interest of the organization. It is rational for workers to increase their effort if they know their input is being monitored. In other words, an organization's expected profit can exhibit increasing gross returns from monitoring systems. A large proportion of employees are now using information and communication technology (ICT) to do their work, it has meant that firms can now use ICT to monitor work. The introduction of enterprise apps into the workplace, has led firms to possess a greater amount of IT. Therefore, as a manager, you can monitor a greater amount of the workforce; as a consequence, employees have a greater motive to increase their effort. For example, technology has enabled users to increase the productiveness of personnel by simplifying the tasks they undertake through using various applications. Apps also make communication between staff much easier, since now everyone is just a click away. Instant access to files that we require allows workers to be able to be more mobile and be closer to work. Even simple reminders such as notifications that pop up on the phone can be extremely useful for employees who might have forgotten about something and are now guaranteed not to miss a deadline or a meeting. Monitoring is costly, since it takes both time and effort to observe the workers (*Wall Street Journal*, 2014).

ICT is an ideal solution to this since it allows for a "costless" observation. Apps are part of the ICT and allow companies to keep records of work processes inexpensively. They also allow the monitoring intensity to be maximized since applications are able to collect data all the time. This large amount of gathered data can then be analyzed easily and at a low cost, making it much more affordable than other methods of monitoring. It is also safe to assume that the cost of monitoring is continuously decreasing with the advance of technology and more and more applications are being launched each year. As a result, the amount of control organizations have over their employees increases.

"Under the right circumstances, monitoring can provide a plethora of positive results for employers" (Katz, 2015). Applications can help employers improve organization structure and even work out when their employees are most productive. It is common for companies to form groups based on the information they have acquired from monitoring their employees. If the organization knows that certain members do not get along, they do not team them up in group projects. Some firms also have been known to change working hours based on productiveness of their employees, information that was gathered through applications from which staff members submit their work electronically. Some apps are used in order to improve workplace safety. UPS vans monitor the seatbelt usage for their employees to be able to improve upon their safety. E-mail apps that are exclusive to the company (each worker has a company e-mail) have many times been used in order to monitor bad behavior among employees. In many cases, there have been cases of sexual harassment that have been discovered by intercepting e-mails from one employee to another, often resulting in the person harassing being relieved of duty, which helps increase workspace security and productivity. That said, managers should take care to ensure they do not rely too heavily on this method of monitoring, as it reduces the level of trust in an organization, and in turn can have negative consequences, one of which is a nonfavorable culture within the organization. As such, if they were able to incorporate an incentive system into the performance of apps it would be more sustainable.

In comparison to office-based workers, teleworkers often have a higher job satisfaction due to the flexibility and autonomy their jobs provide, it is often found that autonomy increased teleworker's gratification by decreasing work-family conflicts (Bailey and Kurland, 2002). Giving employees access to their documents from anywhere via the internet makes telecommuting easier. Using networked applications within a firm can contribute to the work and life balance of employees in various ways. Applications such as cloud computing and web-conferencing particularly work well for employees who choose to work at home and ease their home life by helping them to access, contribute, and connect with work instantly. Telecommuting often improves the workers' job satisfaction, work-life balance, and can even improve work-family conflict.

Training and Worker Skills

Most employees want to do good work; give them the proper tools, and they will succeed. This means clearly letting employees know what they are responsible and accountable for, communicating regularly with workers so everyone is on the same page, and developing opportunities for employees through training and education to better themselves both professionally and personally (Baron and Kreps, 1999). One of the main uses of applications that are being employed in order to make the work process easier are apps that are for training purposes. Perhaps the most common example is call centers where calls are being recorded in order to be used later to train new employees on how to deal with customers. The Lifesaver app is being used in many countries to help driving instructors teach their students first aid, which is a compulsory part of taking a driver's license in some countries. Companies also keep record of logs that are based off employees using different company apps. This is done to have proof if an organization is being sued or intends to sue the employee it has been monitoring.

Companies are also looking to external businesses to build specialized applications for their specific firm needs. Red Robin Gourmet Burgers is a medium-sized restaurant business with over 500 locations within the United States. In order to tackle high labor turnover, they commissioned Fliplet, an application building company, to design an interactive training app for new and existing employees. A specialized app such as this can help employees to further integrate themselves with the desired culture of the firm and, in a multilocation company, help to maintain strategic alignment of core company values and goals to deliver a homogenous service experience. The use of such training apps can also lead to increased efficiency as new employees will have greater access to training resources and will be able to adjust into the firm's working practices more smoothly.

SkillPill (www.skillpill.com) and Udemy (www.udemy.com) are widely recognizable apps for training purposes, the former aiding training in areas like sales, management and marketing and the latter offering a vast number of courses catering those wanting corporate training. Introducing these to the work environment lets employees continually develop and progress without long, expensive training programs. The additional training will increase the productivity of the workers in many ways. Economic theory describes how when training is received, the quality of the labor force is also increased, resulting in greater productive capacity and more physical units of production created. Another idea is that the extra attention to workers can make them feel more valued, which in turn makes them contribute more to the business, "give better service, and even stay in their jobs longer," again positively effecting the output of the firm. A high staff turnover rate is costly, time consuming and can waste resources. So, we can see how easy, cheaper methods of training reachable via apps can boost the potential of businesses and be worthwhile. Yet this depends on the employee's perception of such apps. They may feel the management does not trust their ability, or indirect monitoring is taking place to continually check if workers can perform to a satisfactory standard. Benefits of this training method are reliant on the compliance and expectance of the employees.

Tablets up to date with training software that firms can develop themselves or purchase externally can be distributed among employees to run training programs. This saves both time and money for businesses as they can distribute new information to employees in a simple format and can offer interactive tests on the tablets at the same time (an example of a firm that offers this is Mindflash). They offer their customizable learning programs to be accessed on smartphones with added features which would not be accessible on a PC. One such example is an augmented reality aspect when the camera can be aimed at a new tool for construction workers and the safety features will be highlighted. Apps will mean that businesses can take their training out of the office and will allow employees to top up their training when they are free. This should benefit businesses as employees will quickly and easily be able to refresh their training if needs be. Finally, cloud computing lessens the time to train employees and this is proving to have a positive impact on the bottom line figure of income statements of companies implementing cloud technologies. The ease of updating "apps" gives organizations competitive advantage since workers can be trained quicker and easier. The rises in profits and reductions in training time of workers is beneficial for companies.

On the other hand, companies face with difficulties while training employees who are not familiar with "apps." Organizations may need new experienced workers to train employees having problems with using cloud systems and provide solutions to the problems occurred by apps. Besides training employees to catch up with new technology, they might be struggling to use these technologies if the workers are inexperienced. Consequently, motivation of workers may decrease. An alternative is electronic books that offer deeper levels of content, cover virtually every topic imaginable, and are available for purchase (or on a license basis for organizations and libraries). They are more readily searchable than video or training content, far less rigid and limited in content, provide beginning to end coverage that will suit just about anyone's needs and are portable and downloadable on just about any device. Most corporations ignore this option but some like IBM and Oracle have their own presses; understanding that their customers need a deep understanding of topics that they sell.

Another challenge that workers face is with broadband. Although internet is widely available, there might be places where the workers may not able to access the internet connection. Cloud computing is a technology where users can access data via the internet. Losing internet connection can be a temporary problem; however, it still affects the users since they can not access their documents and share them with their colleagues. Thus, it can cause more serious problems than it seems. Mobile apps are an asset to businesses; a study by Accenture reveals that 82% of executives believe enterprise apps to be essential within their organization. In recent years, many management teams have chosen to use apps to deliver training programs to their employees. Apps can store videos and online questionnaires that allow training to be delivered whenever necessary and potentially from the comfort of the employee's home. Online training could be the simple answer to the problem of scheduling training days and ensuring employee attendance due to the busy nature of management and the restricted time available to deliver relevant training.

Health and Safety

Apps allow company employees to quickly access information that would otherwise take time to find answers to specific questions, whether it is having to either ask a colleague for or spend time pouring over books to find out. This can benefit firms in a number of ways. First, apps can be extremely beneficial from a health and safety perspective. There are numerous apps available, which can quickly tell someone information which could potentially save them from causing or being involved in an accident. One example is Chem Alert (https://rmtglobal.com/chemalert) that contains information about 120,000 different chemicals. This allows people to check the safety procedures, which need to be adhered to for chemicals without having to spend time finding it in books. A similar situation has occurred in hospitals where old fashioned pagers are facing competition from secure mobile applications, which can be used to offer specialized alerts between nurses and doctors. *Smartphone technology can be accessed anywhere and at any time without having to rely on physical space or the availability of other people.* This technology can also help the workforce to be used more efficiently and not be used for unnecessary reasons. For example, a security company in Boston found that troublemakers were disturbing one of their properties but with use of facial recognition software they could know how many guards were needed. The introduction of apps in workplaces such as these offers further examples of how apps can increase the speed of processes in the workplace but also improving health and safety features which are in place. This can help businesses to maintain the wellbeing and productivity of their employees.

Health and well-being, once a chore, is now considered a lifestyle. With "over two-thirds of US organizations offering wellness programs" (Valet, 2015), there is now a need to incorporate a technology-based solution into these programs (Lauby, 2013). Around "50 percent of employers use mobile apps to engage their employees in their health." GetHealth (gethealth.in), which has been adopted by organizations such as General Electric, gives employees the opportunity to engage in exercise contributing to an increased work life balance, while it lets employers monitor performance and track their return on investment (Gethealthapp, 2016). From increased exercise, employees will experience improved physical and mental wellbeing thus decreasing their risk of burnout and giving them greater satisfaction both in and out of their professional lives. Lowering burnout also decreases absenteeism and improves motivation, which is good for the organization, who will benefit from the increased productivity.

In summary, phone and tablet applications can be used by employees in a variety of ways, allowing the business to streamline multiple different key processes and generally perform better. However, it is important for employees to use the right apps and use them appropriately. Businesses should keep up to date with technological trends as apps are sure to change as time goes on. New updates will also become available to apps that can improve their quality but can also lead to temporary bugs which can hinder the apps usage. The way in which information is passed among apps and platforms can also change quite suddenly.

Strategy

Competition is often behind the failure of organizations, so an application that provides an analytics tool to deliver a valuable insight into the market is vital in maintaining market dominance. These tools can offer visibility into consumer behavior and market performance which will provide optimal business strategies for success. With the rise of mobile technologies and the "on demand economy" (Khaleeli, 2016), organizations use apps as their primary business model. Employees use business-end apps in companies like Uber (www.uber.com) and Deliveroo (www.deliveroo.com) to undertake their work. Through the app, Deliveroo employees can choose their work availability, manage their orders and interact with their superiors (Deliveroo, 2016). By promoting increased flexibility and independence, through elements such as no tangible office time, employees can fit "their work to their lifestyle" (Khaleeli, 2016) thus increasing efficiency and effectiveness in the company's business processes.

As businesses are becoming increasingly global, the demand for clear internal communication has never been greater. Companies are turning to applications in order to ensure that employees have access to real-time information to guarantee they are connected and well informed on daily activities within the company. These apps are especially constructive for employees working in project-based groups where relevant information can be posted, and read, in real time by select members of the project or group. In conclusion, mobile applications, or "apps," provide a huge range of benefits to companies. They help to increase productivity by saving time and resources, as they provide useful features, which are accessible in seconds to executives as well as general employees. In the case of Clarks shoe retailers, it is evident that apps have replaced an entire process of measuring a child's foot and brought it forward to the twenty-first century. Digital measurements provide a streamlined process for trained fitters to obtain the most precise measurement possible, while simultaneously helping Clarks to build a huge database of information. This is beneficial in their efforts to obtain as much data about their clientele as possible, while removing the time-consuming process of collecting this information through surveys of vague samples. Through discussing how businesses can also produce their own apps, it suggests that said apps have become a way for companies to promote added incentive and further their relationship with consumers.

For example, the use of loyalty apps, which give consumers the freedom to see their potential rewards quickly and easily, thus benefitting both parties. "Contact us" and general help features within a business' app also allows customers to efficiently find the answers they are looking for, as well as get in contact with the company with minimal effort. This also works around geological obstructions such as being in a different country or region to the business they wish to contact. However, "contact us" type features can be a way of collecting contact information for the seller but an imposition to the customer. These "services" now mostly prevent contact with a company representative of any kind; if you don't fit in to one of their categories, you are out of luck as you will be talking to their computer.

Some parties argue that there are downsides of using mobile app technology in the workplace, suggesting the fact that the use of technology can be addictive and a time-consuming way of communication and task operation (Athey and Ellison, 2014). These uses, however, can be prevented with the right employee education and simple precautions within the workplace. Add to that risk is the ill-behaved phone use and its monitoring and the resulting HR issues and the debate over whether there should be compensation for it. Overall, the use of app technology on mobiles and tablets outweigh the disadvantages and are becoming more fashionable each day. The easy handling of the apps, instant communication availability, and securing the delivery of important notifications are only some of the main reasons behind its success. Also, benefits of using a cloud-based platform for communication and task handling are undeniably major convincing factors that drive companies to resort to app technology.

Chapter 6
Apps and Performance Outcomes

Businesses today use apps to drive their productivity much as they capitalized on the invention of the transistor over seventy years ago. The current technological trend is the use of apps to increase productivity within work processes, largely due to wireless internet connectivity and reliability, with continued improvements foreseen in the future. For example, Ventola (2014) states that the use of apps to share information between medical staff in hospitals is becoming customary. The growth of cloud computing has enabled wireless access to data, offering greater productivity as documents can be located faster. Modern health services employ apps as they offer faster health care to patients, so survival rates increase due to the speed of information. Further examples of the use of apps to streamline work processes include iPresent (www.ipresent.com) and AlphaGuide (www.alphabet.com).

iPresent aims to create greater alignment between marketing and sales for optimized content, better customer engagement, and improved results. It instantly distributes the latest content into the hands of salespeople wherever they are in a fully customizable sales engagement app. The assumption is that feedback from sales and analytics will allow salespeople to measure performance and improve content for better customer engagement. AlphaGuide provides drivers and fleet managers all of the information they need for their business travel. App features include Corporate Car Sharing: customers can book and cancel vehicles in a few simple steps; Mileage Tracker: simple and precise tracking and reporting of vehicle mileage; Point of Interest: allows users to search for the nearest electric car (EV) charging stations and tire partners, using Global Positioning System (GPS). The benefits of these apps will be investigated later in the chapter, together with some drawbacks of these technologies in the workplace.

The modern era is known for many key developments in technology such as the smartphone and tablets. These new technologies allow businesses to gain many advantages. The business can save time, have greater access to information, improve communications, and offer greater benefits to their workforce. This chapter will discuss the benefits of mobile technologies that streamline the workplace environment and impact company performance. It is a subject that evolves quickly along with market demand and has potential effects on many businesses across multiple industries. Outcomes range from significant integration, accessibility, and many more operational aspects, including efficiency and effectiveness. Enterprise mobility has become a global trend with companies focusing on how they can improve key processes through the use of smartphones, tablets, and

DOI 10.1515/9781547400546-006

other mobile devices. Why make this transition? A survey carried out by Canvas in 2015 (383projects, 2015) showed that 81% of service sector organizations in the study demonstrated cost savings between $1,000 and $25,000 resulting from converting manual processes to mobile apps.

Productivity apps symbolize an important transition in the business management's worldview. The way many companies have embraced these apps signifies the strong consumer demand for these features, and their tangible, far-reaching benefits. This also potentially empowers employees as software designers are continually making efforts to turn digital apps into humane technology that reflects positive "post-tech" business transformation, including changes in talent, organizational structure, and products and services.

Productivity

The concept of increased speed of work processes leading to increased productivity is crucial in evolving and growing the business. It is often deemed very difficult to improve productivity in an organizational workforce. There are many incentive and motivation-based theories and schemes used to attain productivity improvements. However, the growth of apps has proven to do exactly that: it streamlines business workplace environments by essentially allowing employees to do more within their working hours. According to a report by *Training Journal* (Robert-Edomi, 2015), 63% of people who use apps at work say that their favorite mobile tools save them time (86 minutes a week), 39% state they enable them to stay on top of tasks, and 17% reveal these apps help to manage finances. If an employee can save almost an hour and a half a week, these minutes can be diverted toward other productive tasks within the organization, further benefiting the operating efficiency of the business.

Furthermore, task management apps are employees' favorite mobile tools, chosen by 44% of workplace app users. This is followed by travel apps (33%) and networking apps such as LinkedIn (26%). The ability and act of improving their own work may result in keenness and agility when responding to situations within the business. By introducing this technology into the workplace, businesses are not only improving and streamlining their own operations, but growing the skill set of their employees, undoubtedly an asset close to the heart of any organization seeking to succeed.

Productivity apps commonly have features like blocking out the sites that distract individuals most or locking them into the "good" work they should be doing. However, can they really achieve these goals? In other words, can apps save people from their tendency to procrastinate? A recent study focused on students taking online courses and investigated how antidistraction apps affect student performance (Patterson, 2018). The experiment separated 657 student subjects into three groups to test different software features that claim to boost focus. These include (1) a commitment device: the tool set a daily limit for time spent on distracting sites, (2) an alert tool: the tool caused a reminder to get back to work to pop up after 30 minutes of slacking, and (3) a distraction blocking tool: the tool blocked distracting sites for a set amount of time. The study tested the impact of these tools in a massive open online course (MOOC), and there was also a control group who had to rely only on good, old-fashioned willpower. The results showed that relative to students in the control group, students in the commitment device treatment spent 24% more time on coursework, submitted 27% more homework assignments, and were 40% more likely to complete the course. They also received course grades that were 0.29 standard deviations higher. On the other hand, outcomes for students in the alert and distraction blocking treatments were statistically indistinguishable from the control.

These findings suggest that productivity apps can achieve their promise of improving "focus" in performance related tasks but they must be designed based on some psychology principles. Dennison et al. (2013) presented four productivity apps that encourage focusing on higher-order writing skills and support cognitive load for use with secondary students. The apps were combined to provide teachers with a step-by-step technique for instructing students to write a quality expository paragraph. They found that technology and software applications can provide a means of academic support for students with disabilities.

There are a multitude of apps that aim to increase productivity within the workplace. Google Sheets, for example, offers the standard spreadsheet feature of condensing data and making sense of numbers. However, it also has a range of add-ons and preinstalled features that aid workers, such as its Explore Tool that automatically makes graphs and extracts insights from individual employee data (Guay, 2016). This makes normally time-consuming and effort-absorbing tasks, such as analyzing data and drawing up graphs easier and faster to accomplish. Other applications, such as Basecamp3 (https://basecamp.com) also work in a similar way to reduce workload by simplifying work processes and allowing for greater productivity. FocusList (focuslist.co) can help employees plan their day, dividing it into a series of timed tasks. It is much more than a to-do list; once users start work a countdown timer appears, encouraging them to follow the "Pomodoro Technique" of working in 25-minute sessions with 5-minute breaks in between. The goal is to keep their brain fresh and productive. Users can then review how much time they spent on each task and track their productivity over weeks and months. Omnifocus (https://www.omnigroup.com/omnifocus/) is a personal task manager and creates location awareness and places and so reinvents the to-do list beyond dates. It sends a reminder when users arrive at a particular location (Context feature helps to see what tasks users can do at work, at the grocery store, on the phone). It can also help to organize by person (if you need to do something for them or help them out).

One of the key motivators behind apps use is time. Data can be entered into a device and immediately sent to where it needs to go. Of course, this can be achieved on a computer or laptop, but the portability of smartphones and the customizability of apps has created a new dimension in the business environment. One such example is when wait staff at a restaurant take orders and input them directly into a mobile device through a particular app. Not only does the staff have a clear view of what is available on that particular day, but they can send the order straight through to the kitchen without having to waste time traveling there themselves. Some restaurants have taken mobile applications to the next level by fitting tables with their very own devices that can be used to order and pay for food. Hours (www.hourstimetracking.com) keeps track of user time in an easy and useful way (keeps a running list of timers that one can switch between with one tap). For example, with respect to accounting-related tasks, it quickly identifies mistakes and makes adjustments by simply dragging the start or end time of a time block. Users can even set a reminder to tell them when to start a timer or to stop one for their work, and adjust their time on their visual calendar.

The increasingly global nature of organizations, meaning new time zones and locations to accommodate, is opening up the workplace to increased after-hours access (Henricks, 2006). Cloud-based applications, such as the Google G Suite, offers a group of programs that can be accessed from anywhere and at any time (Google, 2016), promoting flexibility, no matter the device or location. Working in the cloud is a direct contributor to work-life balance, as global employees have the flexibility to collaborate on work whenever necessary, fitting it in around prior commitments. This collaboration also benefits the organization, as work can be reviewed and changed by multiple users simultaneously. With more people having access to shared documents and to contribute their ideas, the work is completed more quickly and at a higher quality, improving productivity (Salesforce, 2015).

Previously, the organization's intranet was the preferred method for internal communication (Fliplet, 2016), but applications such as Slack (www.slack.com) have altered this. Slack's adoption by organizations, including Lush and The Times, allows improved communication and increased efficiency. The Channel function, which can include public and private groups, allows all parties, internal and external, to converse via a live stream while also integrating other applications as needed, such as cloud-based applications Google Drive and Dropbox (a service that allows users to share files from their own computer or smartphone).

This reduces the need for daily face-to-face meetings and constant e-mails, thus saving time, promoting location flexibility, and adding to an improved work-life balance. Location flexibility is also improved with the adoption of video conferencing applications. Skype for Business (www.skype.com) is an example of a virtual conferencing application that allows up to 250 employees, located globally, to undertake virtual meetings without the need for business trips. Traveling for work can cause employees to experience fatigue, leading to depression and emotional distancing from family members (Espino et al., 2002), upsetting their work-life balance.

However, using applications like Skype or Zoom (www.zoom.uk) improve the work-life balance as employees can communicate effectively without wasting time or being tied to a particular location. Zoom fulfills many businesses' need for video conferencing while improving on areas that Slack can be lacking. Zoom provides high quality video and audio and even has an option to share a screen with presenter setting so one can show exactly what they want while keeping notes and memos off the screen. These factors also benefit the organization as improved communication translates to a more productive workforce, and location flexibility lessens travel-related expenses. Through the use of these tools, travel-related fatigue will also decrease giving employees more energy and motivation both within and beyond their work lives.

Managing time efficiently is something to strive for, especially in a business where time is a valuable resource. Employers promote time management applications to their workforce to encourage productivity both within and outside the work place. Google acquired the scheduling application Timeful for its employees in 2015 (Oreskovic, 2015). The app "notice[s] your scheduling behaviors and intelligently suggest[s] what time to undertake an activity" (Tweedie, 2014). This allows employees to organize their time more effectively, make them less susceptible to burnout and contributes to a better work-life balance. Organizationally, this is beneficial, as less burnout results in a happier and more productive workforce (Schawbel, 2015). Employers can suggest the use of apps such as Be Focused (https://xwavesoft.com) to help focus their employee's efforts on a task for a given amount of time; this limits procrastination via the use of nonwork related sites, such as games and social media, and it enforces intervals of productive work on a set task. The app then allows the employee to take allotted breaks, which enables them to refocus and reflect. The apps are not controlled by the employers, and they give workers control over their allotted work times and tasks. Once the settings are activated, however, the app ensures that it is not easy for the individual to quit (as all actions are recorded). These tasks can be of both a work and personal nature; the aim is to make the most out of their time and ensure they maintain routine and positive habits.

Companies now possess the technology and capacity to be productive in more interesting ways, and this can be seen in the vast number of productivity-tracking apps that are available. Employees are aware that time is scarce and, therefore, a good work-life balance can often be difficult to achieve if workers are stressed-out over the large number of tasks they have to complete. Chrometa (https://chrometa.com) acts as a personal timekeeper by tracking the time spent on applications. Recording application usage can determine where time is being utilized and identify any unproductive periods to encourage employees to use their time more efficiently so that they do not put undue pressure on themselves to work from home after office hours. Along with this, a good work-life balance can be put at risk if employees are overworked, so applications like Chrometa also allow and encourage individuals to take breaks they are entitled to. A minor issue with productivity trackers is that managers can use them to monitor employees unreasonably, causing them to feel a lack of privacy and that they are not trusted by their supervisors.

Portability

Another appeal of these apps is their portability. Along with mobility comes the increase in telecommuting and virtual offices. An advantage of telecommuting for the employer is that it can reduce operating costs by saving on facilities, such as office space, and potentially it can increase employee performance if implemented correctly. The successful execution of mobile computing can be assisted by apps. For example, the project-management app, Asana (https://asana.com) allows managers to supervise employees by tracking their progress and assigning tasks, as well as offering workers the opportunity to share files and respond to each other. Microsoft OneDrive lets employees transfer their data easily and more securely. Saving and transferring data through apps or applications such as these is instantaneous, and it also provides more security when transferring data than through memory sticks or physical paper copies, which can be lost or stolen. The secure and instant transfer of data makes many processes much more efficient. Also, although there are technical limitations with some apps, such as bugs, and the fact that they may not be able to do everything that you need, they are still an improvement over the alternative method of transferring documents and data.

There are also online app builders that allow businesses to create, launch, and maintain their own mobile apps. Bobile (https://bobile.com) is a prime example that allows companies to create their own app, requires no information technology (IT) skills, and provides a platform for sales, marketing, and internal communication. Salesforce, the customer relationship management company, conducted a survey on the use of apps in European workplaces that revealed enterprise apps boost employee productivity by an impressive 34% (Salesforce, 2015). With the increase in international workplaces, and the increase in the number of people working from home or remote locations, apps allow workers to be productive on the go with online collaboration (Salesforce, 2015). Additionally, employees can use their enterprise apps to book specific rooms, equipment, or company resources. This increases their efficiency and helps employees to organize their work, incentivizing them to remain prepared and be in a better position to achieve set goals and progress within the company.

One of the most time-consuming tasks for most organizations is handling paperwork. By utilizing the technology available today to scan and digitally share documents via apps, organizations can reduce the amount of paperwork required and lower their costs for printing and distribution. As a result, employee time is spent more effectively and assets are available to contribute to other organizational budgets or projects. It is also worth considering that this technology may reduce the risk of human error. Despite all of these benefits, some problems can arise from the adoption of these smartphone apps. Older employees, who are less likely to be as technologically minded as their younger counterparts, may lag behind in their adoption of new technology (Smith, 2014). In fact, they may be resistant to such change. This could cause them to spend time outside of work learning about this technology, thus disrupting their work-life balance by causing increased anxiety (Knapton, 2014). Stress levels may also rise with the pressure that results from time management apps (www.messenger.com). The feeling of being monitored can lead to demotivated staff whose work is rushed and, therefore, completed with lower quality. Work may also be completed at home in order to meet deadlines, thus impacting on their work-life balance.

Workplace Efficiency

It is worth mentioning that most apps share a common characteristic—their main goal is to take a very complicated task and simplify it though mobile functionality. This helps to speed up the processes of completing daily multipart tasks, such as store audits. During retail reviews, managers often have to check for the functioning of lights, floor cleanliness, or the state of numerous items related to the daily operations of the business. It takes time to remember, write down, and enter all these matters into a system. Mobile technology allows for use of electronic checklists that save information instantaneously and transfer it to the relevant departments. In effect, it will take only a few minutes to review the store operations via an app as opposed to the time it would take using paper methods.

Thus, significant time is saved, and it is worth noting that additional features can speed up other organizational aspects. However, any extra custom-designed functions might be quite expensive to develop. One way of mitigating these extra costs is to review and choose the most suitable off-the-shelf program that already has the necessary functions available. Taking all aspects into account, mobile technologies can extensively improve the handling of the administrative workload in commerce. Associated costs can easily be decreased while streamlining work processes is a major benefit.

One of the most important ideas of management practice is total quality management (TQM), which is a way of managing a business to increase its overall efficiency and effectiveness, through improved quality throughout all the business processes and operations. This allows businesses to have a competitive advantage over others. The use of technology and mobile e-commerce is a factor of TQM, and in Vox Cinema's case, they have applied this through their application. They have carried out business practices such as online booking and offering a loyalty program all within the app. They can also pre-order food, so that when they arrive it is ready for them, which is Vox's unique selling point. This gives the customers many benefits, such as being able to skip the queue when making a booking online. It also improves the quality of the service, a competitive advantage over other movie theaters, and therefore greater customer satisfaction. In addition, the loyalty program encourages and motivates customers to make repeated returns as they could get special benefits and offers, with the help of the app it is made even easier for them. The app also helps reach a larger target market through easier accessibility of the resources. This is in line with their vision which is to "Create great moments for everyone."

There are many other features in regard to increasing the quality of the service. One of them is that the app collects data on the bookings of movies that the user normally watches, then tries to tailor personalized recommendations when there are new releases with similar genres to the ones the user typically watches. The information overload theory states that increased customer satisfaction can be achieved when recommended content fits user interests (Liang, Lai and Ku, 2006). These recommendations can sometimes come in the form of push notifications, which are a fast and efficient way to communicate with customers. Push notifications can be beneficial, and different to online websites, as they can provide the customer with updates and reminders that get the audience to regularly engage with the brand even if they are not aware of it (Rubygarage, 2019). According to a study by Urban Airship (2017), sending frequent high value push notifications to customers can increase app retention rates by three to ten times, which in turn could increase the possibility of using the service. An advantage of using mobile apps over normal e-commerce websites is that it has the feature of being ubiquitous. They are available anytime, anywhere through mobile phones, online or offline; this is another factor that could encourage frequent interaction with the business.

Another business model that the app implements is the reduction of transaction costs. The app helps monitor which film tickets are sold the most, and whether to increase available show timings of that film. This helps the business have an easy to operate feedback system, which increases the quality of the service to the customers as well as customer satisfaction by responding to demand and giving viewers what they want. In addition, the company can gain more profits if more customers come to the most popular films. Finally, the app benefits the company by taking steps that take into account the company's corporate social responsibility. The use of e-tickets is beneficial as it reduces the use of paper tickets, which in turn can reduce paper waste and pollution and help preserve the trees. When the business is being eco-friendly, the business is seen in a good light; this could enhance the company's name and give it a better reputation. In addition to this, business costs of printing, ink and paper will be significantly reduced.

Overhead Costs

Technological innovation in the modern era has allowed corporations worldwide to streamline their work processes in order to access a wider market, while simultaneously providing a higher level of quality and service. The introduction of smartphone apps is one way firms have incorporated modern technology into their work processes to achieve their goals and business objectives. In addition to the common features of every organization, such as communication and coordination, smartphone apps can benefit more specific processes within a business. For example, the process of inventory management can be a time-consuming and resource-hungry operation if not carried out accurately. The difficulty surrounding inventory management is the need to complete a range of tasks successfully, from providing accurate customer forecasts to maximizing the efficiency of purchasing and production. Multiple technology companies have developed a wide range of applications to suit all types of inventory needs. SOS Inventory (www.sosinventory.com), with prices ranging between $25 and $200 a month, provides a subscription-based service where clients can transfer items between locations and track them in order to enable close monitoring of costs. The advantage of this application is its versatility. It can be used for small or large businesses depending on the price plan chosen. This group of applications gives businesses the means to install a perpetual inventory system (one where inventory quantities are updated continuously after each transaction), which would be very labor intensive without the appropriate technology.

Another benefit of using apps within the workplace is the potential savings generated through fewer overhead costs. One example where this benefit is applied first hand is at HSBC, a global bank (www.hsbc.com). Market research reveals that most customers now do their banking via by computer or smartphone. When customers go to a branch for straightforward transactions, such as balance transfers, the HSBC staff is charged with streamlining the process for these customers by explaining how transactions can be conducted directly via the HSBC app. The effect of this changeover is that customers can now bank from the location of their choice, increasing efficiency from both the bank's and the customers' perspectives. This in turn has led to the closure of approximately 27% of the HSBC branch network. Thus, the reduction of rent paid for branch offices in town centers as well as the decrease in staff wages can be reinvested for further research and development. In the long run, through streamlining the banking process and increasing efficiency for its patrons, it ensures that the bank will maintain a loyal customer base while continuing to attract new customers, both of which will contribute to the bank's profit margins.

Apps that allow workers to be able to work and communicate constantly from any physical location will increase employee efficiency and productivity. The cost and difficulty of communication will no longer be determined by geographical location, known as the *death of distance*. Applications such as WhatsApp and Skype make it very quick and economical to communicate with firms all over the world. Being able to work from any physical location greatly benefits workplace environments where there is a need to communicate constantly and the workers aren't forced to sit behind a desk at a computer all day, such as at building sites. For workers on building sites, using apps such as Evernote, which allows groups of workers to work on and access the same notes, keeps them organized and up to date on all events relating to their job.

Mobility

Apps are desired in the workplace by both employees and management. A recent study undertaken by the Economist Intelligence Unit (https://www.eiu.com) of the Economist Group found that 38% of employees listed utilizing mobile technology for their work have had the greatest impact on their job satisfaction. The study further suggests that companies who support mobile technology have also observed an 18% increase in creativity and a 21% increase in employee loyalty, underscoring the invaluable significance of app utilization for organizations.

Employee mobility is an example of the most significant advantage that results from flexible working conditions. It does more than benefit the firms by allowing employees to work wherever they are located and improve productivity—it also improves the work-life balance of employees and keeps them satisfied in terms of their working conditions. The old way of attending face-to-face meetings is coming to an end, although the majority of meetings within organizations still take place this way.

Mobile applications such as GoToMeeting (www.gotomeeting.com) allows employers, employees, and every businessperson around the world to attend meetings virtually. This decreases travel costs and time and lets employers invest in improving the working environment of employees (although they increase profit first and foremost to their stakeholders). Moreover, by attending the meetings out of the office, employees can use the time saved for their personal lives and improve their work-life balance. Enhanced work-life balance motivates employees and improves their will to produce more and achieve objectives with better results more efficiently. According to research studies done by many businesses and governmental organizations, if firms help their employees to balance work and family responsibilities, the return will be greater productivity and substantial business improvements (Scotland, 2017). Makinson et al. (2012) argue that the use of mobile applications has its benefits and issues for employees and the organization. For example, the benefits are flexibility for work scheduling, remote working, the possibility of fewer health problems, less turnover, and improved staff retention. However, the implication of this is, when employees spend an extended number of hours using these mobile applications, it could conversely have an undesirable effect on their work-life balance.

Collaboration

It is known that companies using apps benefit from the increase in collaboration. Applications enable workers to work more collaboratively by improving the communication among them. Thus companies who foster such collaboration have a better working environment, as employees are more motivated to achieve the same set of goals. According to Salesforce (2015), people perform better when they work in groups and apps enhance the workers' ability to do work together as they can check and share files anyplace and at any time. When employees collaborate with their colleagues, they feel they are a part of the organization and are more motivated as a group to achieve the organization's objectives. Also, outcomes of the group discussions can be improved when team members have stronger collaboration.

The opportunity to collaborate in the workplace can be one of the primary advantages that mobile applications provide. The benefits of Dropbox are not solely limited to fostering file sharing. As stated above, Dropbox can be used as a common server where every employee in every department has access. Applications such as Dropbox and HyperOffice (www.hyperoffice.com) make project management easier by offering collaborative platforms for the organization. This is done by removing intermediary steps, such as an employee from the human resources (HR) department editing a document and forwarding it to the marketing department. HyperOffice is aimed specifically at improved collaboration within enterprises. By using such applications, employees can log into the cloud service used by their organization, edit a document, save it, and make the file available to the rest of the organization in a single place without having to e-mail the document to an employee distribution list. As a result, employees at different locations, even if they are in different countries, have the ability to work together and achieve more by through collaboration. Efficiency is improved, as time is saved, giving employees the chance to take a break or focus on different projects. Accordingly, the profitability of the organization increases through enhanced productivity, and employees have the chance to prove themselves and impress their managers.

Creative Labor

Mobile applications also allow employees to become much more creative. For example, programs like AutoCAD 360 (https://web.autocad.com) or ChemWriter (https://chemwriter.com) use touch-based interfaces that allow users to sketch engineering and chemical structures on a tablet screen or computer monitor. Once drawn, innovative configurations can be rendered as real-world simulations onscreen. As a result, workers can seamlessly obtain and test complicated new structures anywhere they see fit. This aids in creative pursuits, which are taken out of strict working contexts and extended into multiple operational environments. Thanks to the variety of their surroundings, staff become more motivated in their effort to pursue ingenious solutions. Furthermore, this enhanced portability leads to greater job engagement as efforts can easily be joined in by other individuals from different departments. As a result, aspects of a particular design can be transferred to factory floor on the go. As a consequence, this ease of transfer can lead to increased privacy and reduced security risk. Nonetheless, superfluous portability could be open to abuse through commercial espionage that seeks to steal new ideas. Therefore, a company should match these ostensible advantages with a clear set of new rules that protect the organization's information and make sure their employees are aware of them.

The adoption of this new technology can significantly benefit performance in multiple enterprise settings. Commercial improvements affect many operational aspects of the establishment, while the business status quo is challenged. This presents a lot of opportunity for new entrants who instill this new technology in their structure from the very start. Nevertheless, new technological advancements should be applied with appropriate care; that is, following appropriate precautions can fuel understanding and mitigate detrimental effects. Only then will the true value of such technology be utilized to obtain better outcomes. Overall, businesses should embrace mobile applications to restructure their work settings. The sheer variety of improvements provided by mobile applications clearly outweighs any associated risks. At the same time, the potential of tackling such difficulties is considerable, and it only speaks in favor of implementing mobile applications.

To conclude, you have seen how mobile applications can improve the performance of organizations and their employees. Companies can either identify their core organizational processes and choose apps that will enhance them or select specific areas of such processes to focus on, such as communication. Specific stages of the process (for instance, planning) are clarified and made more accessible through apps that create flowcharts. Similarly, apps that let customers provide feedback help companies adjust processes in order to ensure that they stay competitive. The choice of apps to streamline functions within the workplace is virtually limitless. Organizations should take advantage of the world where new emerging technologies are available all of the time in order to secure market share and dominance.

Many companies are using this technology in many different forms in the workplace (Campbell, 2015). There has been an increase in recent years of the use of apps by both consumers and businesses, with around 2.2 million apps available on the Apple App Store in 2017 alone (Statista, 2018). QuickBooks, Trello, PayPal, and Dropbox are just some examples of applications used by businesses that make everything from monitoring to accounting easier and more efficient. There are many benefits to using these types of technology that help businesses improve their efficiency and save costs. One main benefit of using apps in the workplace is to gain improvements in efficiency. Efficiency is used "to show how productively a process is working" (Boddy, 2014); hence, an improvement in efficiency is good for the organization as this saves time and money. Apps make work a lot easier and faster to complete due to their ease of use and convenience. They are much more convenient in recording inventory levels than writing down inventory numbers, as the information keyed into an app can be fed straight into internal databases for analysis as opposed to manually entering data through a written inventory count. In turn, this convenience and ease makes the business more efficient, as it does not take as long to complete activities meaning that the business saves time and money.

One example of software that has been designed exclusively for business use is QuickBooks (https://quickbooks.intuit.com). QuickBooks is a software application aimed at smaller businesses as well as people who are self-employed. The application not only provides businesses with both financial and management accounting reports, but it also allows both employees as well as business owners to access the business' financial records and reports at anytime, anywhere. The app is currently being used by over 2 million businesses around the world (Quick-Books, 2018), which underscores just how large the market is for this type of technology, as well as the number of businesses that use this technology in their workplace. Being able to use applications such as QuickBooks, businesses save time and effort. As QuickBooks reports are produced in seconds, a lot of time is saved when compared to traditional finance and accounting methods. Not only can information be analyzed quickly, the business can spend more time on performing other essential tasks.

The less time spent producing reports, the more time that can be spent on improving business productivity. This in turn improves the efficiency of the business. The convenience of an application such as QuickBooks is also key in understanding why efficiency may increase through the use of this type of technology in the workplace. As an app can be used on a mobile phone or tablet, work does not necessarily have to be limited to the office. Hence, work that can be carried out with ease by employees, internally and externally, means more work can be completed versus the traditional approach of working purely on equipment available in the office. This convenience means time can be saved. Nevertheless, the organization may often experience conflicts with employees who do not want to work outside the office. Incentives can be put into place to try to minimize this conflict. Time is vital in business, and every second counts, whether executing a stock trade or trying to deliver a new product to the market before a competitor. Sufficient time can be saved through the convenience of using an app, as work can be completed much faster than ever before. Using the example of Dropbox employees can now work on projects and reports from anywhere. Hence, if a report is needed fast, it can be worked on and shared more easily than ever before, in turn saving time. This increases the efficiency of the business as the flow of work is faster than ever, meaning projects can be completed a lot faster using app-based technology. Overall, the improvement in efficiency provided by apps, which enhances convenience and saves time, allows the business to complete tasks faster and easier meaning productivity is increased.

In addition, apps can also be used to accomplish simplified monitoring and control. Monitoring and control plays a vital role in business, so much so that these criteria are built into the definition of the organization. Monitoring and control are vital to ensure staff are working effectively and efficiently. Seeking optimal monitoring and control within the organization is one of the main challenges for managers. The use of technology in the form of apps, however, helps mangers reach an optimal level of monitoring and control. An example of an app that helps do this is Inventory+. This app allows auto dealers to have "full control of your inventory right from the palm of your hand" (Google, 2018). Here managers or employees can easily control inventory levels, as well as monitor trends in those levels. By making monitoring and control easier through the use of technology in the form of apps, businesses benefit greatly. Not only do businesses potentially increase their productivity by knowing when an employee or group of employees is not working effectively, it may also benefit the business through cost savings in terms of being able to monitor and control inventory levels more effectively.

Although there are multiple benefits to using technology such as apps in the workplace, there are also some drawbacks. In some cases, the cost of using apps can be daunting, especially for smaller businesses. Many business applications such as QuickBooks require payment of monthly fees for their use. Another drawback is that they can leave the organization open to data theft. Data breaches are on the rise with "1,093 data breaches" (Kharif, 2017) reported alone in the United States in 2016. If certain data stored in such apps falls into the wrong hands, it could potentially compromise the financial viability of the organization. For an example, if a competitor gets a hold of another business's financial records stored in QuickBooks, they could potentially use strategies such as price skimming to force the business out of the market. In addition, one of the main problems in implementing technology in the workplace is when the technology just does not work the way it should. If an app crashes the business can be stymied for anywhere from minutes to days, which can be catastrophic.

Summary

In summary, weighing the benefits and drawbacks of using technology such as apps in the workplace, the potential benefits far outweigh any potential drawbacks. The potential improvements in efficiency through the ease of use as well as the convenience apps, as well as simplifying monitoring and controlling, will greatly benefit the workplace. The business will be able to improve productivity, meaning more products can be sold, increasing revenue for the business, as well as being able to stay on track with ongoing work. Although some workers may not be comfortable with being able to do their work from anywhere, incentives can be put in place by the organization to motivate these employees to comply. With constantly improving technology, the increased use of apps and being able to work from almost anywhere in the world with ease will likely become the norm in years to come. Thus, it is important to get ahead of the market and try to adopt technology such as apps into your business models to get a jump on this trend. For example, recently the use of cryptocurrencies (a digital or virtual currency that uses cryptography for security) has been in the news. The cryptocurrency wave has caught many businesses by surprise; whereas those who explored the benefits blockchain technology in its early forms, for example, have benefited greatly.

Some drawbacks, such as potential data theft, associated with technology such as apps are still quite valid. However, more is being done by governments and app developers every day to help reduce this risk. Beyond this, a cost-benefit analysis on the use of apps would strongly favor the benefits. Although there is a cost to using business software such as QuickBooks, this cost is most often relatively small when compared to traditional accounting approaches. Not only does this save the business money in the long run, but it also makes doing business easier and faster. There are also huge cost savings when it comes to the improvements in efficiency provided by apps and their enhancement of monitoring and controlling processes. The costs saved by spending less money on mistakes and the time spent on doing various tasks can save the organization money. The improvement in efficiency can also help to improve revenues, which in turn will help grow the profits of the organization.

Chapter 7
Mobility and Work-Life Balance

Technology increasingly blurs the lines between an individual's personal and professional life, therefore, an effective smartphone app must create a partition between personal and professional tasks to allow employees to experience a positive work-life balance. The introduction of smartphone apps, however, has resulted in working hours being extended resulting in increased work pressure on employees. In order to improve the work-life balance of employees using smartphone apps, it is important for employers to encourage the use of apps that are designed to reduce the stress levels and the pressure that employees experience, and to keep their personal and work-life independent of one another.

Many people believe that work-life balance means an equal number of hours spent on work activities and personal activities. At the core of an effective work-life balance is daily achievement and enjoyment (Scotland, 2017; Shanafelt et al., 2015). They are, as Bird (2003) states, "the front and back of the coin of value in life." A positive work-life balance can lead to increased productivity, improved staff retention, and a positive working environment. Although, individuals have separate lives and priorities, as work-life balance ranks as one of the most important workplace attributes, it remains essential for employees to find this balance. Striking a healthy work-life balance is a difficult challenge, even in the best of times. It is all the more daunting and essential during times of economic upheaval and uncertainty. Adding to this pressure, today's mobile devices have obliterated the line between work and home; that is, employees are constantly connected to their jobs, often leaving them feeling overwhelmed, discouraged, and depleted. In this chapter, we will examine how companies can use smartphone apps to reverse the effects of this pressure and recover and improve the work-life balance of employees. Using these insights will allow them to recalibrate their schedules to support their ideal work-life balance.

What Is Work-Life Balance?

Work-life balance refers to the process of maintaining equilibrium between work commitments and a fulfilling personal life. When there is a certain incompatibility between both roles, a conflict arises. Work-life balance conflict is described by Harris et al. (2011) as the interference of family and personal life activities in work and vice versa. That is, a good work-life balance is about employees enjoying a flexible working practice that enables them to find a balance between the

DOI 10.1515/9781547400546-007

two important areas of life, work and personal life, and avoid any role conflict (Shanafelt et al., 2015; Hyman and Summers, 2004). These definitions highlight striking a balance between employers' demand for hard work and their employees' nonwork-related responsibilities as work-family conflict can have negative consequences at work, such as a decreased performance, stress, and burnout, as well as in the individual's personal life, such us a reduced life satisfaction.

A study conducted by Amstad et al. (2011) on "a meta-analysis of the work-family conflict," identified some issues that occur as a result of an imbalance when employees fail at an attempt to balance work and life. His study demonstrated that an imbalanced work and personal life could lead to health problems, for example, sleeplessness, eyestrain, mental issues, and depression. Therefore, a balance between work and family is necessary to achieve, as when one outweighs the other, the impact on the individual could be severe. Consequently, companies have a significant interest in improving the work-life balance of its employees (Ho et al., 2013).

Recent studies have proved technology to be a fundamental shift that impacts work and life balance (Scotland, 2017). Technology is a game changer that seems to make professional life easier as it reduces gender inequality in the workplace, supports workers who care for adults and the disabled, and involves parents especially women with childcare responsibilities. The use of technology can ease away the idea of being present in the workplace at all times, therefore, giving employees greater freedom of movement, and a better balance of work and life. Makinson et al. (2012) argued that the use of mobile applications has its benefits and issues for employees and the organization. For example, the benefits are flexibility for work scheduling, remote working, the possibility of fewer health problems, less turnover, and improved staff retention. However, the implication of this is, when employees spend an extended number of hours using these mobile applications, it could conversely have an undesirable effect on their work-life balance.

There are issues, such as, employees feeling secluded from the company's values, and managers not being able to recognize some skills and traits their employees have, which could negatively impact the performance review. This shows that despite the benefits of the use of applications in the workplace it could also have a negative impact. According to a survey by Scotland (2017), 50% of its respondents saw the use of mobile technologies as a mechanism that is adding stress. The use of mobile applications creates more room for employees to be monitored by their employers, increasing additional stress levels. Thus, contradicting Corona and Olivia's (2007) finding that the use of technological applications reduces health issues. Other scholars recognize the use of mobile applications as a potential blur to the limitations between work and personal life (Ho et al., 2013).

Nevertheless, as employees endeavor to have better flexibility, the applications do create a new set of complexities. Hyman and Summers's (2004) study on the practice of work-life in the economy found that from the employees' perspective, despite the increase in demand for an improved well-being and work-life balance for employees, some employers are yet to make the policy a priority. Regardless, many studies have proven mobile technology applications create better flexibility and efficiency for employees (Ho et al., 2013). Several developers have already tried to introduce apps increasing the compatibility of and individual's work and personal life (Brooks, 2012). Companies can indeed use these types of apps to help workers organize their day better, clearly separating work and private life, and allow employees to do things for themselves. As a work-life imbalance can lead to high levels of stress, a lower quality of life, and decreased effectiveness at work, apps can play an important role in helping to reduce this imbalance. For example, a company could offer an app with an individualized timetable for the week, which could help workers structure their week more efficiently. There already exists a variety of such apps as discussed in Chapter 6. To improve the work-life balance, the timetable should contain compulsory breaks and a maximum number of work hours per week. This is especially important for those workers who find it hard to stop working, and hence do not take enough breaks and work too much overtime. Working too much overtime can lead to tiredness and nervousness.

In addition, priorities should be defined, as people often can not accomplish all their assigned tasks (Moser, 2015). Further, there should be compulsory time for private activities only, as research suggests that the lack of personal time can result in a greater number of layoffs (Felstead et al., 2002). To support time for private activities, the company could provide an app that turns off various functions on the phone, so that the individual can focus on their private life. One example of such an app would be Shyft (https://myshyft.com). In addition, a company can implement health management programs through apps. For example, an app with a health training program, including theory and practical exercises for physical activity and nutrition tips, would be very useful. Obtaining a healthy life style is important as a good amount of physical activity, for example, can prevent stress.

A review stated that many mobile phone apps can indeed have positive effects on physical activity and weight (Stephens and Allen, 2013). Furthermore, a company can provide an app with a stress-management program to reduce stress and promote relaxation. An increasing number of companies have already implemented stress management programs for their workers. An app can personalize these programs and lower costs. These health management programs, however, only indirectly influence work-life balance as they focus on the reduction and prevention of stress (Moser, 2015).

Individual Needs and Apps

The general advantages of apps are that they can be individualized to the workers' needs and feedback is possible. Also, apps provide a cost-effective way of improving work-life balance as perhaps companies would not need to invest in sports equipment on their own. Many companies do offer fully-equipped gyms of their own, and using these facilities are undoubtedly a lot more beneficial to a worker's health. On the other hand, smartphone apps provide great flexibility for the worker as they can be used anywhere. Apps are only useful in promoting work-life balance, however, when they are effective. Therefore, the effectiveness of the specific apps must be measured. By encouraging the use of apps that help within the organization and prioritizing different tasks, managers can assist employees in maintaining control of their busy schedules. Todoist (https://en.todoist.com) is an app that helps employees keep track of their daily responsibilities and sends notifications of what tasks should be undertaken and when, depending on their deadline and importance. This app primarily focuses on organizing, encouraging employees to be aware of outstanding tasks, and highlighting the importance of managing time to be productive. Even the basic concept of an interactive to-do list is useful in ensuring that important tasks are not forgotten (although a lengthy list might be overwhelming and leave employees feeling drained at the thought of an endless checklist).

A clearly organized interactive schedule helps to allocate time slots to each task and assists the individual in keeping their workload under control, allowing them to "switch off" once they finish their work day. It is vital for employees to have an opportunity to refuel their body and mindset by having a certain cut-off point each day. This refueling is essentially what prolongs an individual's productivity in the long run (Stawarz et al., 2013). A particular advantage of using apps in business is that on their commute to and from work, even on a cramped train with very little space, employees can do that last bit of work before getting home or arriving at the workplace. This is much easier than having to use a laptop, which due to its relative size and lack of personal space, is not always possible on a train. This means that work can be completed at any time, so working from home is possible and much easier when you are not able to come into an office. There are certain things that a cell phone does well and some that you would be better off not attempting, but people do anyway. There is a loss in productivity by using the wrong device for the job all the time. That is why attempts have been made through apps to try to make the experience better on such a small screen and with such small input options.

For example, the main problem with work-related smartphones is the fact that employees feel obligated to be "on call" at all times. One way in which employers can counter this is through the use of apps that block certain work-related apps and contacts for a certain period of time. These apps give employees a chance to block work-related notifications on their phone and focus on their personal lives, improving work-life balance. For example, the app could be configured to block all work-related calls between 8 p.m. and 8 a.m., giving employees the chance not to feel on call. However, this may frustrate employees when they need to get some work accomplished but are blocked from doing so by their employers. Employers may not want to do this in general.

By improving their work-life balance, employees feel more motivated and less stressed. These benefits can then lead to the organization having less absenteeism (Chimote, 2013). Reduced absenteeism will ultimately lead to a greater return on investment from their employees. However, some employees may be reluctant to use blocking apps, because being unable to respond to e-mails outside of working hours has proven to have a negative effect on an employee's career trajectory as they may miss the opportunity to act instantly on some important new information (*Harvard Business Review*, 2016). This suggests that employees first need to know where their time is going. Apps such as ATracker (www.wonderapps.se) can help them define their daily tasks, and with a simple tap will track how long they spend on each item. Employees can then determine whether they are spending too much or too little time on certain tasks. Therefore, it is up to the employer to encourage employees to use such an app to improve work-life balance without the fear of being penalized for doing so. By encouraging a culture where employees' work-life balance is prioritized, businesses can look forward to a range of benefits including reduced employee absenteeism, improved productivity, and enhanced brand image (Chimote, 2013).

Zirtual (www.zirtual.com) is another example of an app that can be used to improve work-life balance. Zirtual is a virtual assistant app that can carry out simple tasks such as sending e-mails, scheduling meetings, and managing social media accounts. Users of Zirtual can have basic administrative tasks completed for them, meaning they have more free time and a better work-life balance (Brandon, 2016). Video conferencing apps like WebEx and BlueJeans (www.bluejeans.com) allow employees to work from anywhere. Interactions are more collaborative and personal than with a phone call and more convenient for the employee. On the other hand, a major benefit of e-mails is that they provide a record of the conversation. For example, using Notes during a call is not practical. Therefore, the record is important, and retrieval of old Notes or short message service (SMS) on a smartphone are not practical solutions. So, for business communications, e-mail is the best solution for retaining important communications. Research has found that 87% of remote employees "feel more connected to their team and process when using video conferencing" (Coleman, 2013).

For example, LinkedIn, the business/employment social networking service uses the BlueJeans app for interviewing and training employees. The objective is to improve the work-life balance of LinkedIn's employees because it allows for better scheduling and has no travel requirements, which increases productivity and reduces unnecessary costs. However, video conferencing from home also has limitations: technological difficulties with devices or with internet connectivity may occur, which is stressful and also complicates communication. It is also much easier to be distracted outside the work environment, especially if the employee is at home. Reduced participation/engagement may be the result as employees may not feel obliged/pressured to get involved because they are not physically in the room.

The apps discussed above are just a few examples of available apps aimed at improving work-life balance for employees. The flexibility these apps offer has created a shift in our culture, where employees are expected to make use of this technology even when not in the workplace. Recent estimates show that working parents spend an average of 64 hours paid and unpaid per week engaged in activities related to work (Schneider, 2014). Fenner and Renn (2009) describe these unpaid hours as "a form of distributed or remote work where employees engage in job-related activities at home and away from the traditional workplace" (p. 179). These unpaid hours were previously impossible physically before the advancement of smartphone and computer applications.

The main way for employees to regain their work-life balance is through a cultural shift from organizations where unpaid hours are not expected of employees. The current work culture means that employees "feel obligated to be on call at all times"; in some companies, people are outfitted with phones so that they could be available anytime and anywhere. This culture must change before apps such as BlueJeans and Zirtual can be used effectively to improve work-life balance. It is the job of the organization to change this culture and encourage employees to use apps that improve productivity while giving employees more recreational time. Once organizations start to encourage employees to improve their work-life balance through the use of smartphone apps, they will begin to notice benefits such as reduced absenteeism. Overall, smartphone apps can be used to improve work-life balance significantly if the organization as a whole embraces this culture. HelloAlfred (www.helloalfred.com) helps individuals perform all the tasks that need to get done in each day or week. The app has a goal to build intuitive, personal help into the places we live. It balances work and life by taking care of daily household routines, including shopping, cleaning, and delivery.

Although there are many positive impacts of app use on employee work-life balance, there is, however, conflicting research that could suggest otherwise (Scotland, 2017). For example, Sarker et al. (2012) conducted research into managing employee use of mobile devices and proposed that the use of smartphones and tablets (and therefore the apps on them) produce a lack of separation between work and personal life. Employees perceive that they must be available all the time, which ultimately creates stress and confusion about what is expected of them. It was also found that being connected continuously can lead to compulsive behaviors, which even though may benefit the employee's work, may also hinder their health and personal life.

In conclusion, it is clear that, to some extent, the use of digital applications benefit employees in a number of ways; simplifying everyday tasks while optimizing the time that can be used personally and professionally, thus promoting a healthy work-life balance. Nevertheless, as this is a relatively new area, there is limited research into the effects of such technology, so judgment about its effects can not be made conclusively. It is also important to mention there are some disadvantages linked to certain apps. For instance, an app designed to foster physical activity does not necessarily encourage social contact, and people might not be motivated to use all its features on their own. Instead, or in addition to creating an app, a company may also offer physical education classes itself. In that way, the community within the company is supported, and people might be more motivated to take part in the classes when their colleagues are also participating in them.

Even though apps can be useful in promoting work-life balance, they are not the overall solution for the work-life balance conflict. Modern technologies have led to an even greater blurring of the lines between work and private life, as companies often demand constant accessibility of their workers (Kossek et al., 2012). Therefore, the use of apps further contributes to the danger that people will spend even more time on their mobile devices than they already do. Also, workers are tempted to look at their e-mail and other work-related tasks since the same mobile device is used for work and personal use. Moreover, using a smartphone that is also used for work as well as custom apps created by the company reminds workers about of work-related tasks even when they are off the job (Stawarz et al., 2013).

Due to these facts, one can conclude that even though apps can indeed facilitate a good work-life balance, other strategies need to be put into place by the company as well. The company needs to compensate for overtime, though this does not solve work-life conflict directly. Furthermore, a company should discuss with their workers the issue of availability outside of work, as persistent access is sometimes necessary (Sarker et al., 2012). Further strategies include time spent working, flexible hours, and maternity and paternity benefits among others (Arnold and Randall, 2016). Such strategies clearly encourage a work-life balance (Moser, 2015) and can not be conducted using apps, but rather need to be implemented in the policies of the company itself.

Summary

To conclude, apps are beneficial to organizations in terms of logistics and operations. The possibility of managers completing tasks and providing feedback while commuting or traveling is just one of the operational benefits. Due to an apps capacity to download and store information when connected, this work can then be accessed offline without a cellular connection or proximity to a Wi-Fi hotspot on an easily transportable mobile device. The ability of apps to store company data and statistics should also be considered in terms of the increased ease of employee access to this data for meetings and preparation; however, this also poses a great security risk if the device is lost or stolen. Having each employee set up a work profile on the enterprise app is also useful to managers and supervisors in monitoring employee performance and progress and as a mechanism to control and coordinate employee activities. This could be valuable to the managers who are overseeing a particular organizational program. However, employees setting up an app to have themselves monitored is full of moral questions and open to tampering, falsifying records, etc. The other factor is that users on a smartphone can and do have their activities tracked and the next phase is for the corporation to track everything you do; the employee becoming the droid to do what all the others do until they are effectively replaced by robotics.

Nonetheless, the flexibility offered using technology is of benefit to an employee's work, family, and life-related activities. Robey and Cousins (2015) found that mobile users were able to change between work and domestic provinces "by constructing rules governing when mobile technology use was appropriate for one domain but not the other." This goes to show that mobile applications influence work-life balance and the well-being positively. Therefore, as this increases productivity, it reduces absenteeism, and pushes for retention. If work-life balance is struck right, mobile technology can also help build upon that balance and create valuable relationships among workers, their employers, as well as clients. In addition to the benefits of mobile applications, this technology could potentially add some real value to the future, for example, futuristic things like virtual reality. However, as some studies have indicated, some employees may perceive the use of these applications as a cause of stress, as they find the two domains, work and life, still interfering with each other, which is challenging.

Another potential disadvantage of mobile technology is the social impact it has on employees. Employees who may constantly take advantage of mobile apps may at some point feel secluded from their employers and colleagues, which could have a negative impact. The effect could be on the individual and on the firm, as the employee can suffer from depression and other mental issues caused by stress as a result of deciding to take time off work. This is more likely to happen to key figures within the organization. Also, apps could potentially stop employees from reaching the very top of their career. This is supported by Neilan (2017) who found that 95% of males are CEOs compared to 5% of females in the top 100 companies. This shows that women may still prefer to choose their families first due to lack of support for good work-life balance from the workplace.

Chapter 8
New Digital Markets and Emerging Business Models

It is evident that technology has had a significant impact on today's society and the modern workplace. As the smartphone has become an essential possession, it is understandable that the number of available mobile apps has mushroomed, including those designed for the workplace. This increase has caused companies to incorporate mobile apps into their organizational processes. What makes these apps popular is the fact that they cater to a wide range of businesses, from the raw materials sector to the manufacturing sector to the service sector.

As discussed previously, some of the processes that are enhanced through apps include the tracking and managing of inventory, the generation of work orders, and the scheduling and assigning of tasks. Procter & Gamble uses "custom apps to improve productivity and drive sales around the world" (https://us.pg.com) and PepsiCo finds that distribution is "simplified with iPad and iPhone for merchandisers, delivery staff, and managers" (www.pepsico.com). Like the iPad, the Microsoft Surface tablet is also used in many industries, including healthcare, education, and engineering.

In this chapter, we will examine the larger trends in the apps ecosystem, such as the emergence of entirely new business concepts such as ridesharing services; new ways of doing things at the commercial sector level, such as mobile banking; and radical changes occurring in personal lives, such as those brought about by the use of social media.

Sharing Services

Geolocation is the geographic location of an object linked to a global positioning system. Some companies have capitalized on this technology, even basing their entire existence on them. As you learned in Chapter 1, *Uber* (www.uber.com) is a perfect example of a geolocation-based app. Its goal is to provide a ridesharing service that requires little or no investment on the part of the driver. Furthermore, it is extremely convenient and easy to use for passengers. These benefits come from Uber using its excess capacity, in terms of both the driver's empty seats in his or her car and in using a mobile app on their personal smartphones as both a fare meter and GPS navigation system. Thanks to this mobile app, Uber has streamlined its process to the max, and the company requires very little personal

DOI 10.1515/9781547400546-008

contact with the drivers, as they are independent contractors and rely on communication through the app.

The app provides the interface for the driver to interact with passengers who can find their ride, track their route, pay, tip, and rate the driver through the very same mobile app. This business model has permitted Uber to expand much faster than the classic asset-based company, as they did not have to purchase vehicles, or fare meters in the cities in which they operate, thanks to their mobile app and the sharing economy model it followed. Most importantly, they managed to get around the practice of purchasing a "medallion" for the right to drive a taxi that other taxi services have had to purchase.

The sharing economy describes a peer-to-peer, collaborative model that many successful start-ups, such as Uber, are based. Many of these companies are geolocation based, meaning that they use apps to streamline their business process. *Airbnb* (https://airbnb.com) does this for apartment sharing, *ZipCar* (www.zipcar.com) does it for vehicle sharing, and *BlaBlaCar* (www.blablacar.com) does it for carpooling. These are just a few examples of peer-to-peer geolocation-based companies. These companies offer the benefits of easy customer communication, flexible business strategies, and a fast means of expansion. All of these organizations base themselves almost entirely on a mobile app that both the employee and the customer requires in order for them to operate. This is not the case for all companies that use mobile apps to streamline their work processes.

The most common apps used in companies today are communication based. These communications come in several different forms and bring several different benefits to the company using these apps. The most commonly adopted means of app/application-based communication is email, which allows employees to communicate within the company with co-workers, supervisors, customers, and suppliers whenever and wherever. Even though email is already a well-established means of communication, the mobile app form of it brings a new level of connectivity to the workplace, allowing extensive communications, including documents and graphic-based attachments, to reach employees and customers in new places. Instant messaging apps such as *WhatsApp* offer a simple interfaces that makes it easy to have immediate conversations and to transmit document and graphic files.

These apps all offer the benefit of increased communication in the workplace as well as easier access to collective knowledge, which in turn helps the teams function better and boost their effectiveness in the workplace. A lot of mobile apps designed for use in work environments are in fact designed to support collaboration and teamwork. Examples of cloud-based file sharing and collaboration platforms include Dropbox, Google Drive, and OneDrive. These platforms allow several team members to collaborate on a single document and share documents and graphics files. They have been available since before the success of mobile apps, however, the ability to access these platforms through a mobile app has made them even more effective in support of teamwork and collaboration.

Companies are also using apps to make their everyday processes easier to achieve when away from the office. Invoicing apps (such as *Wave,* www.wave-apps.com) are very useful for small businesses or contractors that do not spend a lot of the time in the office. These apps enable billing wherever there is a data connection. They also add mobility to the company's services while also simplifying time-consuming processes employees face every day. Some large companies will also build custom apps for their particular processes. In an effort to simplify the work processes and in turn make the work product of employees easier to understand, companies use helpdesk apps that streamline troubleshooting and problem solving. This in turn makes the employees more productive, as they spend less time fixing technical issues and more time doing actual work. These helpdesk apps can also be linked to training apps that teach new employees aspects of the job with which they might not yet be familiar and help them to get accustomed to the organization's processes without having to assign another employee to train them, in turn saving on training costs.

On top of resolving internal problems, apps are often used to boost the companies' external image and help with employee recruitment. Recruitment apps (such as *Hirevue* [www.hirevue.com] and *Jobscience* [www.jobscience.com]) have increasingly become more common. These apps streamline the employee selection process by filtering candidate profiles, which helps the Human Resource department find suitable individuals more cost effectively. The marketing department can also use mobile apps to boost brand recognition and attract new customers. Innovative marketing strategies have included "mouth-to-mouth" promotion apps that, with the help of a referral program (incentivizing the customer to promote the company), become a tool to showcase the company, allowing potential customers to discover the functions and the operations of the company.

Use of these apps creates a significant amount of data about both the employees and the customers. This data can then be analyzed to understand where the company can improve and therefore increase its competitiveness. Thus, even though these apps have had a huge impact on our private lives and promise to bring a lot of benefits to the workplace if used properly. They are still to be universally adopted, as some security-conscious managers avoid using them for fear of making their companies vulnerable to the security flaws that these apps might contain. This problem should not last for too long, however, as the security of collaboration, messaging, and other business apps get stronger as they gain in popularity in both the professional and private markets.

Uber is a ride hailing service company that is unique in that the use of smartphone apps is central to their business model outside of the technology market. Uber was founded in San Francisco in 2009, and the service is now available in around 53 countries around the world. On its website, Uber declares that they are working to transform the way that the world moves by seamlessly connecting riders to drivers through the use of their smartphone/tablet app, while making cities more accessible, opening up more possibilities for riders, and more business for drivers. This highlights the advantages that Uber holds over traditional taxi services or even public transportation. As a user, you are instantly connected to your driver over the app and are then able to keep track of the exact location and route of your hired driver. The app is easy to use and provides you with step-by-step instructions that you can follow so that you do not feel overwhelmed or intimidated. Uber is a prime example of how apps can benefit businesses by increasing their convenience and increasing their exposure across mobile devices.

Social Media

The development of the social media, mobile, and web-based technologies has led to a reshaping of individual preference and organizational culture in terms of discussion, co-creation, and sharing. Firms have recently taken a significant interest in researching more effective methods to influence, connect with, and learn from customers and employees (Robson et al., 2015; Leclerq et al., 2017; Oprescu et al., 2014). In addition, the ability to inexpensively monitor and track everyday activity, an increase in individual and behavioral analytics, and the successful gamification experiences of companies such as Nike and Foursquare are all thought to have accelerated the emergence of the field of business issued smartphones.

In today's technology-driven world, the role and application of social media have grown exponentially, and its ability to empower the individual to communicate with the masses with such ease has dramatically transformed the business and political landscape. Social media platforms vary in their application, and some are better designed than the others to facilitate the sharing of certain forms of media; videos (e.g., YouTube, Vimeo), images (e.g., Instagram, Pinterest), and audio (e.g. SoundCloud). There is also a growing trend in the number of platforms that allow for cross sharing between platforms. As social media becomes increasingly accessible, organizations are continually innovating with the technology to increase their application within the business world, in both private and public sectors. This increased use can be observed in McDonald's recent recruitment innovation, which allows for candidates to apply for jobs via Snap, previously known as Snapchat. This section seeks to provide further understanding into the emerging realm of social media's relationship with new businesses. It explores social media's uses within the fast progressing, sharing economies and other apps-based businesses that were invented only a few years ago (e.g. Uber and Airbnb).

Airbnb

Airbnb (https://airbnb.com), founded on August 11, 2008, also in San Francisco, is a global community marketplace for connecting hosts and travelers. Like Uber, they have been able to take advantage of the reluctance to regulate companies that have skirted the legal requirements in an industry. In the case of Airbnb, their business is lodging and they have managed to avoid restrictions regarding zoning for businesses and other requirements and responsibilities that hotels by law must adhere to. Airbnb remains poorly regulated and the impact on communities must be considered in any discussion of their business. Airbnb facilitates the listing, discovery, and booking of unique, short and long-term accommodation. Airbnb was initially founded as a local, fledgling start-up company providing air beds, shared spaces, and small living quarters for guests. However, it began to grow rapidly and soon expanded into offering rentals of private rooms, entire properties, and even villas and an exclusive selection of private islands. In 2014, Airbnb was named *Inc.* magazine's "Company of the Year," an unequivocal testament to the exponential success of the less-than-decade-old business.

Airbnb predominantly competes with HomeAway, VRMO, and FlipKey in the fiercely competitive online short-term lodging industry. As of 2018, Airbnb was serving over 2 million guests per night across 191 countries (Airbnb Press Room, 2019), at a price of just over $80 per night and a valuation based on March 2017 funding of $31 billion (techcrunch.com, June, 2018). The long-term success of such companies is highly dependent on the effective implementation of functional and engaging social media strategies to improve the quality of service provided to guests. Customers are arguably the most important and influential stakeholders in terms of their decision-making processes and day-to-day business activities, and therefore they must be provided with a supreme and consistent level of service. Airbnb utilizes strategic social media and content-marketing strategies to communicate, manage, and connect with customers globally in a hospitable and homogenous fashion.

Airbnb managed the launch of their new and improved brand in an adept and stimulating manner, with a particular focus on valuable social media strategies to involve several key stakeholders heavily in the design, development, and inauguration of the brand launch. Airbnb also redesigned and improved the interface and functionality of their online website and mobile application, along with launch of their new brand, in a conscious effort to streamline the overall customer experience. Airbnb completely overhauled and redesigned customer touchpoints and the overall customer experience. Airbnb introduced a platform to gather customers' concepts, encouraging them to submit their own interpretation of the company's logo.

Airbnb also produced a marketing campaign, introduced a new website, released teaser lines, and dropped subtle hints to promote the brand launch and generate interest among customers: "For so long, people thought Airbnb was about renting houses. But really, we're about home. You see, a house just is a space, but a home is where you belong...That is the idea at the core of our company: belonging" (https://airbnb.com). Airbnb informed the media about the brand launch before the official ceremony, inviting them to engage with the founders, discover and learn about the new brand, and fully absorb the planned changes ahead of the public unveiling. However, Airbnb was completely caught off guard by the social media backlash that would immediately follow the brand launch. Observers identified distinct similarities between the new logo and that of another technology company, while others suggested that the new logo was in bad taste. Later, Airbnb announced that the two companies had reached a mutual agreement before the brand launch, and that the other company was in the process of designing a new logo.

Airbnb uses both their captivating, user-friendly website and attractive, intuitive application to lure customers to the company and drive traffic for the brand. Airbnb restructured the design, features, and photos on the website and application, presenting a cleaner, uncluttered design, providing more convenient booking and checkout options, and offering larger, higher-quality photos of listed accommodations. Airbnb also added push notifications to the mobile application to simplify and expedite communications between host and customer. Prior to the introduction of push notifications, e-mail messages were used to communicate between two parties—a sluggish and unproductive method of communication that required constant monitoring and resulted in many inquiries and requests being left unanswered. Users, however, are now able to receive instant notifications for questions and answers, bookings, and travel arrangements directly on their mobile devices.

Airbnb ascertained that push notifications correlated to users responding to more queries and requests, and doing so at a significantly faster rate improved their brand image and recognition. Airbnb recognizes that users expect solutions that enable real-time communication and immediate responses, and that ensuring that these features are available increases and accelerates response rates, boosts customer satisfaction, improves the quality of service provided to guests, and enhances the overall customer experience. Airbnb uses alluring content-marketing strategies, with a particular focus on creating a series of user-centric features to offer convenient solutions for customers. Airbnb connects thoughtful customer service with practical and interesting content and develops synergistic interactions with customers.

Airbnb created a selection of social filters, travel guides, and educational curricula—*Social Connections*, *Neighborhoods*, and *Hospitality Lab*—allowing users to sync social media accounts with an existing *Airbnb* accounts, providing customers with dedicated, destination-specific details and tips, and hosts with both online and offline workshops and hospitality advice. *Social Connections* allows users to link social media accounts to display available accommodations among mutual friends, and it also shows connections to similar top-rated hosts and accommodations that have previously been booked by friends. *Social Connections* supports users in a secure and reassuring search to discover accommodations within their own personal networks.

Neighborhoods provides local information for a wide range of major cities, and it helps customers discover unique cultural experiences based on their specific interests. *Neighborhoods* serves as a great tool for customers in their hunt for their ideal accommodations prior to booking, conveniently equipping them with the resources required for the decision-making process, rather than forcing them to reference external travel guides. *Neighborhoods* also entices prospective customers browsing the travel guides to return to complete a booking using the platform in the near future.

Hospitality Lab provides hosts with specialized training programs to ensure more uniform, consistent guest experiences across the company's entire global network. *Hospitality Lab* trains hosts on fundamental standards for hospitality, including improving response times, accommodation listings, and the cleanliness of properties in order to avoid disparity within the network and maximize guest experiences.

Airbnb highlighted the importance of incorporating valuable features and solutions into their content-marketing strategies to align them with the company's strategic mission and vision, expand and diversify their customer base, and form authentic relationships with customers. However, there are question marks over the company's relationships with the community—there is little mention of "community" in their marketing literature. Airbnb emphasized the significance of delivering interesting content of genuine value, and in return offered a legitimate, trustworthy sources of information, as their customers could be leveraged as brand ambassadors and a loyal community of brand advocates.

Airbnb uses different social media channels—endorsing their brand by providing regular updates on current affairs and events, promoting in-house content, sharing success stories, and encouraging users to partake in creative acts of hospitality. Airbnb also posts a plethora of original content on their social media channels, produced by both the company and the customer base. Guided tours, testimonials, tutorials, host and customer stories, and even a series on living local are a small assortment of the countless videos showcased by the company. Airbnb asks individuals to share their personal experiences and success stories, and it effectively crowd-sources a large portion of their easy-to-consume promotional content and distributes the customer-led content via social media. Airbnb recognizes the power of brand marketing through social media, and it uses these social media strategies to increase engagement with customers.

Mobile Banking and Financial Services

Today most banks have launched their own apps for their customers; the apps have services such as viewing balances, setting up direct debits and standing orders as well as transferring money. This move to mobile banking has had a huge impact on banking companies' business models resulting in less staff being needed in high street bank branches. From 2011 to 2015 a 32% decline in high street branch visits was incurred with now just 71 customer visits a day on average (*The Guardian*, 2016). In this case apps have brought a cost saving benefit for companies and a more efficient service to customers to keep up with increasing pace of life. Business customers of banks have also incurred a large benefit from banking apps as time can be saved because members of staff have to go to and from the bank on a less frequent basis, which has also reduced costs.

The progression in banks' business models has opened a gap in the market for branch free banks, such as Monzo which was founded in 2015 by Tom Blomfield and is an entirely app-based bank (Blomfield, 2017). Tom Blomfield in an interview with Virgin Start Ups said he believes physical banks are a thing of the past and the large quantity of money spent on maintaining buildings is a cost with few benefits and using an app-based service eliminates these costs. Furthermore, lifestyles of customers have progressed with available technology, and today people have less time to visit physical bank branches so working from an app makes Monzo's services accessible to more people and at any time of day and in any location or country (Blomfield, 2017). Unlike most high street banks, Monzo has aimed to target young adults with their service and build confidence in money handling, by offering bespoke auto budgeting for its users, allowing customers to personalize and set limits for different types of spending which is visual on the app (*The Guardian*, 2017). This business aim would not have been accessible without apps, hence apps are significantly benefiting the industry's business models.

Bank customers now regularly use smartphone apps to examine their balances, deposit checks, transfer money, and much more—all at a touch of a button. This makes customers happy, as they do not have to go to the physical bank in order to conduct these transactions. Mobile banking apps can also send customers notifications when their funds are low or when they have received an electronic deposit, for example. Being kept up to date this way increases customer satisfaction meaning they will more likely to keep banking with a particular bank. This is important to the banks as they face increased pressure from new financial technology (fintech) companies offering more personal services, that banks have not. In fact, the traditional banking industry is reacting and the fintech offerings of open source APIs that enable fintech innovations are now being picked up and utilized by traditional banks that are seeking to offer the services that the nimble fintech innovators have brought to market.

Barclays

In 2012, *Barclays* (https://www.home.barclays/) developed an app called Barclays Mobile Banking that, among other things, allows users to transfer money between accounts as well as to keep track of incoming and outgoing funds. Barclays also branched out and adopted a new revenue-generating technique using the app. When customers viewed their transactions using the app, Barclays would occasionally post messages in between transactions that advertised that the customer could borrow a certain amount over a certain period of time, for example.

Interestingly, 49% of 20–24-year-olds still live at home with their parents and pay low rent or none at all, meaning they generally have less need to borrow (Statista, 2016). Barclays therefore targeted an audience of potential customers that may not have considered borrowing money before they were exposed to this idea by the customized advertising on the mobile app. Nevertheless, one of the main objectives of a commercial app is to encourage customers to reuse services due to their speed and convenience. If Barclays were to over-promote to such an audience, this could deter them from using the company in the future due to such unwelcome promotions. To retain and continue to generate interest in the company and its app, as much as possible, organizations must tailor their advertising to suit individual customers and limit the amount of advertising to which they are exposed.

Barclays also launched the *Pingit* app in February 2012. This app allowed users over the age of 18 to transfer money to other *Barclays* account holders. The age limit was then reduced to 16 to include their younger customers. When it was first released, Pingit allowed customers to transfer amounts ranging from $1.30 to $330. This improved the speed of service that Barclays was providing, as transactions could be completed from a smartphone on the go rather than having to log in online. Barclays also included small businesses in this launch, which gave them a competitive edge over other banks. If both an individual and a small business used the app, transactions could take place in under a minute. A personal smartphones then had the ability to transfer money to nearly 50,000 businesses at the touch of a button. Today Pingit is no longer just a Barclays app, now serving customers' banking needs throughout the UK. The service is also free to download, making it very popular.

That being said, there is a security risk of having all banking information available on your smartphone. A significant number of the top 100 paid apps have been hacked in terms of repackaging or the distribution of clones (Statista, 2018). There is therefore a risk to all individuals when disclosing their personal information online, even more so if banking details are exposed. Security is a priority for banks employing such apps for their services, and Barclays and *Santander* (www. bancosantander.es) have adopted similar methods with regard to confidentiality. For example, even if someone gained access to a smartphone or tablet with one of their apps, a 5-digit passcode is needed to open the app, and the user is automatically logged out if the app is unattended for 5 minutes. However, banking apps are free, and several of the Apple App Store's free apps were hacked in 2013 (Statista, 2016).

While Barclays focuses predominantly on speed of service, such as transferring money promptly and paying charges quickly, Santander concentrates more on account management. A popular feature of Santander's app is that you can split a bill with your friends, making it far easier to pay in restaurants and divide utility bills. Thus there are steps that Barclays could take to improve their app to enhance debit or credit card security.

American Express

Over the years, social media has been growing exponentially. While it originally started out with the goal of getting people closer together; some companies saw an opportunity for direct marketing and better customer service. Eventually, they took the plunge and reaped the benefits. One such company is *American Express* (www.americanexpress.com). Although its social media presence started off as a simple customer service for cardholders, the financial services giant eventually decided to bear a bit more risk and develop a service based feature called "couponless deals." This feature gave customers tailored deals based on their "likes," providing interactivity for customers and the company on social media. (Essentially, the company was data mining while providing their customers tailored offers that they would find difficult to resist due to their lowered indifference curves (a line showing all the combinations of two goods which give a consumer equal utility), since they liked the product in first place. At the same time, American Express was generating income for their partner companies.

To get these deals customers had to use an app American Express would advertise. This is the source of revenue from American Express' perspective. They would also take advantage to advertise their pages on social media sites suggesting that more deals are available as long as the customer "likes" their pages. This might seem like American Express was giving out "freebies" for very little in return, but by gathering likes on their pages, it did three things for American Express:

1. It increases the chance of other people joining in due to the "bandwagon effect," since amount of likes are publicly visible.
2. Every individual who has liked their page received news about their new deals, increasing awareness of these deals, hopefully resulting in sales.
3. Social media has certain features that cause heavily visited/liked pages to be promoted on their partner company's home page, thus increasing the effectiveness of the advertisement.

All of these taken together made for a huge increase in brand awareness while satisfying their existing customers at the same time. It also left their clients with a positive experience, as just by being an American Express customer, they got special deals from other companies which made them feel more valued and distinct from the rest of the crowd. Having gained this popularity through their actions on social media, the financial services giant could then push their audience to their partner companies. This is what American Express has done with their "small business Saturday" idea. In exchange, they get even more of a positive brand image that causes people to trust them. When people find a particular brand to be trustworthy and view them as supporting small businesses, they are more likely to choose them in the future because they believe that they are helping smaller companies to succeed as well.

On the flip side, having all of this attention on social media makes American Express much more prone to scrutiny from competitors and the press, thus they have to maintain their good image if they don't want to make those who choose to go with them feel deceived. Since social media is found worldwide, every individual has to be catered to, which naturally is a very difficult task. If not done correctly, it can seriously damage customer satisfaction. In the case of American

Express, their customers are found in approximately 130 countries around the globe. American Express needs people who are able to speak the required languages. This means having to manage each at the same time to make sure everything that is posted online is consistent with what the brand wants to portray about the company, which is no easy task as immediate responses are expected on social media, and also because American Express is a very large company with numerous levels of authority.

Overall, social media can be very useful for increasing customer satisfaction and developing a personal connection with customers, as seen in the American Express example. However, this requires a high degree of organization to make sure that everything appearing on social media is in tune with what the company wants to portray about their brand, which can be difficult for large companies. Social media can also be a company's Achilles heel if not managed properly, considering how fast paced and widespread is the reach of social media: one simple negative post could mark the downfall of a company's image and ultimately destroy current customer satisfaction.

Messaging Apps

Facebook Messenger

The growth and range of apps that have appeared in recent years has greatly benefitted the workplace, mainly through increased communication, productivity, and accessibility. Furthermore, *branded employee apps*, which are those apps tailored specifically for employees within the workplace are growing in number. These too are bringing widespread benefits to the workplace. The *Facebook Messenger* app is highly useful, as notifications can be disbursed rapidly to a large number of employees simultaneously. The app supports unlimited chat, allowing managers to spread information and notifications easily and inexpensively without needing to channel the information throughout multiple levels in the organization—it is simply relayed to everyone. For example, Empire Cinemas utilizes Facebook Messenger to deliver work timetables and notices of staff meetings in advance. This means that employees only have to look at their smartphone to be reminded of these dates, rather than having to check in at work and make notes. This is a great advantage, as it reduces communication problems so that there were fewer employees missing shifts and meetings since they had easy access to the app.

Facebook Workplace

Facebook went a step further and introduced an app called *Workplace*. This app works in a similar manner to the standard Facebook app; however, in this case, employees have their entire profile listed, allowing managers to coordinate with employees more easily. For example, by examining employee profiles, a manager can formulate teams without having to meet with the employees. Furthermore, invites to events and meetings are easy to issue, letting managers see how many employees can attend which promotes improved planning and organization—key aspects of effective management.

Facebook WhatsApp

Apps such as *WhatsApp* have greatly improved communication within the workplace and have also reduced the diseconomy of scale of communication. This has been achieved by improving the flow of information within the organization by breaking down the communication barriers that arise in multi-level companies (vertical span), a wide span of control, and a large number of employees at the bottom level. These organizations may face communication problems as information has to pass through multiple levels until it reaches its intended audience. This means that the information can arrive too late if needed in an emergency, or it can be relayed incorrectly. Hence WhatsApp allows for messages to be sent to people within a group. It can be sent to first-level managers who can then disperse it to their employees, reducing the time required to send and receive messages.

Microsoft Skype

Apps such as *Skype* have also improved communication within the workplace. In this era of globalization, virtual teams have increased with members spread across the planet. Nevertheless, these teams need to communicate key information to each other and to respond rapidly. Skype allows for team members worldwide to communicate beyond simple messages and email. Skype's video call capabilities allow participants to see each other in real time as well as to exchange documents at a low cost, even if meeting participants are in multiple countries, saving the company significant travel expense.

The development of "smart" accessories that can be linked to apps can bring about huge benefits to companies by aiding in monitoring and increasing the flow of information, which reduces asymmetric information conditions (e.g. one manager has more or better information than the other) within the company. One such app *Smart Badge* is used to summarize data from smart badges. A Smart Badge can store a range of information such as identity, access rights, and other key profile data. Companies can use smart badges to monitor employee activities and actions. The smart badge can yield key information such as attendance at meetings and time spent on and off site. Using the app which summarizes smart badge data, the company can monitor individual behavior patterns and act accordingly. Note that the Hawthorne Effect (the tendency of people to work harder in response to their awareness of being observed) may occur when individuals are aware that they are being monitored through their smart badges, and thus they may alter their behavior. This can have a positive effect as employees are less likely to slack off but more likely to become expert at rigging the system. Their responsibilities can also be monitored and slack time reduced through the use of such apps as Google Drive. On Google Drive, an individual's work is displayed by a different color and their name is clearly stated next to their work. This can reduce slacking off as their work product is displayed publicly but may cause employees to deliver low quality work on time. This can be beneficial as it reduces the cost of monitoring and can improve productivity, but its downsides are the impact on employee morale and it may train the employee to do the bare minimum in order to accomplish their responsibilities with a focus on timely delivery.

Social Media Marketing

The Body Shop®

The Body Shop (www.thebodyshop.com) is a company that relies on social media to promote their products to their target market. The Body Shop uses a blog, Twitter, Instagram, Facebook, LinkedIn, Flickr, and Pinterest to name just a few of the ways that they communicate directly with their customers. The use of social media has grown massively in recent years due to the growth in the supporting technology and the unlimited access that we now have to these social media tools. We now have apps that are available to us at the click of a button on our smartphones, tablets and even on some smart TVs. This means that companies have a greater sphere in which they can communicate and interact with their customers in order to promote their brand and products.

Due to its global expansion, The Body Shop's target market has expanded rapidly. This is why it is critical for the company to utilize social media in order to have contact with its customers on a global scale, "with over 2,500 stores in over 60 markets worldwide" (www.thebodyshop.com). The Body Shop continually has access to new markets, and as an established brand it can use to promote their products and communicate with their customers. Nonetheless, there are drawbacks to the way globalization has changed companies' communication with their customers. There are cultural barriers that companies such as The Body Shop now have to recognize as they communicate with their customers. They need to ensure that they are aware of the cultural differences from market to market in order to ensure that they do not alienate any potential customers from their brand. The use of social media is essential in order to be able to have a constant stream of communication with The Body Shop's target market. It also gives the company a large reach and ensures that word-of-mouth brand recognition can be passed along by users in order to expand their target market pool. This is easy to achieve through social media due to the fact that users can share their likes with their friends and family, creating a wider community for the brand.

Recently, The Body Shop created a YouTube channel for its brand. This is a key step in the process of exploiting social media in order to reach customers. On YouTube, The Body Shop posts videos for its customers about beauty hints and tips and which products they should look to purchase. The Body Shop uses experts to give advice to their customers about how to use their products and to suggest products for their customers. This allows The Body Shop to target its customers more effectively, as social media ensures that their customers are exposed to their brand since "YouTube is more popular than cable television" (www.thebodyshop.com). Therefore, The Body Shop is able to have contact with their target market more readily. The use of YouTube as a marketing tool is essential, as it gives a face to the brand and allows The Body Shop to give their customers insights into the company's professionalism and brand image, which they express through their choice of video uploads and content style.

Another strategy is to use social media advertising in order to beat the competition. Within the beauty sector, there are many brands that advertise themselves as being the best option for customers. Within the ethical beauty company category, *Lush* is *The Body Shop*'s biggest competitor. On social media, "although The Body Shop and Lush are two very similar brands, their approach toward social communication is very different. The Body Shop takes on a professional tone, not really encouraging interaction from their social communities. They focus on more informative posts/tweets for their customers, about new products, how-to videos and brand news." This demonstrates that The Body Shop tries to promote its image of being the expert in beauty as well as being an ethical and principled company. "The Body Shop seeks to make a positive difference in the world by offering high-quality, naturally-inspired skincare, hair care and make-up produced ethically and sustainably" (www.thebodyshop.com). This is because The

Body Shop uses their voice on social media to raise awareness of the company's business model and encourage their customers to think ethically when making purchasing decisions. They are able to encourage customers to buy their products as a result of their brand image and also to persuade other users to buy their brand as a result of their positive image as a company due to their ethical business practices.

There are many reasons for companies like The Body Shop to use social media as a key marketing strategy. Social media has become a key element of branding, as it allows customers to get a better insight into the brand and its goals: "The Body Shop is a leader in promoting greater corporate transparency, and we have been a force for positive social and environmental change through our campaigns around our five core Values: Support Community Fair Trade, Defend Human Rights, Against Animal Testing, Activate Self-Esteem, and Protect Our Planet" (www.thebodyshop.com). Through its use of using social media, The Body Shop is creating brand loyalty with its customer base, as customers understand that its advertising campaigns support their values. It also shows that The Body Shop is making an effort to communicate with them and educate them about new products and special offers. Thus customers are more likely to continue to purchase The Body Shop brand.

Social media further allows companies, such as The Body Shop, to gain a better understanding of their target market through social media data mining (data mining is the process of identifying patterns in large data sets). This occurs as a result of customer characteristics that can be identified from social media accounts, which can help companies to identify what their average customer expects from the company. They can assess the effectiveness of their marketing campaigns as well as be able to measure their follower participation. "One of the first things we learned was that our new social media accounts gave us a real-time view of how we could improve" (www.thebodyshop.com). Companies like The Body Shop can also use social media as an outlet for responding to criticism that their brand and products receive; that is, when someone uses social media to voice a complaint about a service or product, "through customers' comments, we started learning about issues with our products and services more quickly than ever before. In response, we set up systems so that a customer who has a question or a problem can get a quick answer from our team" (www.thebodyshop.com), as the company could then use social media monitoring to retrieve this feedback and use it to make improvements. The company could also apologize directly to the customer about their complaint and even offer the customer a form of compensation. This meant that the company was more likely to retain such customers and also establish a better brand image. The fact that The Body Shop can reach out to any of their customers about their comments means that customers have a personalized experience with the brand, making the brand greatly appealing to its customer base.

As a strategy, working with social media is generally productive for successfully marketing a brand. That's why many companies in the service sector are now implementing social media plans to improve the quality of service to their customers due to the broad reach of social media. It allows brands like The Body Shop to convey a personalized approach that attracts customers to purchase their products because the company has been able to shape a sense of community and belonging around the brand. Through social media, customers can directly engage with companies from which they purchase goods and services, and it makes them feel significant to the company's success, which then encourages brand loyalty and repeat purchases. Many customers use social media in order to attain opinions from other product and brand users before they make a purchase, which is why The Body Shop has to ensure that they are providing key knowledge about their products to customers through social media sites such as YouTube. Therefore, the use of social media by companies like The Body Shop will continue to grow.

Spotify

Spotify (www.spotify.com) is a music streaming service that uses social media to promote its products. In the current business environment, the use of social media to communicate with customers is essential. This is because social media helps the organization to achieve greater brand loyalty, higher brand recognition and new customers. It also provides the consumer with a richer experience, as they are able to communicate with the organization and seek out more information.

An example of a service organization that has implemented this strategy is Spotify. When investigating Spotify's use of social media, it is apparent that social media plays a big role in their ability to communicate with and obtain new customers. Early on, Spotify became associated with Facebook, and the way it interacts with Facebook improves the communication between Spotify and its customers as well as communication among its customers. Spotify requires a Facebook connection for new customers, which then allows customers to see what their friends are listening to on a newsfeed. This also allows customers simply to click on a Facebook link and listen to a song using the application. This use of social media improves the quality of service, as it gives their customers a richer experience because they are able to connect with friends and share their taste in music.

Spotify maintains profiles on the three main social media platforms: Facebook, Twitter, and Instagram. Spotify's strategy for setting up profiles on these platforms is that it allows them to communicate easily with consumers. For example, Facebook allows Spotify's customers to comment on Spotify's new features, albums, and so forth. "Spotify's Facebook page has 2.4 million 'likes' and an average of one post per day, primarily about bands who played or visited Spotify offices, and curated playlists for bands performing at festivals and award shows that can be listened to via Spotify" (www.spotify.com). This clearly demonstrates the success of this Spotify strategy when it comes to communicating with its audience, as 2.4 million customers or potential customers are exposed to a Spotify post about their music daily, and this can ultimately lead to customers using Spotify to listen to the various curated albums posted.

Another example would be a Twitter user who tweets Spotify about a certain feature that they are missing. This then allows Spotify to capitalize on this feedback and improve their offering. "Spotify's stream has 264,000 followers and an average of four to five tweets per day. There is a much higher level of engagement than on Facebook. On Twitter, Spotify answers users' questions, retweets music-related tweets by both regular and celebrity users, and even sends users' playlists made for them" (www.spotify.com). Allowing consumers to interact with your organization can improve the quality of service provided. This is due to the fact that any negative feedback provided by a customer can be investigated and the problem fixed in order to improve their service experience. Furthermore, this interaction will yield a richer customer experience, as users see that they are being acknowledged by the company, which ultimately leads to higher brand loyalty.

Another strategy that Spotify has implemented is the use of social media to promote deals and offers to customers, an example of this is Spotify's seasonal offer of three months premium service for 99¢. The use of social media to promote this offer let Spotify communicate it to its large customer base and to attract new customers. This strategy benefits Spotify, as using social media to promote such offers lowers marketing costs. Furthermore, keeping customers well informed about deals through social media improves brand loyalty and recognition, and again this can attract new customers. Additionally, social media can be used to launch advertisement campaigns, and one of Spotify's strategies does just that. Spotify uses social media in order to mass advertise new features of their service. A recent example is the addition of The Beatles catalog to their music library. Spotify created the Twitter hashtag #BeatlesOnSpotify to launch this campaign. The use of social media for this strategy aids Spotify in communicating new albums, artists, tracks, and so on. By doing this on social media, Spotify is able to obtain immediate feedback from customers as they can post their opinions and views on new features. In addition, by using social media, they are able to communicate to customers who they weren't aware existed who might be interested in the newest features enough to become a Spotify customer.

In conclusion, Spotify has become a successful music service partly by using social media to communicate with their customers. Their social media strategy has allowed them to obtain customer feedback by using Twitter to post and reply to customers comments. Moreover, Spotify facilitates the use of their service through Facebook. Customers who are registered with Facebook and Spotify are able to see what their friends are listening to as well as to listen to the same song simply by clicking on the Facebook link by sharing technology. This underscores that a strategy that relies on social media to facilitate the use of a service also aids in customer communication. Finally, Spotify also uses social media platforms to communicate new features as the foundation of their advertising campaigns.

Whole Foods Market (WFM)

Customer perceptions of service value are dependent on the level of employee service productivity and service quality delivered to customers. Hence there is a positive correlation between service value and customer satisfaction, leading to customer loyalty that directly affects organizational revenue growth and profitability. Marketing strategies of companies operating in the service sector are built around customer service, and effectively channeling such communications ensures their success. Internet technology has had a huge impact on organizations, providing them with many opportunities including direct communication with customers through social media. This is the main reason that Amazon purchased Whole Foods in 2017—to be able to send the Whole Food message out to customers and to use their strength as the internet marketplace to capitalize on the goodwill generated by Whole Foods.

Whole Foods Market's (*WFM*) (www.wholefoodsmarket.com) social media strategy has contributed significantly to its growth, making them the leading natural and organic food store. Its strategy is based upon the company website and six supplementary platforms consisting of Facebook, Twitter, Pinterest, Flickr, the WFM blog, and Foursquare. WFM utilizes these platforms as the basis for building brand image and promoting their products. Their primary tool for customer engagement and service is Twitter, responding to individual customer inquiries and requests almost instantly, as well as updating customers with their latest offers. In order to maximize their communication, thus consumer satisfaction, they have social media accounts for most local stores as well as several niche accounts for specific products such as wine and cheese. WFM engages as well as educates their customers through the role of blogs and Facebook platforms, providing consumers with product and health information, recipes, and cooking tips. For example, when food labeling legislation changed, WFM used these platforms as a way to educate shoppers on GMOs and to answer any immediate questions. It used the feedback they received to develop a set of frequently asked questions (FAQs).

One way that WFM enhances their communication is by thinking globally while acting locally. They assign community managers to every store, allowing management of customer engagement through numerous social media platform accounts, emphasizing the local component of focusing on being where the customers are located. This focus on leveraging local store accounts allows them to embrace freedom and initiative, as well as having a more personal connection to their respective shopper communities. Although WFM experiments to see what social media strategies works best, they make sure that each platform concentrates on a given objective, with a continual focus on improving the relevancy of customer engagement and ensuring that it occurs as naturally as possible—listening, observing, and applying new ideas from what they learn.

Despite the role that social media plays to enhance the communication channels between WFM and its customers, it also can have a negative impact on an organization. It offers a platform that enables competitors and customers to espouse their ideas, yet it difficult to regulate as authorship is generally anonymous and sources are rarely supplied. This was demonstrated when WFM was investigated for allegedly mislabeling products and overcharging customers, which resulted in the creation of a "Boycott Whole Foods" page on Facebook, drawing the attention of 30,000 members within two weeks and developing into a national movement throughout social media. Customers were angry, claiming that WFM was favoring conventionally-grown produce over organic foods.

The use of social media, particularly Twitter, can generate value for organizations along the three stages of the marketing process: pre-purchase, purchase, and post-purchase. Social media also allows customers to be involved in the marketing process, essentially enabling organizations to obtain creative ideas free of charge. WFM identified with the creativity of their customers and used Instagram as a source photos from their community. They used the #WFMEarth hashtag, encouraging people to send photos capturing beautiful images of the world, emphasizing the importance of taking care of our planet, with the weekly winner receiving a $100 store card.

The notion of customer knowledge becoming a competitive advantage and the emphasis on collaboration with customers has become increasingly prominent in academic literature. The use of social media platforms such as Twitter allows WFM to integrate customer input into their decision-making processes, as it provides them with easy access to customer feedback. Microblogs also provide

WFM with a unique type of information, as it allows them to analyze customers' feedback in real time, as opposed to summaries of customer analyses over time. They also have the opportunity to study the ethnography of online communities through Kozinets' (2002) method, "netnography" (an online research method used to understand social interaction in contemporary digital communications contexts) allowing them faster, simpler, and less expensive access to customer feedback through a more naturalistic and unobtrusive process.

WFM capitalizes on this real-time phenomenon through their use of Twitter account, reinforcing their brand messages and sales promotions. They use this platform to connect with customers about product recalls, health tips, and special promotions, awarding a $25 "Tweet of the Day" gift card and organizing tweeting contests about Whole Foods' philosophies.

Ultimately, WFM can use their social media presence to improve their customer service and complaint-management process, as it allows them to respond to dissatisfied customers rapidly and professionally (e.g. they use status updates). A WFM online community manager identifies any issues or negative comments highlighted by customers through daily analysis of their Twitter account, answering questions within 24 hours. Alternatively, WFM engages with consumers who are referring to them as "Whole Paycheck," a negative connotation built upon the boycott referring to their high prices, in a bid to understand better their unfavorable impressions and underlying concerns. Organizations in general need to be aware of the formality of the language they use to address their customers through social media. WFM believed that quality was one of their competitive advantages. However, they behaved lackadaisically with their followers, misrepresenting their upscale brand, thus leading to outrage and discussion concerning the appropriate use of language in social media.

WFM has positioned itself as embracing corporate social responsibility (CSR), espousing core values such as "caring about our communities and our environment," sourcing their produce organically and sustainably, as well as devoting 5% of their annual profits to various social causes. Their stance on CSR could potentially magnify the efficiency of the communication they maintain with their customers. This can also put WFM in a risky position, as customers may not just buy into their CSR messages, but rather on the authenticity of WFM endeavors. This emphasizes the importance of alignment between actual CSR activities versus CSR messages. Due to the emergence of social media, however, external communication channels have arisen that are not entirely controlled by the company, making it extremely difficult for WFM to control such messages. In contrast, consumers can also serve as a highly credible form of a CSR communication channel. This positive use of social media empowers customers, magnifying word-of-mouth through virtual channels, thus allowing companies to use customers as their CSR advocates.

The use of social media is also an imperative for WFM in order for them to remain competitive as a global company. Customers appreciate global companies that exert influence on the well-being of society, and expect them to have a duty to tackle social issues. Social media allows WFM to communicate their CSR messages, as well as managing their brands and perceptions of what consumers expect them to be. Global brands often have negative connotations associated with them due to the instability of global markets highlighted by the media and discussions that are spread over the internet. Social media is a way of monitoring and challenging these perceptions in real time in order to maintain brand image and a competitive advantage over other global companies and even smaller firms. Ultimately, the use of social media is a form of total quality management (TQM), hence WFM is continuously improving by responding to customer needs and expectations.

As the service industry is becoming ever more competitive, with 80% of all United States economic activity taking place in the service sector, it is imperative that companies focus on what drives customer loyalty and customer satisfaction. This continuous focus on customer service is improved through monitoring communication channels between the organization and consumers, hence the importance of social media. One of the main benefits of WFM using social media is the ability to draw feedback from customers in real time, allowing them to develop more insightful communication techniques, such as a set of FAQs more tailored to their customers. WFM also cleverly uses social media to include customers in the decision-making process, enhancing their competitive status through the notion of collaboration and generating customer value, as well as conveying their CSR messages and promotional material—particularly important when competing in a global market. Still, WFM needs to ensure that they monitor their social media carefully, as customers also have the ability to subject their ideas to scrutiny, ultimately putting WFM's reputation and brand image in jeopardy.

Netflix

Social media has become a powerful communication and marketing tool among companies and consumers. If social media is used correctly, companies are able to connect with a new and wider audience, resulting in strong personal relationships among their current and potential future customers. Implementing a social media strategy in your business has many benefits which will improve the quality of your service. Businesses learn more about their audience using services such as Google Analytics, which helps track information from your website. For example, it tracks the types of users who visit your website so that you are able to adapt your products and services according to their age, sex, and location. It is also a very useful way to generate feedback on a product or service, or the company in general. Twitter is a great example of receiving feedback and complaints on a service or product quickly, which the company can use to improve on the existing product or service. Finally, it is a very cost-effective method of marketing.

Netflix (www.netflix.com) is involved in many social media platforms. One of the effective ways they market is through YouTube. Netflix sponsors popular "YouTubers" to promote the brand on their YouTube channel. This is an effective method of promotion as these YouTubers have a massive fan base and they are able to spread the word to a huge audience. It is also similar to a celebrity endorsement—when fans see their favorite YouTubers use a certain product or service, they are most likely to try it out too. Netflix also has their own YouTube channel, where they post trailers of shows airing on their streaming service, which is a great way to market their services. Today, more and more people are watching shows and videos on their computers and smartphones at the expense of traditional TV. Netflix is able to create relationships with a community of loyal customers through YouTube, by making reviews of their shows available and by giving news updates on what films and shows are going to be offered on Netflix soon.

Netflix also uses Twitter, Facebook, and Instagram to communicate with their customers, and they have recently joined Snapchat. All of these platforms offer an easy and quick way to respond to their customers and to receive feedback from them. Twitter is a great platform for Netflix to increase brand awareness through quirky tweets. Take a look at the examples here:

As you can see in the above image, Netflix is witty in their tweets and replies. This attitude towards its customers makes them feel more connected to the brand, and by building brand loyalty it encourages people to talk about the brand further. This increases its marketing reach without significant expense, and this benefits the company as a whole. Netflix personalize their responses to customers as well as using puns with them. This is a great way to raise brand awareness, and it also makes customers feel special. These people are then more likely to attend the event or even follow Netflix on Twitter. On Instagram, Netflix is able to promote their brand to a large social media market. Again, this is great way to create awareness. On Snapchat, Netflix is able to send and receive photo messages to and from their customers, as the loyal customers are the ones who tend to follow the company.

Personalized communication is a major factor in social media that should be used to market or promote goods or services. Netflix excels at doing this. As mentioned above, Netflix sends personalized responses on social media sites and through email. This makes the customer feel as if they are speaking to real human beings, not just dealing with an automated computer response in a corporate tone. Also as mentioned above, Netflix embraces a playful persona successfully in their communications. Netflix maintains a "Recommended for You" tab on their website that creates a personalized playlist of TV shows and movies, allowing for greater consumer engagement based on the user's taste.

Netflix has two sets of blogs. One is a tech blog where they post information about technical issues, the decisions and challenges they face regarding the software, and how they implement these on the Netflix service. The other blog that Netflix maintains is Tumblr—a microblogging and social networking website, which is a friendly and visually-appealing one, aimed at millennials. Tumblr is in the top-15 most visited sites in the United States. It is an easy way for fans of Netflix to share blog posts among millions of users. Netflix knows exactly who their target market is and how to communicate with them through the right social media platforms. Getting involved with platforms such as Twitter, Tumblr and Facebook gives consumers an opportunity to share their posts, thereby increasing viewers and brand awareness at little or no cost.

Netflix also knows exactly what their customers want through their market research. Netflix carried out a survey to find out what people thought about so called "binge viewing." They found out that 61% of their users binge watch regularly and 73% of their users claimed that they have positive feelings towards binge viewing. This means that they watch two–six episodes consecutively.

On the whole, Netflix's social media strategy is one of a kind, as their main method of marketing is via word of mouth. Social media is a great platform to spread the word, with features such as "shares" and "trending topics" (which are relatively more valuable to the reader) on Twitter and Facebook. This significantly cuts down marketing costs as social media is, in essence, free. Netflix has taken full advantage of the popular social media platforms that are used by a large number of people.

Southwest Airlines

Customer service has always been at the heart of *Southwest Airlines'* (www.southwest.com) communication and advertising strategies, starting from the early days when Southwest Airlines was the first U.S. airline to launch a website. Southwest Airline's approach to a successful communication strategy is to engage all functions within the organization and for the employees in charge of handling social media to bear the responsibility for listening and replying to customers in a friendly and engaged manner. In fact, the fit between Southwest's communication strategy and its overall approach to business is what makes its social media approach so viable, with over 6 million likes on its Facebook page. Its mission of enthusiastic, high-quality customer service very much reflects this same approach to communication. Moreover, Southwest aims to continue developing its brand personality of "fun loving," by communicating about the brand across all social media in order to boost the brand image with current and future customers. It also seeks to design superior multimedia information to share with its social media users. Probably, however, the communication strategy most directly related to its profits is communicating with its customers to inform them about new products and services as they launch. This is likely to increase customer brand loyalty and attachment.

Social media enables extra services to be delivered to customers, such as informing them of flight delays, gate changes, weather conditions, and so on, hence improving customer services and adding value by keeping customers informed and up-to-date about their flights and travel plans. Give that Southwest Airlines is a low-cost carrier; social media is used extensively to achieve its communication strategy at low cost.

Southwest's social media communication strategy focuses on using online platforms to communicate better with customers through a mutual relationship, while giving both the employees and customers a chance to raise their views and continue to deliver an excellent customer service, consistent with Southwest's overall organizational objectives. The social media platforms that Southwest Airlines currently uses includes Facebook, Twitter, Flickr, YouTube, and its own blog called "Nuts about Southwest," staffed by a team of 30 bloggers. This blog mainly features employees sharing posts about their lives at Southwest. This helps in two ways:

1. It enhances the customer experience by providing an opportunity to speak with real employees talking about their lives.
2. It increases intrinsic employee motivation and hence serves Southwest's customers better.

Southwest understands that customers use these platforms to engage with the company and to submit inquiries and feedback. In return, they expect timely and appropriate responses. Consequently, Southwest organized a Social Media Committee that oversees communications, marketing, and customer relationships. One of the major communication strategies employed by Southwest is to include employees in every aspect of communications, for instance by arranging internal social media meetings.

According to Anne Murray, director of marketing communications, a critical aspect of this strategy is to understand the customer and tailor their offers according to each customer's needs. This increases customer satisfaction, as they are treated as individuals. This personalization of communication between Southwest Airlines and its customers is the reason they have several local Facebook pages rather than just one, decentralizing responsibilities to each of its geographical units. The airline also maintains a "Listening Center," where customer service is enhanced through social media by listening to and acting upon complaints. Customers can even communicate with the listening center while in flight and get their problems addressed immediately. The communications team undergoes customer service training to ensure that they understand how to best serve Southwest's customers.

Southwest has a very strategic approach to social media by insisting that every department participate in it. Better communication allows for better decisions to be made at Southwest Airlines. Their main objective in using social media and associated communication technologies is to stay ahead of the competition by targeting a wider audience and reaching customers directly through a variety of media. Their communication strategy is about creating an experience for customers through exchanges between employees and customers that in turn fosters better customer service. Southwest also uses social media to communicate news about events to the customers in order to keep them informed and to handle any crisis effectively.

While engaging with customers, Southwest employees always follow its policy of keeping communication concise in order to ensure that the customers are provided with the most effective service through clear information sharing. Southwest involves its employees in their communication with customers. Southwest aims to be forward thinking and open with customers by providing information about problems (for instance, a flight delay or mechanical issue) through social media instead of allowing the customers to have to discover the problems by themselves, where the issues may only worsen. Hence, social media is used as a tool to deliver clear information in a transparent manner to prevent small problems from becoming larger ones.

Southwest Airlines tries to stimulate interaction with customers on a regular basis and seeks to use all types of multimedia, ranging from photos to videos. For example, it may post a picture and ask customers to identify the airport at which the photo was taken. By supporting such features, Southwest Airlines aims to add personality to its social media pages. Southwest also tries to reflect its "friendly" culture in its social media presence. Understanding the personality of the audience is very critical for Southwest Airlines to establish a personal relationship with its customers. Southwest Airlines maintains a close relationship with its customers through its employees, wherein Southwest employees maintain a blog about their daily life at the company on "Nuts about Southwest," sharing their stories, which increases participation and interaction with their customers. Southwest Airlines retweets its customers posts in an effort to show its appreciation.

Southwest Airlines has a clear policy responding to all of the inquiries submitted by its customers, as opposed to those companies that leave many customer inquiries unanswered. In fact, Southwest Airlines seeks to benefit from criticisms raised by customers and views them as an opportunity to improve its services, as opposed to viewing them as a threat to its brand image. This approach of listening, caring, and assisting customers in resolving their problems results in an enhanced brand image. Accordingly, Southwest Airlines utilizes social media not only to communicate with customers, but also to assist it in handling operational issues that customers may experience. Southwest Airlines uses social media to remedy the damage that can be caused by a given issue by reaching out and listening to customers. If customers have a problem, they are guided to ask for support through Twitter, which also provides enhanced value to customers as they do not have to wait in long queues.

Southwest is transparent not only through social media, but through other communication avenues as well, for example by informing customers about flight delays on its website. Southwest purses consistency in its communications not only through a variety of social media platforms, but also through email, public reports, and its website, emphasizing the supportive customer service of Southwest Airlines. Even its symbol on the New York Stock Exchange is LUV, stressing the friendly and caring aspect of the airline. Southwest continues to communicate its attractive fares outside of social media as well, for example, on

DING (Southwest Airlines App), where it provides customers with unique discount offers. Even Southwest's older advertisements reflect communication of its low prices, great service, fun, and love. Southwest Airlines uses email in a more personalized manner to reach its customers effectively; that is, in an approach similar to its use of social media to respond individually to each customer. The airlines' chief marketing officer, explains that it is important for the company's message to stand out among its competitors, whether communicating through TV, social media, or any other communication channel. Southwest's entertaining culture is communicated to customers even during the safety announcements where flight attendants use humor, often greeted with customer applause, further reducing stress on short trips. Thus Southwest uses social media in a consistent and complementary manner to its other forms of communication.

Southwest Airlines has shifted from traditional methods of customer service to use of social media over time. The airline uses social media both to gain insights about its customers and to inform them about the company. As customers are becoming more and more well-informed, they demand additional personalized service and sincere interaction with brands such as Southwest Airlines seeks to provide. Southwest Airlines tries to reflect its culture to its customers when it communicates with them. Southwest Airlines also increases its sales revenue through social media and also enhances its brand awareness. Southwest Airlines manages to utilize social media extensively as a tool to communicate its mission and culture while complementing its other communication strategies, achieving greater compatibility between its communications and its corporate practices.

Chapter 9
The Case for Business Issued Smartphones

The use of technology at work is becoming more popular on a daily basis. In fact, some smartphone users consider these mobile devices extensions of their physical selves. The main reason for the rapid growth in business-issued smartphones (BIS) is due to the fact employees can work from home if they choose to. With ever increasing technological advancement and development of new software apps, it comes as no surprise that many companies are looking for ways to implement these resources in order to attain a competitive advantage and streamline work processes. Successful companies understand that there is a constant need to improve their business processes—to become more productive and efficient and to respond to changes in the market quickly while providing better service to customers. Technology acquisition, innovation, and implementation play important roles in achieving this goal. There is undoubtedly an ever-increasing abundance of smartphone and tablet apps that companies are implementing not only for their cost and performance benefits, but also to benefit the employees and the overall workplace environment and culture.

Organizational Control and Coordination

To understand organizations, measures must be in place to observe the work that is being performed by employees. Managers should be able to control and monitor their work easily so that they can legitimately say that they know what is happening in their organization.

There are two main methods of monitoring; a manager can either observe an employee's input or output (i.e. effort or units produced). In some cases, there will be a direct link between the input and output, so a manager can observe the employee's effort without having to constantly watch them, due to the fact that it can be deterministically calculated using the output. This will often be very cost-effective, given that many organizations will already have systems in place to measure output. However, it is sometimes hard to establish an easy link between input and output. This can be the case if goods are produced in a team, where it is not always apparent who has performed which tasks, or how much team members have contributed. A solution to this problem is presented in Taylorism; divide up tasks into small, standardized, closely specified subtasks so as to achieve predictability of job performance. By decomposing tasks, it can become easier to trace output to a particular person, as the link between input

DOI 10.1515/9781547400546-009

and output becomes more transparent. Once there is transparency between input and output, the costs involved with monitoring are reduced for a company.

The most common way monitoring takes place now is through the use of business-issued smartphones (BIS). Using BIS systems in organizations makes information such as employee performance quickly and easily available. Using this, line managers and senior management staff can see in more detail how the organization and their departments are performing, and, if they are under-performing, they can identify the areas for improvement.

Although BIS-based control and coordination has many advantages, it can also have negative impacts on a company's workforce. Employees can often feel that they are under constant supervision when BIS-based control is used, and they can feel as though they are being spied on. Many employees like to feel as though their managers can trust them to do their job, so if managers are continuously monitoring their performance, employees can become less motivated. In the past, when BIS was less readily available, appraisal-based control systems were often used. Monitoring could be performed by appraising employees, which gives a more personal feel. This became, however, less and less common as BIS-based monitoring systems became cheaper and quicker.

An efficient monitoring method was required as financial incentives for employees became more common practice. Financial incentives are often given as a reward for hitting certain targets, whether it is a production target or customer satisfaction target, for example. As was often the way, though, if a worker was given a production target, it was likely that they would compromise on quality in order to produce as many units as possible, therefore increasing their bonus. This in turn costs the company more money as customers will then require refunds or a replacement product if their purchase is faulty. BIS-based control allows companies to monitor not only employee performance, but production quality. Whether it is a factory manufacturing car parts, or a telephone call center, performance measuring systems can be designed in order to monitor quality of production or service.

Although BIS-based control can have negative impacts on employees, employees need to be trained on how the monitoring is carried out, and also how they can help in the monitoring process. It is not simply about spying on them by monitoring emails and phone calls, for example. It is about much more than this; by monitoring effectively, organizational problems can be found and worked on, benefitting everyone in a company. The use of BIS streamlines many processes, including data analysis. Data can be instantly collected and analyzed, which in turn can produce innovative solutions when it is viewed by employees, resolving organizational issues. Involving employees in the monitoring process, through analyzing results and giving them the opportunity to offer ideas for solutions if needed, they can feel a much more important part of the firm.

Purely analyzing data, however, is often not enough to really understand an organization. Assessing financial results and performance data, while useful and provides an insight into how a company is performing, does not show the underlying problems that a firm may have. A company could theoretically have brilliant profits in the short term, but problems deep inside the firm could be either stopping these profits from progressing, or even reducing them in the long term. If one has a comprehensive understanding of the company though, these problems can be identified and resolved. This is the view that managers need to have. It is not enough for them just to know how many units of a good their department is producing, or how much profit their team has made. They need an in-depth understanding of the organization, and this will come through involving employees. Employees can often know much more about how a specific section of the organization works than a manager will. An employee may have great insights into what problems a firm might have, and by involving them in the monitoring process, the procedure can be improved, along with employee morale.

In conclusion, if the monitoring-based control and coordination mechanism is going to be a useful concept for understanding organizations, it needs to be realized that quantitative measuring is not sufficient; qualitative measuring is also hugely important. "Surveillance," or spying, needs to be limited, otherwise employees can lose their trust in managers. The monitoring needs to be shown to be being used for the best interests of the organization, and that it is not just for keeping tabs on employees. Lastly, employees must be involved in the monitoring process, and they should receive personal feedback, allowing them to improve, and improve the company's performance, while approaching and resolving any underlying problems that a company may be facing. Business issued smartphones can be an excellent method of achieving employee participation, while also receiving detailed feedback and performance information, all the while saving time and money for the company.

Benefits of Smartphone Apps

There are many benefits for companies who implement smartphone apps to support their business operations. One of the main benefits is that such apps allow employees to work from anywhere—be it at home, from a coffee shop, in another city, or even in a foreign country. When employees can work from anywhere, they are often more productive. For many employees, it cuts down on the time spent traveling to the office and gives them more flexibility with their personal schedules. When employees can work from anywhere, it opens up their schedules to work flexible hours throughout the day. Thus it allows for a better work-life balance and means that employees aren't stuck behind a desk for a fixed number of hours. This greater freedom and empowerment results in higher employee satisfaction, which contributes to greater productivity and efficiency overall. This can only be beneficial to the employee. Also to the benefit of the company, as more employees work from anywhere, it means the work space required for each individual is lowered. Thus the amount of office space required is reduced resulting in a cost savings for the company.

Another benefit, of course, is the fact that the use of apps can streamline workplace processes and activities, making them easier and faster to accomplish. There are many third-party, general-use apps that can be implemented by companies in the workplace, some of which may already be in use by employees on their personal mobile devices. Apps such as *Cisco WebEx* (www.webex.com) allows employees to share their desktop while delivering a presentation online and to conduct video conferencing and meetings (businessinsider.com, 2014). Thus co-workers and teams can deliver presentations and attend meetings online even though they may be in different locations.

There are also innovative smartphone apps developed by companies themselves for internal use by their own employees. These too are designed to streamline work processes, but the benefits often extend to the customers who, as time moves forward, also demand and favor a technological approach that allows for them to access services wherever and whenever.

Another benefit of using apps is they allow for better customer service, providing quicker response times and resolutions. An example of this app is the one offered by LGT Group, a private banking and asset management group. LGT's goal was to make their current and future banking services available on mobile devices anywhere, at any time. They wanted to create a service that prioritized their customers changing digital needs, and in addition they wanted to provide their employees with a portal that gave them access to customized information and company services. This led to the creation of the *LGT SmartBanking app* (https://smartbanking.lgt.com). The app integrates with legacy systems and allows for long-term development and growth in the future. By using the app, employees are able to perform company services, view customer data, connect with higher management, and carry out daily business needs—all from their mobile devices. The public version of the LGT SmartBanking app, which customers can use, allows them to perform all necessary transactions on their smartphones, as well as providing an improved communication experience with LGT representatives. Thus the introduction of the app not only benefitted the employees in managing and accessing work, but so too their customers who now have access to a better service as well.

Drawbacks of Smartphone Apps

Conversely, there are some concerns relating to the implementation of apps experienced by some employees and app users in general. One major issue relates to security. The issue with apps and the smartphone or tablet devices on which they are installed is that they are somewhat easily hackable by those with the necessary skill to do so. This could put sensitive company information at the risk of being lost, stolen, or compromised if sufficient security precautions aren't in put into place to prevent such attacks. This is particularly the case when companies allow employees to use their own personal devices for work. Devices and apps are not only susceptible to being hacked, but if an employee is careless and their device is lost or it is stolen, confidential company information may be at risk.

Thus companies using apps need to take precautions and either provide devices for employee use with necessary security in place, or should employees be allowed to use their personal devices, provide the security software and check these devices to ensure that the required security software is installed properly and in use. Either way, this is an extra and ongoing expense for the company, as they need to be certain that the security software is kept up to date in order to ensure maximum protection. Furthermore, companies do not have control over the development of third-party apps that may cause security-related risks.

Another potential issue is that of the reliability of these apps. Like all technology, when apps go down, it means that employees can not do their work, either in the office, at home, or on the road. For app use to be considered a success, companies need to ensure that such occurrences are rare and can be quickly resolved. Again, this all costs extra, so a company needs to assess whether a particular app is affordable and worth implementing. Another point to consider in relation to employees working from anywhere is that for it to work it requires a certain type of employee for a certain type of work. Therefore, employees require a reasonable skill level and degree of trustworthiness in order to ensure they do the work properly.

One more concern is the fact some employees may not like/want apps to be forced on them as they are used to the processes and systems already in place and do not want change. Overall, it is evident that there are many benefits to be had from the implementation of apps in the workplace. Undoubtedly, the workplace in general is changing as a result of technology. For many employees, no longer is the workplace an office, as the implementation of apps has resulted in employee homes becoming the main place of work. Even in a traditional workplace environment, for those who are unable to work from anywhere, their work processes are becoming streamlined and easier to manage because of mobile device apps. The major downside, of course, is the not insignificant issue of security. However, if companies are willing to invest in the right security software, then the use of mobile device apps is the clear way forward. This trend is in line with the rapidly changing use of technology in our society, as people demand the implementation of such technologies so that they can have easier and greater access to goods and services.

Work Organization and Management

The main benefit of introducing apps in the workplace is that greater productivity is achieved, offering economic benefits to businesses. Apps allow quicker access to information and promote faster communication among individuals.

Formal vs. Informal Communication

Apps also streamline work processes by providing greater communications between individuals and groups. This communication is boosted through *instant messaging* applications such as Google Hangouts and Facebook Messenger. These applications allow faster communications between employees and therefore can speed-up work processes. Where instant messaging exists, companies like to monitor the communications in order to ensure that communications are appropriate for the workplace. In contrast, some see the existence of informal channels of communications as beneficial for companies where innovation and creativity is encouraged. *AlphaGuide* (www.alphabet.com) is an application whereby organizations can communicate with individuals who often travel on business, such as sales representatives. This application is a formal channel of communication, and it is used to remind or direct employees to certain locations. The use of *AlphaGuide* would be seen by many companies as an effective use of technology; this needs to be seen in the context of Facebook Messenger, which is a purely social media application that allows users to communicate informally (Messenger, 2015).

Acceptance of Technology

The use of mobile applications in the workplace has encouraged greater worker motivation, as apps have allowed greater job enrichment and enlargement, and this can lead to improved working conditions. Job enrichment is facilitated through the introduction of technology, such as a mobile application that can help an individual learn a new work process. Job enlargement can occur as the implementation of apps can lead to improved time management within the firm so that more tasks can be carried out. Apps can also improve working conditions, with instant messaging meeting the social needs of individuals. An academic perspective that interprets the effectiveness of this is called the "Technology Acceptance Model." Although what has been stated above is positive, in reality, many individuals do not readily adapt to new technologies and work processes (IGI Global, 2018). What has been identified in the extant literature is that the individual must see the technology as useful and easy to use. Utility and ease of use of technology are two of the most critical factors in the acceptance of technology by individuals.

One application, mentioned at the start of Chapter 6, that empowers employees is iPresent (www.ipresent.com). This is an application that allows salespeople, or those who present information to others, to deliver high-quality presentations from data that is either be stored on a mobile device or stored on a cloud platform (iPresent, 2018). This app empowers salespeople, as they are able to access data without needing to ask the permission of managers or other colleagues. The data that they require is quick and easy to find, improving their efficiency and their presentations. Both of these improve the final outcome and provide additional motivation to these employees.

Monitoring Workers

In modern-day work environments, there are many tools that businesses can use to ensure that they recruit the right people and that they work effectively while on the job. Business may believe they have more control, but they will lose the trust of workers if they misuse this technology, causing a loss in motivation. Thus, the business must decide whether it would rather continue monitoring its workers, or try to increase productivity in some other way. One major way of doing this is by being able to keep track of a worker's movements to make sure they are producing effectively. Amazon loading dock workers have their movements tracked when they are unloading stock at the ship yard (Data and Society Research Institute, 2014). The modern era of technology has given rise to a business mindset that monitoring employees will lead to better results. Businesses now have the ability to see which workers are most productive and to remove the ones who are not. Through the use of computers and technology in the workplace, it is also now possible to monitor what exactly employees are doing with their time in the office when they are not working (webcams/videos are also used to monitor workers, and pose ethical issues).

Studies show that 40% of businesses actually screen their employees' email (Ferguson, 2009), often for things not related to work. 66% of employers are said to keep track of a worker's internet history (Employee Surveillance and the Modern Workplace, 2016). Businesses now track their employees in what might be viewed as a personal space. Thus, they can determine whether the employee is wasting time or not. In terms of personal communication, it is not just email that can now be monitored but phone calls as well, as call centers can screen worker's phones with calls being fed into a central feeder every three–four minutes (Data and Society Research Institute, 2014). The level of personal expression in a phone call is very high, and this action shows the level of a business's potential for control over their employees.

In business, there are many different types of managers. Some managers believe that the employee can not be trusted and is naturally work adverse. These managers are likely to forfeit a worker's trust for the sake of gathering a vast amount of information about them. A company should have a comprehensive understanding of who someone is before they enter the company through by conducting background checks. A business can simply check an individual's Facebook page. Many large employers carry out drug tests on potential employees even though there is a risk of false positive results if a candidate has certain conditions such as pregnancy or diabetes (Employee Surveillance and the Modern Workplace, 2016).

Related Management Theory

Using such procedures in the workplace is part of managing the business in a certain way. This is Theory X management, where it is believed that the worker is naturally lazy and will try to get out of working (McGregor, 1960). This follows suit on the ideas of Taylor which did have some merits. Taylor was helping to manage a pig iron plant in Bethlehem when the price of pig iron suddenly rose leading the company to sell at a lot of it in a sale. For this effort, a piece rate was implemented and when the wages were put far above those of everyone else in the factory, the average number of pieces of pig iron that a worker moved in a day rose from 13 pieces a day to 75 (Nelson, 1977). People are largely motivated by money, and more pig iron was moved when piece rates were increased. This was an over simplified strategy, however, as the workers who moved this much pig iron were exhausted afterward. For this, a new piece rate was implemented where workers who could move up to 45 pieces of pig iron were given wage increases. It should be noted, however, that even Taylor admitted that a very small number of workers would actually earn this amount of money, and there would be many workers who would actually earn less than they did when they worked in the main factory (Nelson, 1977).

Motivating Employees

Due to improvements in technology, businesses can monitor most aspects of work-life and see what the employees are actually doing. This follows certain beliefs about an organization and the ways in which a worker should be treated. It should be noted, however, that there are other things to consider that can motivate employees and that people are not such simple creatures. Hertzberg suggested that a safe working environment or a standard wage would be something considered customary or a hygiene factor (Buchanan and Huczynski, 2016). However, other things can be used in order to motivate the worker. These ideas were influential to the extent that they are still being used at Kellogg's today. For example, Kellogg's has an initiative where their employees are given free healthcare and free gym memberships. They call it "Fit for Life." Caring about a worker's well-being will make them feel like they are more a part of the business and may motivate them to work harder thereby reducing a company's turnover, which can greatly affect costs in the long-run.

Many businesses now see the need to motivate their workers with things beyond money. Kellogg's also had its version of summer hours where a worker can go home on Friday at lunchtime if they have completed all of their work hours for the week. This allows workers to spend some time away from the office and better their work-life balance, which may make the worker more motivated. Kellogg's also includes workers in decision-making processes that affect their jobs and delegates some responsibility to them. Having a worker participate in the decision-making process can make them feel more important to the company's mission and further motivate them. Finally, Kellogg's holds end-of-the-week meetings to discuss the week's achievements and review any suggestions. This makes their workers feel noticed and their suggestions appreciated.

These are some of the examples of how BIS attempts to encourage "good" decision-making. This concept is similar to the concept of "choice architecture" from behavioral economics. It is a mild form of paternalism that attempts to improve decision-making processes by designing decision points where beneficial biases are encouraged, and detrimental biases are discouraged (Thaler, 2015). Self-determination theory states that an action is either *intrinsically* or *extrinsically* motivated (Deci and Ryan, 2008). Intrinsic motivation involves performing an activity because it is enjoyable or engaging while extrinsic motivation is defined as performing an activity for the sake of outside motivators in the form of financial compensation or obligatory deadlines. Intrinsic motivation is more strongly associated with a higher standard of work in terms of both quality and quantity, and this has been shown to lead to effective learning outcomes and increased creativity across various applications (Hamari et al., 2014). Motivation and creativity researchers (e.g. Deci and Ryan, 2008) contend that extrinsic motivation is detrimental to innovation or adoption of new technology as it redirects attention away from the heuristic aspects of the innovative or creative task and toward the technical or rule-bound aspects of task performance.

However, in a meta-analytic review of the effects of incentives on workplace performance, Condly, Clark and Stolovithc (2003) showed that irrespective of whether the goal was to improve quantity of performance or quality of performance, incentives had a positive effect. Financial incentives produced performance gains more than double of the average gains produced by non-monetary but tangible gifts. Furthermore, incentives had a significant positive effect on getting people to persist at a job once they start it. A recent meta-analysis by Cerasoli et al. (2014) found that when incentives were present and were only indirectly salient to performance, intrinsic motivation was a better predictor of performance. On the other hand, when incentives were directly salient to performance, intrinsic motivation became a poorer predictor of performance.

Incentives and Productivity

Motivation is a key aspect of management theory and in order to gain maximum effort and commitment from the workforce it may be possible to incentivize some aspects of the work. An incentive system is a scheme used within an organization to provide control and coordination in some desirable way. It helps to promote or encourage specific actions or behavior within the employees, as well as keep them motivated. Incentives may be offered to employees in order to help and achieve certain objectives set by the manager. These objectives can be about increasing productivity of the organization, retaining the services of efficient workers or increasing the quality of production. Depending on the type of organization and type of employee, different sorts of remuneration may be appropriate. Some include pay by effort exerted, pay by results or output, promotion and bonuses for top performance. When providing incentives, the organization bear the costs, therefore they will want to ensure they are getting the best return from their employees.

With increased productivity, a company can gain higher profits and have more potential for growth, which are good long-term objectives. Besides, a company may want to retain the services of the efficient workers which they currently have, and if there is a chance that the workers may choose to find work elsewhere, they need to be offered incentives which will influence them to stay. Increasing the quality of production can also help to increase profits; as if a company is offering a product of a higher quality then they will be able to sell it at a higher price. Quality is not always easy to measure, as it can not always be directly observed and is down to a subjective view of the manager.

The type of remuneration used bears different risks to company and worker, so when deciding which objective to focus on, this needs to be remembered. For example, pay by results may give the workers full marginal returns, but it does also impose risk upon them (Lazear and Gibbs, 2014). However for a fixed wage rate, the risk is imposed on the company, but this does reduce the worker's returns. If a company decided to focus on the objective of increasing productivity, pay by output is a way in which a company can try to entice their employees into producing more, however a consequence of this is that the quality of production can drop, if the employees are focusing on quantity rather than quality. Offering bonuses or prizes to the best performers is another incentive which can motivate employees to work harder and increase their productivity. Maslow believed via his hierarchy of needs theory that the root of engaging an employee at work began with pay and security (Buchanan and Huczynski, 2016). If the worker sees the new incentive scheme as a way to enhance earnings, they are likely to increase their efforts. On the other hand, this may be perceived as a shift away from secure earnings by the worker and lead to them either leaving the company which will affect labor turnover rates and the cost associated with labor. Alternatively, they could lose interest in the work if the incentives were seen as unachievable and therefore lead to lower job satisfaction and consequently lower productivity.

Measuring quality of production can sometime prove difficult. For example, if measuring a teacher's performance was based on the scores their students received, it would not be a true measurement of the teacher's efforts as they may have chosen to only teach the subjects which they knew would be on the test, in order for them to look good. With an example such as this, balanced incentives for both quality and quantity need to be provided. When quality can be directly observed, it is easy to introduce an incentive system for quantity. Williamson (1985) said that low powered incentives are a common occurrence in organizational environments. Therefore, in this situation, an idea would be to give the teacher low powered incentives, such as a flat rate wage, and their efforts can be measured both objectively and subjectively. However, where quality can be directly measured, incentives such as pay by effort exerted or pay by results may be offered.

Depending on what the organization is offering has a big influence on which objective should be focused on, and also what the overall aims of the company are. However, in general, the objective of increasing productivity is the one which the incentive contract should aim to help achieve. If deciding to go from fixed rate wages to pay by output, this shift heads toward high powered incentives, therefore should have a high effect on the increase of effort exerted from the employee.

Productivity is a quantitative measure of how well an organization uses its resources in order to produce goods and services. Although this means the increase in production will be easy to measure, the manager must ensure the quality does not decrease, and depending on what is being produced, this is not always easy to measure. Also, companies must be aware of the multi-tasking problem, if there is more than one task to be measured in order to receive the incentive; employees may direct their efforts only into the measurable task such as amount produced, and ignore the un-measurable, yet still important tasks, such as quality. This is why both subjective and objective measures are required. This does not mean that the organization can not choose an incentive scheme that incorporates both high productivity and high quality production. As long as there is a set way in which the quality of production can be measured, bonuses or the pay by results scheme can be introduced if a certain amount of the product or service is produced; however, it must be produced at a particular standard. This would then make employees motivated to focus on both increased productivity, but they would not let the quality of production drop. The company could use an app to check the quality and standards of what they have produced, so the employee can then ensure they are reaching the level required and therefore produce more at that standard, and receiving the remuneration they are aiming for.

An engaged employee will be easier to manage as they will be striving toward the objectives of the organization. By having a more engaged workforce it is likely that the company will be more responsive to change which would be of paramount interest if the company was in the process of acquiring another company or the market environment was subject to constant change. The objectives that companies should focus their apps upon will be dependent on what is necessary for them to grow as an organization and enable comparative advantages against their competitors. A company that is labor intensive will be more likely to focus its attention on productivity advancements through app implementations so as to drive down the labor cost per unit of their product. Alternatively, a manufacturer of a luxury good will place a higher impetus on quality and incentivizing aspects of this—again using relevant apps. It is evident that incentive schemes that incorporate employee engagement via app implementations can increase the productivity, quality and interest of the workforce and therefore must be designed with their needs and aspirations taken into account so that the worker strives toward the objectives set by management. On the other hand, ill-conceived schemes can result in decreased job satisfaction which may lead to increased expenditure on labor, a fall in productivity levels or a disapproving culture developing from within. When designing these schemes management must take into account all relevant information they have and assess what areas can be improved without adverse effects on other factors relating to the business.

Cloud Computing

The introduction of mobile apps into the workplace has led to greater productivity, higher perceived quality of output, and increased worker participation. The drawbacks of using mobile apps, however, need to be considered and acted upon to make the introduction of these applications into the workplace more successful, especially concerning security arrangements. Disadvantages attributed to the use of mobile apps include distractions at work, idleness, high maintenance costs, and counterproductive workplace relationships.

Cloud computing offers an almost unlimited access to data. The cloud is a virtual storage area where individuals can upload and download files. This results in greater productivity as users can access files faster. However, there are key issues surrounding cloud computing, including the increasing cost of maintaining and setting up the system as data becomes more complicated. This also is connected to the issue of cyber security, as there is increased potential for cybercrime to occur.

Information is valuable, whether it be payment information, personal addresses, health information, and so forth. Medical staffs use apps to access data faster than ever before, offering better service to patients. However, all organizations are susceptible to data hacking, and so to benefit most from these technologies, companies must protect their information as much as possible. There are several factors that may influence the adoption of cloud computing: cost reduction, ease of use, convenience, reliability, security, and privacy. For example, use of cloud can reduce a business' start-up costs. Rather than having to pay to set up costly IT infrastructure before they can function, new businesses can simply pay a fee to cloud computing providers. Using third-party cloud services rather than investing in their own infrastructure significantly reduces the up-front capital needed to start a business. Cloud offers a cost-effective alternative for SMEs (small-

and-medium enterprises) that may not have the necessary resources on start-up to acquire in-house computers and the necessary security. Once businesses are up and running, cloud computing use can still lead to cost reductions because again they do not need to invest in their own infrastructure, instead commissioning cloud services on a short-term basis.

For many companies, IT requirements vary over time. An online retailer might see seasonal variance. Ensuring they have sufficient systems to handle peak activity may be inefficient if their systems are under-utilized for long periods as businesses will likely waste resources during nonpeak times. Investing too much in IT may be inefficient, but investing too little could cause disruptions or even outages during peak times. Cloud resources can be deployed very fast as new requirements arise in a "pay-as-you-go" system, ensuring companies only pay for what they need when they need it. This is especially advantageous for SMEs that may not be able to afford to maintain their own IT infrastructure. The elasticity and flexibility of cloud services help businesses reduce the costs of both overestimating and underestimating IT demand.

Moreover, cloud systems are run by the providers, so the consuming businesses will not need to worry about maintenance or updates. The benefit is the convenience for the business of not having to maintain the IT systems themselves. However, IT systems are vulnerable to external threats. These could involve "traditional" hacking attempts, as mentioned above, or "social engineering" whereby a malicious external individual persuades an unwitting employee to give up key security details. Cloud computing services are provided through the internet, making them vulnerable to attack. However, no practical IT system is truly secure, so cloud services are not inherently less safe than traditional IT systems. Cloud data is often stored in multiple data centers, which limits the damage of attacks. Providers such as Microsoft have security systems beyond the capabilities of many other providers or consumers of cloud computing. They can invest in cyber-security to a level beyond any SME and thus, in theory, can provide better security.

External security threats aren't the only potential cause for concern. Businesses need to be able to trust that their provider will respect the privacy of their data, and not tamper or alter it, or share it with any other parties. Likewise, due to its online nature, the reliability of cloud services is raised as a potential issue as any interruptions in the internet could render these services temporarily unusable. Sufficient disruption in the connection could render the services unavailable to the user, which is obviously an issue for businesses that rely on their IT systems. The storage systems used by cloud computing providers are often proprietary and unstandardized, meaning consumers may not be able to easily transfer their data from one provider to another. This risk of data lock-in may be off-putting to potential consumers, as companies need to know that they will retain access to their data in the event of changing a cloud provider, and the terms of this should be laid out in the agreement between the provider and the customer. There is also a risk of services becoming unavailable in the event of the cloud provider declaring bankruptcy, meaning consumers could lose access to their data or applications if the infrastructure that stores their data becomes the property of the provider's creditors. Again contractual measures need to be in place to guard against these eventualities. Finally, there are potential regulatory issues such as whether the cloud provider might be required to allow governments access to customers' data under certain circumstances.

Performance Impacts

The introduction of mobile applications into the workplace has had major benefits, revolutionizing the way people work in modern companies. There are, however, drawbacks to introducing technologies, such as mobile applications to the workplace, many of which have already been addressed above. The biggest concern regarding mobile applications are the potential security risks to the business and customer data. Just as shopkeepers lock up their shops in order to prevent thieves from stealing their goods, companies need to protect valuable business and customer data from hackers. This is especially prevalent in the health sector and banking industry, as information on both health and finances is extremely valuable. Data breaches in these two sectors are extremely harmful to customers and businesses.

In the banking industry, many work processes, such as transferring finances between accounts and identifying the balances within the accounts, can now be done via mobile applications specifically created by banks to be used by their customers. These apps have been created to improve the efficiency of making transactions, and it offers customers greater flexibility and utility. This change over has largely been a successful use of technology, as the speed of processing transactions has rapidly increased in recent years, with contactless payments being a key innovation in this sector.

Nevertheless, wherever customer information is stored online, there is the potential for hackers to locate and exploit information. Nisar and Prabhakar (2017) identify and investigate key customer perceptions about online banking. They identify security, privacy, usability, and reputation as the keys to success in motivating customers to use online banking. This argument corroborates the technology acceptance model mentioned earlier, as usability is observed as a key factor in the acceptance of new technologies by customers in this case. Security is the most important factor, though, so banks and other businesses that deal with the sensitive customer information need to address these security risks to their fullest extent.

One example where customer data was accessed illicitly was via the WannaCry ransomware attack that occurred in 2017 (Graham, 2017). Over 300,000 mobile devices worldwide were affected by WannaCry, with major organizations such as Telefonica, FedEx, and the NHS being hit. In the case of the NHS, files were encrypted by the attackers, meaning that they couldn't be opened properly, and the attackers would request ransom in exchange for the decryption of the files, allowing them to be restored back to their original state. Though many organizations were able to remove the virus instead of paying the ransom; this type of cybercrime is occurring more frequently as an increasing amount of valuable data is being stored online due to the spread of mobile apps throughout business in their work processes. Businesses that wish to use mobile apps in their work practices need to understand how to prevent and deal with cybercrime, as cyberattacks can drastically affect their business in a negative manner.

As employees communicate through smartphones, text messages, email, or video conferencing tools, this type of communications technology eliminates many face-to-face meetings. Interpersonal communications are essential in building workplace relationships, as employees get to know each other in person. Communications technology tools eradicate this type of interaction, as employees become more reserved and self-absorbed, becoming engrossed in their work. This can potentially be of great harm to a business. In addition, businesses should consider the technology acceptance model discussed earlier to improve the positive impact of the use of mobile applications in the workplace.

Overall, mobile applications have been successful in streamlining work processes, but there are unintended byproducts of introducing apps, such as the formation of informal channels of communication. This can be seen as a negative in that such channels can foster procrastination in the workplace. Nonetheless, it can also be seen as a positive in that technologies such as instant messaging help fulfill worker social needs in the workplace. This last point epitomizes the issues surrounding the introduction of mobile technologies, as the ability to maximize the positive and minimize the negative will determine the success of a business doing this.

Chapter 10
Maximizing Productivity in the Smartphone Enabled Workplace

Mobile applications can have a measurable impact on productivity within the workplace. That statement is a two-edged sword. Used for strictly business purposes it is clear that there are benefits in reducing costs, increasing sales, and improving communication and connectivity throughout the company. However, mobile phones and apps in particular are not without their downsides. The most significant of those is the negative impact of cell phones in the workplace on productivity. In particular, studies show that time wasted in social media can be significant. There are jobs where having a cell phone and answering calls, text messages and so on likely have a negative impact on productivity. A partial solution to this problem is for companies to issue guidelines for employees. The guidelines should be different for different jobs. If a person is a front line sales person working at customer locations, the cell phone is an effective tool for this scenario. On the other hand, a person working in the kitchen of the same company has less of a work need for a phone and the phone could end up damaging productivity.

Over the last decade, with the increased use of smartphones and tablets around the world, a smartphone performs many of the functions of a laptop computer, typically having a touch screen interface, internet access, and an operating system capable of running downloaded apps. Smartphones have increasingly been integrated into the work environment. The number of smartphone users is estimated to be 2.5 billion worldwide in 2019 (Statista, 2019), meaning that at least 2.5 billion people have access to mobile applications. In the U.S. alone, smartphone use as of 2017 was over 75 percent penetration; whereas 98 percent of the U.S. marketing sector use smartphones in their daily work (Work Place Insight, 2017). Therefore, there is a considerable market for firms offering apps on a global scale. The use of smartphone and tablet apps offers many benefits, such as the sharing information and gaining new knowledge, encouraging autonomy, improving monitoring and control, and, in some instances, strengthening the relationships between employees and their supervisors. These benefits will ultimately increase efficiency and job satisfaction in the workplace; if the rules surrounding these phones are truly effective in suppressing the downside.

DOI 10.1515/9781547400546-010

Smartphones in the Workplace

With the invention of the smartphone, the use of applications, or "apps," has become increasingly pervasive in both personal and professional settings. In 2013, there were an estimated 2.4 billion internet users around the world (Meeker and Wu, 2013; Dogtiev, 2015). In 2015, people in the U.S. on average spent 2.8 hours a day using mobile devices to run apps. Subsequently, companies that rely heavily on information technology have seen the benefits of adopting enterprise-level apps. Technologies such as these are a valuable control and coordination mechanism for managers in the workplace.

Companies are taking advantage of this opportunity for an increasingly mobile and flexible workforce. Mobile apps in the workforce streamline and create solutions in many businesses, such as in the areas including communication, coordination and control, worker efficiency, and workforce and team alignment. There are challenges to using mobile apps in the workforce, however, as concern grows about the decline in the work-life balance as a result of the near universal adoption of smartphones and apps as well as the security threat their widespread use poses.

In this book, I have highlighted specific workforce applications in use in practical settings and explain their benefits. I have also pointed out the reasonable concerns about the use of apps in workplace environments.

Technology and Society

In the twenty-first century, technology provides a fundamental assist to almost every business, governmental department, educational institution, and medical organization. As computer technology is integrated into every aspect our everyday life, helping us to handle various tasks more rapidly, our society has become more efficient as a whole, just as have a variety of workers in different organizations around the world. Yet the evolution of technology does not stop there. For nearly a decade now, more and more people are equipped with "smart" devices, including smartphones, tablet computers, intelligent personal assistants, and so on that allow us to redefine simplicity in communication and, more importantly, interact with various services worldwide. In fact, apps that run on these smart devices have turned our day-to-day tasks into merely performing a few clicks or issuing voice commands. Every day, thousands of new apps are being developed and deployed and used for banking, making travel bookings, conducting international phone calls, and many other services. Moreover, this invention not only helps us perform the casual activities mentioned, it also improves the efficiency of workers and entrepreneurs every day in the workplaces around the world as these devices have become an essential tool.

Monitoring Workers

Modern businesses have many tools that can be used to monitor and keep track of their workers. One major way they do this is by being able to view a worker's output in order to make sure that they are producing effectively. Modern technology has enabled organizations to run a business in a certain way with the belief that monitoring will lead to better results. Through the use of BIS (business-issued smartphones) in the workplace, it is also now possible to monitor what employees are doing with their time in the office when they are not working. Studies show that 40% of businesses actually screen their employees' email, sometimes for things unrelated to work. Sixty-six percent of employers are said to keep track of a worker's internet search history. Businesses now even track their employees into what might be seen as a personal space, so they can know whether the employee is wasting time or not. They can even find out what is being said in emails to outside bodies.

Business Communications

The most important task for a manager is to be able to communicate effectively and efficiently. Email has been the most effective way to communicate within the organization for many years now, but with the emergence of mobile apps allowing businesses to create an organization-wide network of texting and instant messaging, email is declining in use. This is due to the fact that texting and instant messaging is much faster and easier to use on a phone. It allows users to send messages rapidly to each other, or to conduct group chats, although care must be taken when texting messages to someone you do not know well. This method also allows more frequent communication between the upper management and workers (via the channels of "briefings" and joint committees), easing decision-making and enabling better communication about projects and problems. Texting and instant messaging is available on any device, allowing convenient communication anytime and anywhere. It is important to note however that for messages that need to be referenced in the future, important decisions and the like email history remains an important business asset. The need for you and your company to have a record of your communications is important and so using multiple apps to accomplish the same task can be counter-productive. Your company should have a policy about the use of texting and the other methods of communicating. That policy should consider methods of addressing the chain of command in the organization, the importance of history, the deletion of text messages, emails and the other standard options of communication, including phone calls, fax, voice messaging, and videoconferencing.

Monitoring Performance

There are now many apps available to monitor daily tasks with the organization, such as production output, sales, inventory levels, and so forth. These apps create graphs or charts evaluating how well a business is doing within a specific sector and what adjustments the business can make. These apps can be used by almost any management level when it comes to monitoring performance. For example, an app (*Things 3*) has been created that searches your mobile device for any events and pulls them all together to create an event calendar. This app makes the life of managers much easier, as they are informed in advance about all of the upcoming events without doing the monitoring-related work themselves. The app will search your whole phone even for calls that need to be made and remind you of those beforehand. Another extremely useful app for teams in the workplace is Trello (https://trello.com/). This app is used for electronic document transfer and sharing with your colleagues, allowing for comments and prompt improvements. You can drag and drop desired notes, pictures, and so forth and even show your progress to your managers in order to apprise them on your progress on projects. With new apps being introduced at a rapid pace, chances are that whatever the business needs, it already exists.

Leisure-Based Applications

Since smartphones and tablets are multi-functional devices, several different leisure applications are available to occupy an individual's time. For instance, individuals can spend their time browsing social media, messaging, and gaming. It was reported that smartphone ownership in America is now 77%, up from just 35% in Pew Research Center's first survey of smartphone ownership conducted in 2011 (Pew Research Center, 2018). Accordingly, time spent on leisure smartphone applications showed an upward trend too. This trend begs the argument of whether or not individuals are becoming addicted to their smartphones and its apps, spending so much of their time on such leisure activities. Additionally, the survey indicated that 44% of smartphone owners would experience tremendous anxiety if they lost their phone for just a week.

These survey results demonstrate that addiction to mobile devices and their apps will affect work processes negatively if there is a discrepancy in their work-life balance. Furthermore, such an imbalance would potentially diminish work efficiency as employees are distracted by participation on social media platforms and other non-work-related activities that they conduct with their devices. To combat this issue organizations can recommend the use of collaborative tools such as *Slack*, for group communications, *FaceTime* and others for live video interactions and include a policy for smartphone use for their employees to deter the negative impact of productivity that web surfing and the like can have at work.

It is important for a business to decide whether or not certain mobile applications are appropriate and profitable for them to use. For example, a small local company might not have the need to support employee access to social media platforms, while a large business can afford to develop its own applications for whatever needs they must fulfill.

Risks of Mobile Communications

It is clear that apps have had many beneficial impacts on the workplace, especially in terms of communication and productivity. Employees who are armed with powerful mobile apps will not only increase their self-management skills, but having such technology at their disposal also adds a sense of importance to their work. Nonetheless, the risks must also be examined. The ease of using apps for certain work processes can result in the loss of skills to an extent, as employees who rely on such apps do not have to learn how to do some skills "manually," as the app does it automatically for them instead. While this may reduce training costs and time, it could lead to a less skilled workforce. There may also be employees who are uncomfortable or unfamiliar with certain applications, and their motivation may decline due to the difficulty that they have while using them.

Further, although communication is more fluid and accessible, improving coordination especially within tall organization structures, the loss of face-to-face communication is an issue. Face-to-face communication contributes to stronger relationships as people may react more immediately and can express their feelings more easily (The Business Communication, 2015). This can strengthen teamwork and even relations between employees and their supervisors, bolstering mutual respect, which can result in increased authority and control.

Employee Surveillance

One particular risk may be the loss of employee trust due to possible surveillance by the company. Work product and movements can easily be logged by employers when devices that employees are using are connected to the company's server. Employees may feel threatened by the feeling of being constantly monitored, and a culture of distrust might develop within the organization. Employees may also feel that they are not achieving potential job enrichment, as management monitors every aspect of their work, causing a feeling of oppression. Thus management may have to take a more hands-off approach and allow their employees to be more autonomous in their actions, or employees may not use apps to their full advantage.

Legal Implications

There is also relatively little legal protection against firms surveilling their employees, especially if the employees have agreed to such monitoring in their employment contracts. Not much can be done from the employee's point of view, and such surveillance can cause a loss of employee participation and trust and raise the potential of conflict. Nevertheless, the apps that employees use in the workplace should only aid in their job performance and help them be more productive and effective. Depending on the workplace, there may be employee organizations (e.g. joint committees, works councils) that work with management on all issues related to employment. These are far more prevalent in Europe where that role is often formalized, but is common in labor unions in the US. Employees without such institutional support may be reluctant to ask what kinds of surveillance are in use.

Work-Life Imbalances

Apps that enable constant access to work and email can most certainly intrude on the work-life balance. The ability to be contacted by colleagues at any time, anywhere can create a mindset of constantly being focused on work, which can then lead to anxiety, increased stress levels, and a breakdown of social life from feelings of isolation and depression (Knapton, 2014). Moreover, another possible downside to automating some tasks is that employees will take on more responsibility in that the concentration of labor for each individual is increased. This occurs because employees will be expected to oversee multiple facets of business functions, as management may no longer see a need to hire individuals with specific skills for specific jobs. This could heighten stress levels within the workplace. Employers can combat this by providing constant app-based feedback on work performed and ensuring that their employees understand what is expected of them so that there is less confusion.

Data Security

Another concern is the issue of data governance, mainly in the realm of data security. Businesses must use trusted applications that have the built-in infrastructure necessary to manage their level of use to avoid potential data loss and protect them from cyber attacks. Despite this, there is clear evidence that this industry will continue to grow and help business large and small improve their communications, giving them a competitive edge over companies who choose not to embrace this technology.

Smartphone Addiction

An increasing problem with smartphones is that they are linked to addiction. Car (2011) describes research showing that apps have been developed in such a way as to keep us coming back to use them by "hijacking our dopamine sensors." This addiction to non-work-related apps like social media not only detract from time spent on work, but also decrease the attention level of workers. In other words, they diminish a worker's ability to focus on that which is directly correlated with their output. Further, asking an employee to use this omnipresent device for work processes may encourage a blending of reality and work for that person. As such, they may find it hard to separate the time they are at work from the time they spend outside of work. This in turn can lead to work-related stress which can have repercussions on the worker's overall well-being. While adopting mobile technologies can be the start of a better and more compelling work process, if not well-integrated it can have a detrimental impact when the use of such apps is not carefully monitored. Be that as it may, if apps are allowed into the workplace, there will be a net benefit to the company, as they are a practical mechanism to drive individuals to new heights.

It is apparent that the advantages of mobile technologies outweigh the disadvantages for the following reasons:

1. Applications that are available by smartphone and small devices enable workers to work better as a team so that collaboration between colleagues increases and thus they become more motivated to achieve business goals.
2. Productivity rises as staff can work both as individuals and in a team structure with the flexibility to do so at any time and location.
3. Managers can monitor work processes and output, so that a hard-working employee's motivation may increase when incentivized by rewards for achieving given tasks.
4. The bottom line of the company can be improved as the staff is trained more quickly and easily.

Thus in conclusion, in an environment where the less desirable influences of smartphone use can be contained, apps are very effective tools within the work environment. They not only help promote a more creative environment, but also a more energized and efficient one. Apps allow employees and managers to accomplish tasks a lot faster by sorting through information for them, allowing for better communication and help to form a closer employee network.

Since apps are developed and updated constantly, this means that any issues experienced by users are fixed promptly and at no cost. Overall, the sophistication and utility of apps is still rising, so the future potential of apps in the workplace is substantial.

Bibliography

Aaker, D. and Keller, K. (1990). Consumer evaluations of brand extensions. *Journal of Marketing*, 54(1), 27.

Adjei, T., Noble, M. and Noble, H. (2010). The influence of C2C communications in online brand communities on customer purchase behavior. *Journal of the Academy of Marketing Science*, 38(5), 634–653.

Adler, P., Du Gay, P., Morgon G. and Reed, M. (2014). *The Oxford handbook of sociology, social theory, and organization studies.*

Agag, G. and El-Masry, A. (2016). Understanding consumer intention to participate in online travel community and effects on consumer intention to purchase travel online and WOM: An integration of innovation diffusion theory and TAM with trust. *Computers in Human Behaviour*, 60, 97–111.

Agarwal, R. and Prasad, J. (1998). A Conceptual and Operational Definition of Personal Innovativeness in the Domain of Information Technology. *Information Systems Research*, 9(2), 204–215.

Agarwal, R. (2000). Individual Acceptance of Information Technologies. *Educational Technology Research and Development*, 40, 90–102.

Ailawadi, K., Lehmann, D. and Neslin, S. (2003). Revenue Premium as an Outcome Measure of Brand Equity. *Journal of Marketing*, 67(4), 1–17.

Ailawadi, L., Lehmann, R. and Neslin, A. (2001). Market response to a major policy change in the marketing mix: Learning from Procter & Gamble's value pricing strategy. *Journal of Marketing*, 65(1), 44–61.

Ajabre, A. (2012). Cloud computing for increased business value. *International Journal of Business and Social Science*, 3(1), 2012–234.

Ajzen, I. and Fishbein, M. (1980). *Understanding Attitudes and Predicting Social Behavior*. Englewood Cliffs, NJ: Prentice-Hall.

Ajzen, I. and Fishbein, M. (2005). The influence of attitudes on behavior. *Handbook of attitudes and attitude change: Basic principles*, 173–221.

Ajzen, I. (1991). The theory of planned behavior. *Organizational Behavior and Human Decision Processes*, 50(2), 179–211.

Akerlof, A. (1970). The market for "Lemons": Quality uncertainty and the market mechanism. *Quarterly Journal of Economics*, 84(3), 488–500.

Albuquerque, P., Pavlidis, P., Chatow, U., Chen, Y. and Jamal, Z. (2012). Evaluating promotional activities in an online two-sided market of user-generated content. *Marketing Science*, 31(3): 406–432.

Alchian, A. and Demsetz, H. (1972). Production, Information costs and Economic Organization. *American Economic Review*, 62, 777–795.

Algesheimer, R., Dholakia, M. and Herrmann, A. (2005). The social influence of brand community: Evidence from European car clubs. *Journal of Marketing*, 69(3), 19–34.

Allen, W., Walker, L., Coopman, J. and Hart, L. (2007, November). Workplace Surveillance and Managing Privacy Boundaries. *Management Communication Quarterly*, 21(2), 172–200.

Ally, M. and Tsinakos, A. (2014). *Increasing Access through Mobile Learning*. Commonwealth of Learning Available at: http://en.copian.ca/library/research/commonwealth_of_learning/perspectives/perspectives.pdf#page=210. [Accessed December 24 2017].

DOI 10.1515/9781547400546-011

Ally, M. and Tsinakos, A. (2014). Increasing Access through Mobile Learning. Commonwealth of Learning: http://en.copian.ca/library/research/commonwealth_of_learning/perspectives/perspectives.pdf#page=210. [Accessed January 2, 2018].

Ally, M., Samaka, M., Ismail, L. and Impagliazzo, J. (2013). Use of Mobile Learning Apps in Workplace Learning. *Bulletin of the IEEE Technical Committee on Learning Technology*, 15(4), 6.

Alphabet (2018). *AlphaGuide*. Available at: https://www.alphabet.com/en-gb/alphaguide. [Accessed January 6, 2018].

Alvesson, M. and Willmott, H. (1992). *Critical management studies*. New York: Sage.

Amabile, M. (1993). Motivational synergy: Toward new conceptualizations of intrinsic and extrinsic motivation in the workplace. *Human Resource Management Review*, 3(3), 185–201.

Amedeo, D. (2010). *Person-Environment-Behavior Research*. 1st ed. New York: Guilford Publications.

American Marketing Association (2003). *AMA Dictionary of Marketing Terms*, Available from: http://www.marketing-dictionary.org/Advertising [Accessed July 29, 2018].

Amstad, F., Meier, L., Fasel, U., Elfering, A. and Semmer, N. (2011). A meta-analysis of work–family conflict and various outcomes with a special emphasis on cross-domain versus matching-domain relations. *Journal of Occupational Health Psychology*, 16(2), 151–169.

Andaleeb, S. and Conway, C. (2006). Customer Satisfaction in the Restaurant Industry: An Examination of the Transaction-specific Model. *Journal of Services Marketing*, 20(1), 3–11.

Anderson, E. (2012). *Why We Hate Giving Feedback - and How to Make It Easier*. Available from: https://www.forbes.com/sites/erikaandersen/2012/06/20/why-we-hate-giving-feedback-and-how-to-make-it-easier/#6997fb565518 [Accessed January 10, 2018].

Andrade, R., Araujo, G., Cronemberger, J., Pereira, R., Albuquerque, B. and Mendonca, C. (2015). Improving business by migrating applications to the cloud using cloud step. In Advanced Information Networking and Applications Workshops (WAINA), 2015 IEEE 29th International Conference (pp. 77–82). IEEE.

Andreadis, G., Fourtounis, G. and Bouzakis, D. (2015). Collaborative design in the era of cloud computing. *Advances in Engineering Software*, 81, 66–72.

Anon. (2012). Mobile application (Mobile App). https://www.techopedia.com/definition/2953/mobile-application-mobile-app. [Accessed January 3, 2018].

Ansari, S. and Mela, C. (2003). E-Customization. *Journal of Marketing Research*, 40(2), 131–145.

Antweiler, W. and Frank, Z. (2004). Is all that talk just noise? The information content of Internet stock message boards. *Journal of Finance*, 59(3): 1259–1294.

Apple (2017). Urban-outfitters. https://itunes.apple.com/us/app/urban-outfitters/id358821736?mt=8. [Accessed January 2, 2018].

Aral, S. and van Alstyne, M. (2011). The diversity-bandwidth tradeoff. *American Journal of Sociology*, 117(1, July), 90–171.

Aral, S. and Walker, D. (2011). Creating social contagion through viral product design: A randomized trial of peer influence in networks. *Management Science*, 57(9), 1623–1639.

Arazy, O., Kumar, N. and Shapira, B. (2010). A theory-driven design framework for social recommender systems. *Journal of the Association of Information Systems*, 11(9), 455–490.

Ariely, D. (2008). *Predictably irrational: The hidden forces that shape our decisions*. New York: HarperCollins.

Armstrong, M. and Taylor, S. (2014). *Armstrong's handbook of human resource management practice*. London: Kogan Page Publishers.

Arnold, J. and Randall, R. (2016). *Work psychology* (6th Edition). Pearson.

Arnold, T. (2001). *An electronic citadel a method for securing credit card and private consumer data in e-business sites.* Washington, D.C.: Software & Information Industry Association.

Arrow, J. (1996). *Social Choice and Individual Values.* New York: Wiley.

Arxan. (2013). Arxan Discovers Top 100 Android Apps Hacked in 2013. Retrieved from: https://www.arxan.com/arxan-discovers-top-100-android-apps-hacked-in-2013/ [Accessed January 2, 2018].

Astea International (1979). *Alliance Mobile Edge – The New Standard in Workforce.*

Athey, S. and Ellison, G. (2014). Dynamics of Open Source Movements, *Journal of Economics & Management Strategy*, 23(2), 294–316.

Athey, S., and Gans, J. S. (2010). The impact of targeting technology on advertising markets and media competition. *AER Paper and Proceedings*, 100(2), 608–613.

Avram, G. (2014). Advantages and challenges of adopting cloud computing from an enterprise perspective. *Procedia Technology*, 12, 529–534.

Bacon, D. (2015). There's an app for that. http://www.economist.com/news/briefing/21637355-freelance-workers-available-moments-notice-will-reshape-nature-companies-and [Accessed December 9, 2017].

Bagozzi, P. and Dholakia, M. (2006). Antecedents and purchase consequences of customer participation in small group brand communities. *International Journal of Research in Marketing*, 23(1), 45–61.

Bahtar, Z. and Muda, M. (2016). The impact of user-generated content (UGC) on product reviews towards online purchasing—A Conceptual Framework. *Procedia Economics and Finance*, 37, 337–342.

Bailey, E. and Kurland, B. (2002). A review of telework research: findings, new directions, and lessons for the study of modern work. *Journal of Organizational Behavior*, 23(4), 383–400.

Baiman, S., May, H. and Mukherji, A. (1990). Optimal employment contracts and the returns in a principal-agent context. *Contemporary Accounting Research*, 6(2), 761–799.

Baker, P., Jensen, C. and Murphy, J. (1988). Compensation and Incentives: Practice vs. Theory. *The Journal of Finance*, 43(3), 593–616.

Bakker, B. and Schaufeli, B. (2008). Positive organizational behavior: Engaged employees in flourishing organizations. *Journal of Organizational Behaviour*, 29, 147–154.

Balaji, M., Roy, S. and Sadeque, S. (2016). Antecedents and consequences of university brand identification. *Journal of Business Research*, 69(8), 3023–3032.

Baldwin, C. and Hippel, V. (2011). Modeling a paradigm shift: From Producer innovation to user and open collaborative innovation. *Organization Science*, 22(6), 1399–1417.

Ball, K. (2010). Workplace Surveillance: *An overview. Labor History*, 51(1), 87–106.

Banerjee, S. and Dholakia, R. (2012). Location-based mobile advertisements and gender targeting. *Journal of Research in Interactive Marketing*, 6(3), 198–214.

Barclays. (2016). Barclays Mobile Banking app. Retrieved from: http://www.barclays.co.uk/BarclaysMobileBanking/MobileBankingapp/P1242609123821 [Accessed January 2, 2018].

Barker, R. and Sewell, G. (2006). Coercion versus Care: Using Irony to Make sense of Organizational Surveillance. *The Academy of Management Review* 4, 934–961.

Baron, N. and Kreps, M. (1999). *Strategic human resources,* Wiley.

Başgöze, P. and Özer, L. (2012). Effects of brand credibility on technology acceptance model: Adaption of the model to the purchase intention, *International Journal of Humanities and Social Science*, 2(20).

Bauer, H., Barnes, S., Reichardt, T. and Neumann, M. (2005). Driving Consumer Acceptance of Mobile Marketing: A Theoretical Framework and Empirical Study. *Journal of Electronic Consumer Research*, 6(3).

Bauer, H., Sauer, E. and Becker, C. (2006). Investigating the relationship between product involvement and consumer decision-making styles. *Journal of Consumer Behaviour*, 5(4), 342–354.

BBC (2014). *Flappy Bird creator removes game from app stores—BBC News*. Available at: http://www.bbc.co.uk/news/technology-26114364 [Accessed January 10, 2018].

BBC (2015). *Why Clarks is measuring feet with iPads—BBC News*. [online] Available at: http://www.bbc.co.uk/news/business-32738088 [Accessed January 10, 2018].

BBC News (2017). *NHS cyber-attack: GP's and hospitals hit in ransomware*. Available at: http://www.bbc.co.uk/news/health-39899646 [Accessed January 6, 2018].

Bean, S. (2017). *Over three quarters of UK employees use their smartphone in workplace* Insight. Available From: http://workplaceinsight.net/over-three-quarters-of-uk-employees-use-their-smartphones-in-the-workplace/ [Accessed December 29, 2017].

Bedini, I., Farazi, F., Pane, J., Tankoyeu, I., Leoni, D and Leucci, S. (2014). Open government data: Fostering innovation. *JeDEM-eJournal of eDemocracy and Open Government*, 6(1), 69–79.

Belbin (2012). *Belbin Team Roles*. Available from: http://www.belbin.com/about/belbinteam-roles/ [Accessed January 6, 2018].

Bell, J. (2009). Government Transparency via Open Data and Open Source. *Open Source Business Resource* (February 2009).

Bellman, S., Potter, R., Treleaven-Hassard, S., Robinson, J and Varan, D. (2011). The Effectiveness of Branded Mobile Phone Apps. *Journal of Interactive Marketing*, 25(4), 191–200.

Bennett, D. and Harvey, A. (2009). Publishing Open Government Data. Available from: http://www.w3.org/TR/2009/WD-gov-data-20090908/ [Accessed July 14, 2018].

Bergemann, D. and Bonatti, A. (2011). Targeting in advertising markets: Implications for online vs. online media. *RAND Journal of Economics*, 42(3), 417–617.

Berrigan, J. and Finkbeiner, C. (1992). *Segmentation marketing: New methods for capturing business markets*. New York: Harper Business.

Besanko, D., Dranove, D., Shanley, M. and Schaefer, M. (2003). *Economics of Strategy*. Wiley.

Besieux, T. (2017). Why I hate feedback: Anchoring effective feedback within organizations. *Business Horizons*, 60 (4), pp. 435–439. Available from: https://www.sciencedirect.com/science/article/pii/S0007681317300253 [Accessed January 7, 2018].

Bianco, S. (2016). *Parallels*. [Online]. Available at: https://www.parallels.com/blogs/ras/citrix-receiver/ [Accessed December 4, 2017].

Bickart, B. and Schindler, M. (2001). Internet forums as influential sources of consumer information. *Journal of Interactive Marketing*, 15(3), 31–40.

Bird, J. (2003). Work Life Balance Defined. www.worklifebalance.com/work-life-balance-defined.html [Accessed December 22, 2017].

Blair, I. (2018). *4 Ways Your Business Can Benefit From Having a Mobile App - BuildFire*. BuildFire. Available at: https://buildfire.com/ways-business-benefit-having-mobileapp/ [Accessed November 28, 2018].

Blanchard, L. (2008). Testing a model of sense of virtual community. *Computers in Human Behavior*, 24, 2107–2123.

Blau, P. and Schoenherr, R. (1971). *The Structure of organizations*. Basic Books.

Blom, J. and Monk, A. (2003). Theory of personalization of appearance: Why users personalize their PCs and mobile phones. *Human-Computer Interaction*, 18(3), 193–228.

Blomfield, T. (2017). "How I Made it: Tom Blomfield, Monzo." Interview with Tom Bloomfield. Interviewed for Virgin Start-up. Available at: https://www.virginstartup.org/how-i-made-it/how-i-made-it-tom-blomfield-monzo [Accessed December 22, 2018].

Bloom, N., Garicano, L., Sadun, R and Van Reenen, J. (2010). The distinct effects of information technology and communication technology on firm organization. *Management Science*, 60.

Bloom, N., Lemos, R., Sadun, R and Van Reenen, J. (2014). *Does Management Matter in Schools?* Centre for performance economics, 1312, Available from: http://cep.lse.ac.uk/pubs/download/dp1312.pdf [Accessed December 20, 2017].

Boddy, D. (2014). *Management: An Introduction*, 6th ed. Harlow: Prentice Hall Europe.

Boomsworth, D. (2015). Mobile marketing statistics 2015. [online] Smart Insights. Available at: http://www.smartinsights.com/mobile-marketing/mobile-marketing-analytics/mobile-marketing-statistics/ [Accessed January 7, 2018].

Bosa, D. (2019). Airbnb booked more than $1 billion in third-quarter revenue. CNBC. Available at: https://www.cnbc.com/2018/11/16/airbnb-booked-more-than-1-billion-in-third-quarter-revenue.html [Accessed January 4, 2019].

Bosomworth, D. (2015, July 22). Mobile marketing statistics 2015. http://www.smartinsights.com/mobile-marketing/mobile-marketing-analytics/mobile-marketing-statistics/ [Accessed January 7, 2018].

Bottomley, P. and Doyle, J. (1996). The formation of attitudes towards brand extensions: Testing and generalising Aaker and Keller's model. *International Journal of Research in Marketing*, 13(4), 365–377.

Bouty, I. (2000). Interpersonal and interaction influences on informal resource exchanges between R&D researchers across organizational boundaries. *The Academy of Management Journal*, 43, 50–65.

Boyd, C. (2010). *Consumer psychology*. Maidenhead: Open University Press.

Brand, F. (2014, September 23). Say It Again: Messages Are More Effective When Repeated. The Financial Brand: http://thefinancialbrand.com/42323/advertising-marketing-messages-effective-frequency/ [Accessed January 7, 2018].

Brandon, J. (2016). Zirtual's personal assistant service: A great idea that still needs more polish. *Inc.com* [Accessed January 23, 2018].

Braverman, H. (1974). *Labor and Monopoly Capital: The Degradation of Work in the Twentieth Century*. New York: Monthly Review Press.

Brignall, M. (2012, February 2012). Contactless payments. The Guardian: http://www.theguardian.com/money/2012/feb/16/barclays-pingit-money-sending-smartphone. [Accessed January 24, 2018].

Brignall, M. (2014, January 10). Yodel voted worst Parcel delivery service for the second year running. The Guardian: http://www.theguardian.com/money/2014/jan/10/yodel-worst-parcel-delivery [Accessed January 17, 2018].

Brooks, C. (2012). 10 apps for achieving work-life balance. *Business News Daily*. http://www.businessnewsdaily.com/2779-apps-work-life-balance.html [Accessed January 17, 2018].

Brown, J. and Reingen, H. (1987). Social ties and word-of-mouth referral behavior. *Journal of Consumer Research* 14(3), 350–362.

Brown, R. and Carasso, H. (2013). *Everything for sale?* Milton Park, Abingdon, Oxon: Routledge.

Brustein, J. (2014). Apple Users Spent $10 Billion on Apps in 2013. http://www.bloomberg.com/bw/articles/2014-01-07/apple-users-spent-10-billion-on-apps-in-2013 [Accessed January 18, 2018].

Buchanan, D. and Huczynski, A. (2016). *Organization Behaviour, An Introductory Text*. London: Prentice Hall.

Burgoon, J. K. (1982). Privacy and communication. *Annals of the International Communication Association*, 6(1), 206–249.

Burke, M., Kraut, R and Marlow, C. (2011). Social capital on Facebook: Differentiating uses and users. *ACM CHI Conference Human Factors Computer Systems* (ACM, New York), 571–580.

Business Insider (2014). *The 11 Most Popular Apps Employees Use at Work*. Available at: http://www.businessinsider.com/most-popular-apps-employees-use-at-work-2014-10?IR=T/#sco-webex-for-online-meetings-6 [Accessed December 21, 2017].

Businesscasestudies.co.uk. (2016). Herzberg—Building a better workplace through motivation—Kellogg's | Kellogg's case studies, videos, social media and information | Business Case Studies. Available at: http://businesscasestudies.co.uk/kelloggs/building-a-better-workplace-through-motivation/herzberg.html#axzz3wZfT1fXm. [Accessed January 7, 2018].

Buzzell, D. (1983). Is Vertical Integration Profitable? *Harvard Business Review*, January 1983. Available at: https://hbr.org/1983/01/is-vertical-integration-profitable [Accessed December 11, 2017].

Byrne, J. (2010). *Healthcare Apps exploding in mobile, are you ready?* Available from: http://www.vfluence.com/blog/459/healthcare-apps-exploding-in-mobile-are-you-ready [Accessed December 1, 2017].

Cabinet Office (2012). Open data white paper: unleashing the potential. London: TSO.

Cai, Y., Lau, K., Liao, Y., Li, C., Leung, F. and Ma, K. (2014). Object Typicality for Effective Web of Things Recommendations. *Decision Support Systems*, 63, 52–63.

Cameron, F. and Webster, J. (2005). Unintended consequences of emerging communication technologies: Instant Messaging in the workplace. *Computers in Human Behavior*, 21(1).

Campbell, A. (2015). *What the Heck is an "App"?* Available at: https://smallbiztrends.com/2011/03/what-is-an-app.html [Accessed January 9, 2018].

Campbell, L., Hollingsworth, R. and Lindberg, N (1991). *Governance of the American economy*. Cambridge University Press.

Campbell, W. (2007). A cross-cultural comparison of perceptions and uses of mobile telephony. *New Media and Society*, 9(2), 343–363.

Canalys (2016). *Media alert: Over 1.5 billion smart phones to ship worldwide in 2016*. Available from: http://www.canalys.com/newsroom/media-alert-over-15- billion-smart-phones-ship-worldwide-2016 [Accessed July 5, 2018].

Canvas (2015). *Blog*. https://383project.com/blog/canvas-2015-the-full-talks.

Carroll, R. and Hannon, T. (2004). *The Demography of Corporations and Industries*. Princeton University Press.

Carter, L. (2009). Digital Britain: final report / Department for Culture, Media and Sport and Department for Business, Innovation and Skills. London: The Stationery Office, 2009.

Casaló, V., Flavián, C. and Guinalíu, M. (2007). The role of security, privacy, usability and reputation in the development of online banking', *Online Information Review*, 31(5), 583–603.

Casaló, V., Flavián, C. and Guinaliu, M. (2008). Promoting consumer's participation in virtual brand communities: A new paradigm in branding strategy. *Journal of Marketing Communications*, 14(1), 19–36.

Casas, I. and Delmelle, E. C. (2017). Tweeting about public transit – Gleaning public perceptions from a social media microblog. *Case Studies on Transport Policy*, 5(4), 634–642.

Castro, S., Zhang, D., Chen, C., Li, S. and Pan, G. (2014). From taxi GPS traces to social and community dynamics: A survey. *ACM Computing Surveys*, 46(2), 1167–1182.

Chaffey, D., Ellis-Chadwick, F., Mayer, R. and Johnston, K. (eds.) (2009). *Internet Marketing: Strategy, Implementation and Practice*, 4th ed. Essex: Pearson Education Limited.

Chai, G. (2009). A Review of Marketing Mix: 4ps or More? *International Journal of Marketing Studies*, 1(1).

Chaiken, S. (1980). Heuristic versus systematic information processing and the use of source versus message cues in persuasion. *Journal of Personality and Social Psychology*, 39(5), 752–766.

Chandler, A. (1962). *Strategy and structure*. MIT Press.

Chang, C. and Tung, C. (2008). An empirical investigation of students' behavioural intentions to use the online learning course websites. *British Journal of Educational Technology*, 39(1), 71–83.

Chang, T., Chen, W. and Tan, C. (2012). Advertising effectiveness in social networking sites: Social ties, expertise, and product type. *IEEE Transactions on Engineering Management*, 59(4), 634–643.

Chellappa, R. and Sin, R. (2005). Personalization versus privacy: An empirical examination of the online consumer's dilemma. *Information Technology and Management*, 6(2–3), 181–202.

Chen, L. (2015). Continuous delivery: Huge benefits, but challenges too. *IEEE Software*, *32*(2), 50–54.

Chen, Y. and Xie, J. (2008). Online consumer review: Word-of-mouth as a new element of marketing communication mix. *Management Science* 54(3), 477–491.

Cheong, J. and Morrison, A. (2008). Consumers' reliance on product information and recommendations found in UGC. *Journal of Interactive Advertising*, 8(2), 1–29.

Chesbrough, H. and Rosenbloom, S. (2002). The role of the business model in capturing value from innovation: evidence from Xerox Corporation's technology spin-off companies.

Chesbrough, H., Vanhaverbeke, W. and West, J. (2014). *New frontiers in open innovation*. Oxford University Press.

Chesbrough, W. and Appleyard, M. (2007). Open innovation and strategy. *California Management Review*, 50(1), 57.

Chesbrough, W. (2003). *Open innovation : the new imperative for creating and profiting from technology*. Boston, Mass: Harvard Business School, c2003.

Chesbrough, W. (2006). *Open business models: how to thrive in the new innovation landscape*. Boston, Mass: Harvard Business School Press, 2006.

Chesbrough, W., Vanhaverbeke, W. and West, J. (2006). *Open innovation: researching a new paradigm / edited by Henry Chesbrough, Wim Vanhaverbeke and Joel West*. Oxford: Oxford University Press, 2006.

Chevalier, A. and Mayzlin, D. (2006). The effect of word of mouth on sales: Online book reviews. *Journal of Marketing Research* 43(3), 345–354.

Chimote, N. (2013). Work-life balance benefits: From the perspective of organizations and employees. *Journal of Management Research*, 12(1), 62–73.

Chintagunta, K., Gopinath, S. and Venkataraman, S. (2010). The effects of online user reviews on movie box office performance: Accounting for sequential rollout and aggregation across local markets. *Marketing Science*, 29(5), 944–957.

CIO (2016). *7 ways small businesses can benefit from mobile apps*. CIO. Available at: http://www.cio.com/article/3064234/small-business/7-ways-small-businesses-can-benefit-from-mobile-apps.html. [Accessed January 10, 2018].

Citrin, V., Sprott, D., Silverman, S. and Stem, D. (2000). Adoption of Internet shopping: the role of consumer innovativeness. *Industrial Management & Data Systems*, 100(7), 294–300.

Claro, D., Claro, P. and Zylbersztajn, D. (2009). Relationship marketing strategies: When buyer and supplier follow different strategies to achieve performance. *Rev. Adm. Contemp. Revista De Administração Contemporânea*.

Clemons, K., Gao, G. and Hitt, M. (2006). When online reviews meet hyper differentiation: A study of the craft beer industry. *Journal of Management Information Systems*, 23(2), 149–171.

Click Software (2015). *Mobile Apps in the Workforce: Overcoming Challenges to Reap the Benefits of a Fully Mobile Workforce*. Available at: https://www.clicksoftware.com/blog/mobile-apps-in-the-workforce-overcoming-challenges-to-reap-the-benefits-of-a-fully-mobile-workforce/ [Accessed December 21, 2017].

Coase (1960). The Problem of Social Costs. *Journal of Law and Economics*. 3, 1–44.

Cohen, M. and Levinthal, A. (1990). Absorptive capacity: A new perspective on learning and innovation. *Administrative Science Quarterly*, 35 (1), 128–152.

Cohen, M., Nelson, R. and Walsh, P. (2002). Links and impacts: The influence of public research on industrial R&D. *Management Science,* 48(1), 1–23.

Coleman, A. (2013). Authority, power, leadership: Sociological understandings. *New Theology Review*, 10(3).

Collins, N. (1996). Working models of attachment: Implications for explanation, emotion, and behaviour. *Journal of Personality and Social Psychology*, 71(4), 810–832.

Competition and Markets Authority (2016). *Tell the CMA about a competition or market problem*. Available at: https://www.gov.uk/guidance/tell-the-cma-about-a-competition-or-market-problem [Accessed January 6, 2018].

Comscore, Inc. (2017). *Mobile's Hierarchy of Needs*. Available at: https://www.comscore.com/Insights/Presentations-%20and-Whitepapers/2017/Mobiles-Hierarchy-of-%20Needs? [Accessed March 31, 2018].

Comscore, Inc. (2018). *2017 U.S. Cross-Platform Future in Focus*. Available at: https://www.comscore.com/Insights/Presentations-and-Whitepapers/2017/2017-US-Cross-Platform-Future-in-Focus [Accessed November 28, 2018].

Conlin, M., O'Donoghue, T. and Vogelsang, J. (2007). Projection bias in catalogue orders. *The American Economic Review*, 97(4), 1217–1249.

Conosco, C. (2015). A Fresh Approach to IT Support and Services. Available at: https://www.conosco.com/conosco-blog/it-support/advantages-challenges-mobileworkforce/. [Accessed December 4, 2017].

Constantinedes, E. (2011). Potential of the social media as instruments of higher education marketing: a segmentation study, *Journal of Marketing for Higher Education*, 21(1).

Consumer data privacy in a networked world a framework for protecting privacy and promoting innovation in the global digital economy. (2012). *Washington D.C. The White* House. Available from: http://www.nova.edu/ssss/QR/WQR/interviewing.pdf.

Cooke, P. (2005). Regionally asymmetric knowledge capabilities and open innovation: Exploring 'Globalisation 2. A new model of industry organization. *Research Policy*, 34 (8), 1128–1149.

Coronas, T. and Oliva, M. (2007). *Encyclopedia of Human Resources Information Systems*. 1st ed. Hershey: IGI Global.

Crandall, D., Cosley, D. and Huttenlocher, D. (2008). Feedback effects between similarity and social influence in online communities. *In Proceedings of the 14th ACM SIGKDD International Conference on Knowledge Discovery and Data Mining*. Las Vegas, Nevada: ACM Press, 160–168.

Cropanzano, R. and Mitchell, S. (2005). Social exchange theory: an interdisciplinary review. *Journal of Management*, 31, 874–900.

Crosby, A. Evans, R. and Cowles, D. (1990). Relationship Quality in Services Selling: An Interpersonal Influence Perspective. *Journal of Marketing*, 54(3), 68–81.

Crosby, A. and Stephens, N. (1987). Effects of relationship marketing on satisfaction, retention, and prices in the life insurance industry. *Journal of Marketing Research* 24(4), 404–411.

Culnan, J., Mchugh, J. and Zubillaga, I. (2010). How large US companies can use Twitter and other social media to gain business value. *MIS Quarterly Executive*, 9, 243–260.

Curtis, G. (2011). *Business information systems: Analysis, design, and practice*. Wokingham, England: Addison-Wesley.

Cvijikj, P. and Michahelles, F. (2013). Online participation factors on Facebook brand Pages. *Social Network Analysis and Mining*, 1–19.

Dahlander, L. and Gann, M. (2010). How open is innovation? *Research Policy*, 39(6), 699–709.

Dartey-Baah, K. and Amoako, K. (2011). Application of Frederick Herzberg's Two-Factor theory in assessing and understanding employee motivation at work: A Ghanaian Perspective. *European Journal of Business and Management*, 3(9).

Das, R. and Chen, Y. (2007). Yahoo! for Amazon: Sentiment extraction from small talk on the Web. *Management Science* 53(9), 1375–1388.

Data and Society Research Institute (2014). Workplace Surveillance. Future of Work Project.

David, O., Salleh, M. and Iahad, N. (2012). *The impact of e-learning in workplace: focus on organizations and healthcare environments*. 2nd ed.

Davis, D. (1989). Perceived Usefulness, Perceived Ease of Use, and User Acceptance of Information Technology. *MIS Quarterly*, 13(3), 319–340.

Davis, D., Bagozzi, P. and Warshaw, R. (1989). User Acceptance of Computer Technology: A Comparison of Two Theoretical Models. *Management Science*, 35(8), 982–1003.

Davis, F. (1989). Perceived Usefulness, Perceived Ease of Use, and User Acceptance of Information Technology. *MIS Quarterly*, 13(3), 319.

Davis, F., Bagozzi, R. and Warshaw, P. (1989). User Acceptance of Computer Technology: A Comparison of Two Theoretical Models. *Management Science*, 35(8), 982–1003.

Davis, M. (2015). Average person now spends more time on their phone and laptop on than sleeping: http://www.dailymail.co.uk/health/article-2989952/How-technology-taking-lives-spend-time-phones-laptops-SLEEPING.html [Accessed December 2017]

Dean, D., Arroyo-Gamez, R., Punjaisri, K. and Pich, C. (2016). Internal brand co-creation: The experiential brand meaning cycle in higher education. *Journal of Business Research*, 69(8), 3041–3048.

Debanjan, M. and Peter, N. Golder (2006). How Does Objective Quality Affect Perceived Quality? Short-Term Effects, Long-Term Effects, and Asymmetries, *Marketing Science*, 25(3), 230–247.

Deliveroo. (2016). *Deliveroo apply.* Available at: https://deliveroo.co.uk/apply [Accessed December 9, 2017].

Dellarocas, C. (2003). The digitization of word of mouth: Promise and challenges of online feedback mechanisms. *Management Science* 49(10), 1407–1424.

Dellarocas, C. (2006). Strategic manipulation of Internet opinion forums: Implications for consumers and firms. *Management Science*, 52(10), 1577–1593.

Deloitte (2018). *Understanding the Bring-Your-Own-Device landscape.* Available From: https://www2.deloitte.com/content/dam/Deloitte/uk/Documents/about-deloitte/deloitte-uk-understanding-the-bring-your-own-device%20landscape.pdf [Accessed January 4, 2018].

Dennis, C., Papagiannidis, S., Alamanos, E and Bourlakis, M. (2016). The role of brand attachment strength in higher education. *Journal of Business Research*, 69(8), 3049–3057.

Dennison, L., Morrison, L., Conway, G., and Yardley, L. (2013). Opportunities and challenges for smartphone applications in supporting health behavior change: qualitative study. *Journal of Medical Internet Research*,15(4): e86. doi: 10.2196/jmir.2583.

Derek, T. (2014). How the World Consumes Media—in Charts and Maps. The Atlantic. https://www.theatlantic.com/business/archive/2014/05/global-mobile-media-smartphones-tvmaps/371760/ [Accessed January 28, 2018].

Derks, D., Lieke, L., Brummelhuis, D. and Bakker, A. (2012). *Switching on and off. Does smartphone use obstruct the possibility to engage in recovery activities? European Journal of Work and Organization Psychology.* Available from: http://www.tandfonline.com/doi/abs/10.1080/1359432X.2012.711013 [Accessed November 29, 2017].

Dey, A. K. (2001). Understanding and using context. *Personal and Ubiquitous Computing*, 5, 4–7.

Dhar, V. and Chang, A. (2009). Does chatter matter? The impact of user- generated content on music sales. *Journal of Interactive Marketing*, 23(4), 300–307.

Dholakia, M. and Algesheimer, R. (2009). Brand communities. Social Science Research Network. Retrieved from: http://ssrn.com/abstract=1444833 [Accessed May 2017].

Dias, B., Locher, D., Li, M., El-Deredy, W and Lisboa, G. (2008). The Value of Personalised Recommender Systems to E-Business: A Case Study. *Proceedings of the 2008 ACM Conference on Recommender Systems, ACM, Lausanne, Switzerland*, 291–294.

Dickinson, E., Ghali, K., Cherrett, T., Speed, C., Davies, N and Norgate, S. (2012). Tourism and the smartphone app: capabilities, emerging practice and scope in the travel domain. *Current Issues in Tourism*, 17(1), 84–101.

Diefendorff, M. and Seaton, A. (2015). Work motivation IN: Wright, J. D. (ed.) *International Encyclopedia of the Social & Behavioral Sciences,* 2nd ed. Unknown: Elsevier, 680–686.

Dietrich, D., Gray, J., Mcnamara, T., Poikola, A., Pollock, R., Tait, J. and Zijlstra, T. *The Open Data Handbook.* Available from: http://opendatahandbook.org/guide/en/ [Accessed July 24, 2018].

Dogtiev, A. (2015). *App Usage Statistics: 2015 Roundup.* Available from: http://www.businessofapps.com/app-usage-statistics-2015/ [Accessed December 20, 2017].

Douma, S. and Schreuder, H. (2014). *Economics approaches to organizations.* Harlow(Essex): Prentice Hall.

Dredge, S. (2011). Most branded apps are a flop says Deloitte. But why? *The Guardian*. Available at: https://www.theguardian.com/technology/appsblog/2011/jul/11/branded-apps-flopping. [Accessed April 3, 2018].

Drucker, F. (2011). *The age of discontinuity: Guidelines to our changing society*. Transaction Publishers.

Duan, W., Gu, B. and Whinston, B. (2008). Do online reviews matter?—An empirical investigation of panel data. *Decision Support Systems*, 45(4), 1007–1016.

Duggan, M. and Brenner, J. (2013). The demographics of social media users. Pew Research Centre.

Dushinksi, K. (2013). The Mobile Marketing Handbook: A Step by Step Guide to Creating Dynamic Mobile Marketing Campaigns, 2nd Edition, Information Today, Medford, NJ.

Dwyer, C., Hiltz, S. and Passerini, K. (2007). *Trust and privacy concern within social networking sites: A comparison of Facebook and MySpace.* IN: AMCIS 2007 proceedings, 339.

Eagly, A. and Chaiken, S. (1993). *The psychology of attitudes.* 1st ed. Fort Worth, TX: Harcourt Brace Jovanovich College Publishers.

East, R., Wright, M. and Vanhuele, M. (2013). *Consumer Behaviour: Applications in Marketing*, 2nd ed. London: Sage.

eMarketer (2017). Available at: https://www.emarketer.com/Report/UK-Digital-Users-eMarketer-Forecast-2017/2001988 [Accessed March 21, 2018].

Employee Surveillance and the Modern Workplace (2016). Available at: http://scholar.rhsmith. umd.edu/sites/default/files/pitesa/files/pitesa_surveillance_chapter_2012.pdf. [Accessed January 6, 2018].

Englmaier, L. (2015). Reciprocity in Organizations. Retrieved from personal umich: http://www-personal.umich.edu/~leider/Papers/WERS.pdf [Accessed January 5, 2018].

Erdogan, Z. (1999). Celebrity endorsement: A literature review. *Journal of Marketing Management*, 15(4), 291–314.

Ericson, L., Herring, L. and Ungerman, K. (2014). *Busting mobile- shopping myths.* McKinsey & Company. Available at: https://birdseyevieweu.wordpress.com/2015/01/14/busting-mobile-shopping-myths-mckinsey-company/ [Accessed September 18, 2018].

Escalas, E. (2007). Self-referencing and persuasion: Narrative transportation versus analytical elaboration. *Journal of Consumer Research*, 33(4), 421–429.

Espino, C., Sundstrom, S., Frick, H., Jacobs, M. and Peters, M. (2002). International business travel: impact on families and travelers. *Occupational and Environmental Medicine*, 59(5), 309–322.

European Commision (2011). *Open data: An engine for innovation, growth and transparent governance.* Brussels. Available from: http://eur-lex.europa.eu/LexUriServ/LexUriServ. do?uri=COM:2011:0882:FIN:EN:PDF [Accessed April 1, 2018].

Eustice, K. (2011). *How to build a university mobile application: best practice and insight.* The Guardian. Available at: https://www.theguardian.com/higher-education-network/2011/dec/08/building-university-mobile-apps. [Accessed October 7, 2018].

Evans, J. (2016). *Quality and Performance Excellence.* 8th Edition ed. Boston (MA): Cengage Learning.

Evans, M. and Moutinho, L. (2010). *Applied consumer behavior.* Harlow, England: Addison-Wesley Pub.

Evans, M., Jamal, A. and Foxall, G. (2009). *Consumer behaviour*, 2nd ed. Chichester: John Wiley.

Evernote (2018). *Customer Story: Guayaki | Evernote Business.* Available at: https://evernote. com/business/customer-stories/guayaki [Accessed January 11, 2018].

Evernote (2018). *Evernote Business: Use Cases.* Available at: https://evernote.com/business/use-cases [Accessed January 11, 2018].

Ewoldt, K.B. (2017). Productivity apps supporting higher order writing skills for secondary students with learning disabilities, *Intervention in School and Clinic*.

Farooq, F. and Jan, Z. (2012). The Impact of Social Networking to Influence Marketing through Product Reviews. *International Journal of Information and Communication Technology*, 2(8), 627–637.

Felstead, A., Jewson, N., Phizacklea, A. and Walters, S. (2002). Opportunities to work at home in the context of work-life balance. *Human Resource Management Journal*, 12(1), 54–76.

Feng, X., Fu, S. and Qin, J. (2016). Determinants of consumers' attitudes toward mobile advertising: The mediating roles of intrinsic and extrinsic motivations. *Computers in Human Behavior*, 63, 334–341.

Fenner, H. and Renn, W. (2009). Technology-assisted supplemental work and work-to-family conflict: The Role of instrumentality beliefs, organizational expectations and time management. *Human Relations*, 63(1), 63–82.

Ferguson, C. (2009). Corinna Ferguson: Liberty Clinic: Your rights with respect to surveillance in the workplace. the Guardian. Available at: http://www.theguardian.com/commentisfree/libertycentral/2009/mar/30/surveillance-work-privacy [Accessed January 6, 2018].

Ferro, E. and Osella, M. (2012). Business models for PSI re-use: A multidimensional framework *Using Open data: Policy Modeling, Citizen Empowerment, Data Journalism Workshop, European Comission*, Brussels.

Ferro, E. and Osella, M. (2013). Eight business model archetypes for PSI Re-Use. *Open Data on the Web Workshop*, Google Campus, Shoreditch, London.

Fielding, M. (2006). *Effective Communication in Organizations*, 3rd ed. South Africa: Juta Academic.

Fincham, R. and Rhodes, P. (2005). *Principles of Organizational Behavior* (4th ed.). New York: Oxford University Press.

Fishbein, M. and Ajzen, I. (1975). *Belief, attitude, intention and behavior: an introduction to theory and research*. Reading, MA: Addison-Wesley.

Fishbein, M. and Ajzen, I. (1975). *Belief, attitude, intention, and behaviour*. 1st ed. Reading, MA: Addison-Wesley Pub. Co.

Flanagan, J. (2015). Workplace chat apps to keep your team in sync, *The Huffington Post*, 28th March. Available from: http://www.huffingtonpost.com/fueled/7-workplace-chat-apps-to_b_6548914.html [Accessed January 8, 2018].

Flanagin, J. and Metzger, J. (2013). Trusting expert-versus user-generated ratings online: The role of information volume, valence, and consumer characteristics. *Computers in Human Behavior*, 29(4), 1626–1634.

Fligstein, N. (1990). *The transformation of corporate control*. Harvard University Press.

Fling, B. (2009). *Mobile design and development: Practical concepts and techniques for creating mobile sites and web apps*. USA: O'Reilly.

Fliplet (2016). *Goodbye intranet. Hello internal communication apps*. Available at: http://fliplet.com/blog/goodbye-intranet-hello-internal-communication-apps/ [Accessed November 30, 2017].

Flynn, L. and Goldsmith, R. (1993). Application of the personal involvement inventory in marketing. *Psychology and Marketing*, 10(4), 357–366.

Forbes, P. and Vespoli, M. (2013). Does social media influence consumer buying behavior? An investigation of recommendations and purchases. *Journal of Business & Economics Research*, 11(2), 107–112.

Forman, C., Ghose, A. and Wiesenfeld, B. (2008). Examining the relationship between reviews and sales: The role of reviewer identity disclosure in electronic markets. *Information Systems Research*, 19(3), 291–313.

Forrester Research (2014). User-Generated content's impact on brand building. Cambridge, MA: Forrester Research. Available from: http://media2.bazaarvoice.com/documents/ Bazaarvoice+-+Forrester+study+-+User-generated+content's+impact+on+brand+building. pdf [Accessed July 10, 2018].

Foster, A. and Rosenzweig, M. (1995). Learning by doing and learning from others: Human capital and technical change in agriculture. *Journal of Political Economy*, 103(6), 1176–1210.

Fournier, S. and Lee, L. (2009). Getting Brand Communities Right. *Harvard Business Review*, 105–111.

Frank, T. (2015). 10 Essential Productivity Apps for iOS and Android. Retrieved from: https:// collegeinfogeek.com/essential-productivity-apps/

Frey, S. and Oberholzer-Gee, F. (1997). The cost of price incentives: An empirical analysis of motivation crowding-out. *The American Economic Review*, 87(4), 746–755.

Fried, C. (1968). Privacy. *Yale Law Journal*, 77, 475–493.

Fullan, M. (2014). *Leading in a culture of change personal action guide and workbook.* Hoboken, John Wiley & Sons.

Furedi, F. (2009). *Now is the age of the discontented*. Times Higher Education (THE). Available at: https://www.timeshighereducation.com/features/now-is-the-age-of-the- discontented/406780.article [Accessed October 9, 2018].

Furst, A., Reeves, M., Rosen, B. and Blackburn, S. (2004). Managing the life cycle of virtual teams. *Academy of Management Executive*, 18(2), 6–20.

Gallini, T. (2002). The economics of patents: Lessons from recent US patent reform. *Journal of Economic Perspectives*, 131–154.

Gao, T., Rohm, J., Sultan, F. and Pagani, M. (2013). Consumers un-tethered: A three-market empirical study of consumers' mobile marketing acceptance. *Journal of Business Research*, 66(12), 2536–2544.

Gard, S. (2014). *How apps could improve business performance for your SME.*

Gassmann, O. and Enkel, E. (2004). Towards a theory of open innovation: three core process archetypes. *R&D management conference.* 1–18.

GeekWire (2014). *Study: Americans spend 162 minutes on their mobile device per day, mostly with apps.* GeekWire. Available at: http://www.geekwire.com/2014/flurry-report-mobile- phones-162-minutes/ [Accessed January 10, 2018].

Gefen, D. and Straub, D. (1997). Gender Differences in the Perception and Use of E-Mail: An Extension to the Technology Acceptance Model. *MIS Quarterly*, 21(4), 389.

Gethealthapp. (2016). *GetHealth, Complete workplace wellness package.* Available at: http:// gethealthapp.com. [Accessed December 8, 2017].

Ghose, A. and Ipeirotis, G. (2011). Estimating the helpfulness and economic impact of product reviews: Mining text and reviewer characteristics. *IEEE Transaction Knowledge Data Engineering*, 23(10), 1498–1512.

Ghose, A. and Ipeirotis, G. (2012). Designing ranking systems for hotels on travel search engines by mining user-generated and crowdsourced content. *Marketing Science*, 31(3), 493–520.

Giaglis, G. M., Pateli, A., Fouskas, K., Kourouthanassis, P. and Tsamakos, A. (2002). *On the potential use of mobile positioning technologies in indoor environments.* The Proceedings of the 15th Bled Electronic Commerce Conference-e-Reality: Constructing the e-Economy, June. 17–19.

Giles, F. (1977). Volunteering for job enrichment: A test of expectancy theory predictions. *Personnel Psychology*, 30(3), 427–435.

Gilly, C., Graham, L., Wolfinbarger, F. and Yale, J. (1998). A dyadic study of interpersonal information search. *Journal of Academy of Marketing Science*, 26(2), 83–100.

Go Canvas (2015). *How Businesses are Using Mobile Apps - 2015 Canvas Survey Results.* Available at: https://www.gocanvas.com/content/blog/post/how-businesses-are-using-mobile-apps-2015-canvas-survey-results [Accessed January 10, 2018].

Godes, D. and Mayzlin, D. (2004). Using online conversations to study word-of-mouth communication. *Marketing Science*, 23(4), 545–560.

Godes, D. and Mayzlin, D. (2009). Firm-created word-of-mouth communication: Evidence from a field test. *Marketing Science*, 28(4), 721–739.

Goes, B., Lin, M. and Au Yeung, M. (2014). Popularity effect in user-generated content: evidence from online product reviews. *Information Systems Research*, 25, 222–238.

Goetsch, L. and Davis, B. (2014). *Quality management for organizational excellence.* Upper Saddle River, NJ: Pearson.

Goh, Y., Heng, S. and Lin, Z. (2013). Social media brand community and consumer behavior: Quantifying the relative impact of user-and marketer-generated content. *Information Systems Research*, 24, 88–107.

Goldsmith, E. and Freiden, B. (2004). Have it your way: consumer attitudes toward personalized marketing. *Marketing Intelligence & Planning*, 22(2), 228–239.

Goldsmith, E. and Hofacker, F., (1991). Measuring consumer innovativeness. *Journal of the Academy of Marketing Science*, 19(3), 209–221.

Goldsmith, E. and Horowitz, D. (2006). Measuring motivations for online opinion seeking, *Journal of Interactive Advertising*, 6(2), 1–16.

Gomes, L. and Murphey, J. (2003). An exploratory study of marketing international education online. *International Journal of Educational Management*, 17(3), 116–125.

Google (2016). *Google drive.* Available at: https://www.google.com/drive/. [Accessed December 7, 2017].

Google (2018). Inventoryplus. https://play.google.com/store/apps/details?id=com.ecarlist. android.truetarget&hl=en [Accessed July 12, 2018].

Grahl, J., Rothlauf, F. and Hinz, O. (2014). *The impact of user-generated content on sales: A randomized field experiment.* Research Paper, TU Darmstadt. Available from: http://www.emarkets.tudarmstadt.de/fileadmin/user_upload/download/Working_Papers/grahl.pdf [Accessed July 6, 2018].

Greenhaus, H. and Beutell, J. (1985). Sources of conflict between work and family roles. *The Academy of Management Review*, 10, 76–88.

Greenhaus, H., Collins, M. and Shaw, D. (2003). The relation between work-family balance and quality of life. *Journal of Vocational Behavior*, 63, 510–531.

Gröger, C., Silcher, S., Westkämper, E. and Mitschang, B. (2013). Leveraging apps in manufacturing. A framework for app technology in the enterprise. *Procedia CIRP*, 7, 664–669. Available from: https://www.sciencedirect.com/science/article/pii/S2212827113003193 [Accessed January 7, 2018].

Grossman, S. and Hart, O. (1989). The costs and benefits of ownership: A theory of vertical and lateral integration. *Journal of Political Economy*, 94.

Grover, R. and Srinivasan, V. (1992). Reflections on "a simultaneous approach to market segmentation and market structuring." *Journal of Marketing Research*, 29(4), 474.

Gu, B., Konana, P., Rajagopalan, B. and Chen, M. (2007). Competition among virtual communities and user valuation: The case of investing-related communities. *Information Systems Research*, 18(1), 68–85.

Guay, M. (2016). *20 web apps that ruled the workplace in 2016.* Available from: https://zapier.com/blog/fastest-growing-apps/ [Accessed January 8, 2018].

Guillen, F. (1994). *Models of Management: Work Authority and Organisation in Comparative Perspective.* Chicago University Press.

Guiney, P. (2015). *E-learning in the workplace an annotated bibliography.* 1st ed.

Gupta, S. and Chaudhari, S. (2015). Big Data: Issues and Challenges. *International Journal on Recent and Innovation Trends in Computing and Communication* (Feb 2015), 3(2).

Gupta, S. (2013). *For Mobile Devices, Think Apps, Not Ads.* Harvard Business Review. Available at: https://hbr.org/2013/03/for-mobile-devices-think-apps-not-ads [Accessed April 3, 2018].

Haddadi, H., Hui, P., Henderson, T. and Brown, I. (2011). *Targeted advertising on the handset: Privacy and security challenges.* In: Müller, J., Alt, F. and Michelis, D. (ed.) *Pervasive Advertising*, Human-Computer Interaction Series, Springer, Heidelberg, Germany, 119–137.

Han, S., Kim, L. and Cha, W. (2012). Computing user reputation in a social network of web 2.0. *Computing and Informatics*, 31(2), 447–462.

Harper, J. (2015). Americans now spend five hours a day—on their phones. Retrieved from http://www.washingtontimes.com/news/2015/feb/10/smart-phone-nation-americans-now-spend-five-hours-/ [Accessed December 30, 2017].

Harper, N. (2018). *The disadvantages of technology in the workplace. Chron.* Available from: http://smallbusiness.chron.com/disadvantages-technology-workplace-20157.html [Accessed January 4, 2018].

Harris, D. (2015). Use of 'over-the-top' communication apps in the workplace industry view. Software Advice. Available at: https://www.softwareadvice.com/voip/industryview/otc-apps-report-2015/ [Accessed January 4, 2018].

Harris, K., Marett, K. and Harris, R. (2011). Technology-related pressure and work-family conflict: Main effects and an examination of moderating variables. *Journal of Applied Social Psychology*, 41(9), 2077–2103.

Haselmayr, M. (2014). Here's why your business needs its own mobile app. Retrieved from http://www.forbes.com/sites/allbusiness/2014/11/17/heres-why-your-business-needs-its-own-mobile-app/ [Accessed December 30, 2017].

Haubl, G. and Trifts, V. (2000). Consumer decision making in online shopping environments: the effects of interactive decision aids. *Marketing Science*, 19, 4–21.

Heathfield, M. (2017). *What are incentives at work?* Available from: https://www.thebalance.com/what-are-incentives-at-work-1917994 [Accessed January 7, 2018].

Henkel, J. (2006). Selective revealing in open innovation processes: The case of embedded Linux. *Research Policy*, 35(7), 953–969.

Henricks, M. (2006). *How time zones affect global businesses.* [Online] Entrepreneur. Available from: https://www.entrepreneur.com/article/160228 [Accessed December 8, 2017].

Herrera, F. (2010). *The digital workplace: Think, share, do Transform your employee experience.* Available at: https://www2.deloitte.com/content/dam/Deloitte/mx/Documents/human-capital/The_digital_workplace.pdf [Accessed January 12, 2018].

Herzberg, F. (1987). One more time: How do You Motivate Employees? *Harvard Business Review*, 5–16.

Herzberg, F., Mausner, B. and Snydermann, B. (1959). *The motivation to work.* New York: Wiley.

Hew, J., Badaruddin, M. and Moorthy, M. (2017). Crafting a smartphone repurchase decision making process: Do brand attachment and gender matter? *Telematics and Informatics*, 34(4), 34–56.

Hills, C., Ryan, S., Warren-Forward, H. and Smith, R. (2013). Managing Generation Y occupational therapists: Optimising their potential. *Australian Occupational Therapy Journal*, 60, 267–275.

Hirschman, E. (1980). Innovativeness, novelty seeking, and consumer creativity. *Journal of Consumer Research*, 7(3), 283.

Ho, M., Chen, X., Cheung, F., Liu, H. and Worthington, E. (2013). A dyadic model of the work–family interface: A study of dual-earner couples in China. *Journal of Occupational Health Psychology*, 18(1), 53–63.

Ho-Dac, N., Carson, S. and Moore, W. (2013). The effects of positive and negative online customer reviews: Do brand strength and category maturity matter? *Journal of Marketing*, 77(6), 37–53.

Hoeffler, S. and Keller, K. (2003). The marketing advantages of strong brands. *Journal of Brand Management*, 10(6), 421–445.

Hofer T., Schwinger W., Pichler M. Leonhartsberger G., Altmann J. and Retschitzegger W. (2003). Context-awareness on mobile devices – the hydrogen approach. Proceedings of the 36th Hawaii International Conference on System Sciences.

Holland, J., Cooper, B. and Hecker, R. (2015). Electronic monitoring and surveillance in the worplace: The effects on trust in management, and the moderating role of occupational type. *Personnel Review*, 44(1), 161–175.

Holland, P. (2015). Electronic monitoring and surveillance in the workplace: the effects on trust in management, and the moderating role of occupational type. Monash University. Melbourne, Australia: Brian Cooper; Rob Hecker.

Holton, N. (2012). *A Mobile Workforce: Looking into the Benefits and Risks*. Available at: http://www.glcpu.com/_blog/Green_Line_Solutions_News/post/A_Mobile_Workforce_Looking_into_the_Benefits_and_Risks/ [Accessed December 30, 2017].

Homburg, C., Ehm, L. and Artz, M. (2015). Measuring and managing consumer sentiment in an online community environment. *Journal of Marketing Research*, 52(5), 629–641.

Hoos, E., Gröger, C. and Mitschang, B. (2015). Mobile apps in engineering: A process-driven analysis of business potentials and technical challenges. *Procedia CIRP*, 33, 17–22. Available from: https://www.sciencedirect.com/science/article/pii/S2212827115006484 [Accessed January 9, 2018].

Horibe, F. (2016). *Creating the innovation culture: Leveraging visionaries, dissenters, and other useful troublemakers in your organization*. Ontario, VisionArts Inc.

Hosmer, T. (1995). Trust: the connecting link between organizational theory and philosophic ethics. New York, NY: *Academy of Management*.

Hsee, K., Yu, F., Zhang, J. and Zhang, Y. (2003). Medium maximization. *Journal of Consumer Research*, 30, 1–14.

Hsiao, C. and Chiou, S. (2012). The effect of social capital on community loyalty in a virtual community: test of a tripartite-process model, *Decision Support Systems*, 54, 750–757. https://doi.org/10.1177/1053451217736868.

Hu, P., Chau, P., Sheng, O. and Tam, K. (1999). Examining the Technology Acceptance Model Using Physician Acceptance of Telemedicine Technology. *Journal of Management Information Systems*, 16(2), 91–112.

Huhtala, M., Tolvanen, A., Mauno, S. and Feldt, T. (2015). The associations between ethical organizational culture, burnout, and engagement: A multilevel study. *Journal of Business and Psychology*, 30(2), 399–414.

Hui, S., Inman, J., Huang, Y. and Suher, J. (2013). Estimating the effect of travel distance on unplanned spending: Applications to mobile promotion strategies. *Journal of Marketing*, 77(2), 1–16.

Hyman, J. and Summers, J. (2004). Lacking balance?: Work-life employment practices in the modern economy, *Personnel Review*, 33(4), 418–429.

IBM (2016). *IBM business analytics products training—e-learning*.

IGI Global (2018). *What is Technology Acceptance Model (TAM)*. Available at: https://www. igi-global.com/dictionary/technology-acceptance-model-tam/29485 [Accessed January 6, 2018].

Ilicic, J. and Webster, C. (2011). Effects of multiple endorsements and consumer–celebrity attachment on attitude and purchase intention. *Australasian Marketing Journal*, 19(4), 230–237.

Industrial Democracy Group (1993). *Industrial Democracy in Europe Revisited*. (Oxford: Oxford University Press.

Intense School (2014). *Project Management—Improving Bottlenecks within Organizations Part 1*. Available from: http://resources.intenseschool.com/project-management-improving-bottlenecks-within-organizations-part-1/ [Accessed January 11, 2018].

Jacobs, A. (2009). The Pathologies of Big Data. *Communications of the ACM*, 52(8), 36–44.

Jahn, B. and Kunz, W. (2012). How to transform consumers into fans of your brand. *Journal of Service Management*, 23(3), 344–361.

Jank, W. (2013). *Business Analytics for Managers*. Springer-Verlag GmbH.

Jansen, B., Moore, K. and Carman, S. (2013). Evaluating the performance of demographic targeting using gender in sponsored search. *Information Processing & Management*, 49(1), 286–302.

Janssen, K. (2011). The influence of the PSI directive on open government data: An overview of recent developments. *Government Information Quarterly*, 28(4), 446–456.

Janssen, M. and Zuiderwijk, A. (2014). Infomediary Business Models for Connecting Open Data Providers and Users. *Social Science Computer Review*, 32(5), 694–711.

Janssen, M., Charalabidis, Y. and Zuiderwijk, A. (2012). Benefits, Adoption Barriers and Myths of Open Data and Open Government. *Information Systems Management*, 29(4), 258–268.

Jhuang, S. Y. (2009). Tuekcell launched a new mobile advertising service model, greatly improve the click rate. *Market Intelligence and Consulting Institute*, Available from: http://www. find.org.tw/find/home.aspx?page=news&id=5591 [Accessed September 13, 2018].

Joachims, T. (1999). Making large-scale SVM learning practical. In B. Schölkopf, C. Burges & A. Smola (Eds.), *Advances in Kernel Methods—Support Vector Learning* (pp. 41–56): MIT Press.

Johns, G. (2006). The essential impact of context on organizational behavior. *Academic Management Review*, 31(2), 386–408.

Johnson, G. and Scholes, K. (2009). *Exploring corporate strategy* (5th Ed.). London: Prentice Hall Europe.

Johnson, G., Whittington, R., Scholes, K. and Johnson, G. (2011). *Exploring strategy*, 9th ed. Harlow: Financial Times Prentice Hall.

Johnson, L. (2013). Consumers are driving need for contextual mobile experiences: Token exec. Mobile Commerce Daily. Available at: https://www.retaildive.com/ex/

mobilecommercedaily/proximity-presence-%20portability-preferences-are-new-pillars-of-mobile-marketing%20-token-exec [Accessed August 28, 2018].

Johnson, R. and Creech, C. (1983). Ordinal measures in multiple indicator models: A simulation study of categorization error. *American Sociological Review*, 48(3), 398–407.

Johnston, S. (2005). *Headquarters and Subsidiaries in Multinational Corporations*. UK: Palgrave Macmillan. Available from: http://www.palgrave.com/gb/book/9781403936240?wt_mc=ThirdParty.SpringerLink.3.EPR653.About_eBook#otherversion=9780230511002 [Accessed January 5, 2018].

Jonas, O. (2010). Source credibility of company-produced and user generated content on the internet: An exploratory study on the Filipino youth. *Philippine Management Review*, 17, 121–132.

Kaasinen, E. (2003). User Needs for Location-Aware Mobile Services. *Personal and Ubiquitous Computing*, 7(1), 70–79.

Kahneman, D. and Tversky, A. (1979). Prospect theory: An analysis of decision under risk. *Econometrica*, 47(2), 263–291.

Kahneman, D. (2012). *Thinking, fast and slow*, London: Allen Lane.

Kaikkonen, A., Kekäläinen, A., Cankar, M., Kallio, T. and Kankainen, A. (2005). Usability testing of mobile applications: A comparison between laboratory and field testing. *Journal of Usability studies*, 1(1), 4–16.

Kaisler, S., Armour, F., Espinosa, A. and Money, W. (2013). Big Data: Issues and Challenges Moving Forward. *2014 47th Hawaii International Conference on System Sciences*, 995–1004, IEEE.

Kalafatis, P., Ledden, L., Riley, D. and Singh, J. (2016). The added value of brand alliances in higher education. *Journal of Business Research*, 69(8), 3122–3132.

Kalyanam, K. and McIntyre, S. (2002). The e-Marketing mix: A Contribution of the E-Tailing Wars. *Journal of the Academy of Marketing Science*, 30(4), 487–499.

Kang, M., Mun, M. and Johnson, P. (2015). In-store mobile usage: Downloading and usage intention toward mobile location-based retail apps. *Computers in Human Behavior*, 46, 210–217.

Kaplan, M. and Haenlein, M. (2010). Users of the world, unite! The challenges and opportunities of Social Media. *Business Horizons*, 53(1), 59–68.

Katz, M. (2015). *Monitoring employee productivity: Proceed with caution*. Available at: https://www.shrm.org/hr-today/news/hr-magazine/pages/0615-employee-monitoring.aspx [Accessed January 13, 2018].

Kavanagh, J. and Johnson, D. eds. (2017). *Human resource information systems: Basics, applications, and future directions*. Thousand Oaks, Sage Publications.

Keenan, A. and Shiri, A. (2009). Sociability and social interaction on social networking websites. *Library Review*, 58(6), 438–450.

Kelman, C. (1961). Processes of attitude change. *Public Opinion Quarterly*, 25, 57–78.

Kenny, D. and Marshall, F. (2000). Contextual marketing: The real business of the Internet. *Harvard Business Review*, 78(6), 119–125.

Kernevez, E. (2015). How to use apps to optimize and streamline your business. Retrieved from http://realbusiness.co.uk/article/32089-how-to-use-apps-to-optimise-and-streamline-your-business [Accessed December 29, 2017].

Khaleeli, H. (2016). *The truth about working for Deliveroo, Uber and the on-demand economy*. The Guardian. Available at: https://www.theguardian.com/money/2016/jun/15/he-truth-about-working-for-deliveroo-uber-and-the-on-demand-economy [Accessed December 9, 2017].

Kharif, O. (2017). *2016 Was a Record Year for Data Breaches.* Available at: https://www.bloomberg.com/news/articles/2017-01-19/data-breaches-hit-record-in-2016-as-dnc-wendy-s-co-hacked [Accessed January 9, 2018].

Kim, J. and Ah Yu, E. (2016). The Holistic Brand Experience of BMA Affects Brand Loyalty. *Social Behavior and Personality. An International Journal*, 44(1), 77–87.

Kim, N., Han, K. and Srivastava, K. (2002). A dynamic IT adoption model for the SOHO market: PC generational decisions with technological expectations. *Management Science*, 48(2), 222–240.

Kim, S., Wang, R. and Malthouse, E. (2015). The effects of adopting and using a brand's mobile application on customers' subsequent purchase behavior. *Journal of Interactive Marketing*, 31, 28–41.

Kivetz, R. and Simonson, I. (2000). The effects of incomplete information on consumer choice. *Journal of Marketing Research*, 37(4), 427–448.

Knapton, S. (2014). *High-fliers at risk of isolation and depression from Internet addiction.* Telegraph.co.uk. Available at: http://www.telegraph.co.uk/news/health/news/10557025/High-fliers-at-risk-of-isolation-and-depression-from-Internet-addiction.html [Accessed December 8, 2017].

Kohn, A. (1993). Why incentive plans cannot work. *Harvard Business Review*, 71, 54–63.

Koike, K. (1994). Learning and Incentive Systems in Japanese Industry IN: Aoki, M. and Dore, R. (eds.) *The Japanese Firm: Sources of Competitive Strength: The Sources of Competitive Strength.* USA: Oxford University Press, 41–65.

Koolwaaij, J., Tarlano, A., Luther, M., Nurmi, P., Mrohs, B., Battestini, A. and Vaidya, R. (2006). Context Watcher-Sharing context information in everyday life. IN: Proceedings of the IASTED conference on Web Technologies, Applications and Services (WTAS), July 4.

Kossek, E., Ruderman, M., Braddy, P. and Hannum, K. (2012). Work-nonwork boundary management profiles: A person-centered approach. *Journal of Vocational Behavior*, 81, 112–128.

Kotler, P. (1997). *Marketing Management: Analysis, Planning, Implementation and Control*, 9th ed. Upper Saddle River, NJ: Prentice Hall.

Koufaris, M. (2002). Applying the Technology Acceptance Model and Flow Theory to Online Consumer Behaviour. *Information Systems Research*, 13(2), 205–223.

Kozinets, R. (2002). The field behind the screen using netnography for marketing research in online communities. *Journal of Marketing Research*, 39, 61–72.

Kreps, P. (eds) (1990). Corporate Culture and Economic Theory. *Perspectives on Positive Political Economy.* Cambridge University Press.

Kuhn, S. (1968). *The structure of scientific revolutions,* Chicago : Chicago University Press.

Kumar, A., Bezawada, R., Rishika, R., Janakiraman, R. and Kannan, K. (2016). From social to sale: The effects of firm-generated content in social media on customer behavior. *Journal of Marketing*, 80(1), 7–25.

Kun, L., Shiyu, W., Ling, X., Zhen, W. and Mingchu, L. (2016). A dynamic reward-based incentive mechanism: Reducing the cost of P2P systems. *Knowledge-Based Systems*, 112, 105–113.

Kylander, N. and Stone, C. (2012). The role of brand in the nonprofit sector. The Hauser Center for Nonprofit Organizations Harvard University. Available at: https://ssir.org/articles/entry/the_role_of_brand_in_the_nonprofit_sector [Accessed March 8, 2018].

Lacais, R. (2016). *Mobile Apps Can Transform Business Processes - Enterprise Apps Today*. Enterpriseappstoday.com. Available at: http://www.enterpriseappstoday.com/crm/ mobile-apps-can-transform-business-processes.html [Accessed January 3, 2018].

Lal, R. and Sarvary, M. (1999). When and How Is the Internet Likely to Decrease Price Competition? *Marketing Science*, 18(4), 485–503.

Landry, B., Griffeth, R. and Hartman, S. (2006). Measuring Student Perceptions of Blackboard Using the Technology Acceptance Model. *Decision Sciences Journal of Innovative Education*, 4(1), 87–99.

Lane, L. (2005). *By All Means Communicate: An Overview of Basic Speech Communication*. 2nd ed. Resource Publications.

Latane, B. (1981). The psychology of social impact. *American Psychologist*, 36(4), 343–356.

Lauby, S. (2013). *5 Social Apps to Encourage Employee Health and Wellness*. Mashable. Available at: http://mashable.com/2013/02/09/social-health-wellness/#cQazT858ukq2 [Accessed November 30, 2017].

Laursen, G. (2011). *Business analytics for Sales and Marketing Managers How to Compete in the Information Age*. Hoboken, NY: John Wiley & Sons.

Lawrence, R. and Lorsch, W. (1967). *Organization and environment*. Addison Wesley.

Lay-Yee, L., Kok-Siew, H. and Yin-Fah, C. (2013). Factors affecting smartphone purchase decision among Malaysian generation. *International Journal of Asian Social Science*, 3(12), 2426–2440.

Lazear, E. and Gibbs, M. (2015). *Personnel Economics in Practice*, 3rd Edition, John Wiley & Sons.

Leclerq, T., Hammedi, W., and Poncin, I. (2017). Engagement process during value co-creation: Gamification in new product-development platform. *International Journal of Electronic Commerce*.

Lee, P. and Talbot, E. (2016). *Global Mobile Consumer Survey: UK Cut*. 5th ed. [eBook] p.4. Available at:https://www.deloitte.co.uk/mobileuk/assets/pdf/Deloitte-Mobile-Consumer-2016-There-is-no-place-like-phone.pdf [Accessed December 7, 2017].

Lee, Y., Hsieh, Y. and Hsu, C. (2011). An investigation of employees' use of e-learning systems: applying the technology acceptance model. *Behavior & Information Technology*, 32(2), 173–189.

Legris, P., Ingham, J. and Collerette, P. (2003). Why do people use information technology? A critical review of the technology acceptance model. *Information & Management*, 40(3), 191–204.

Lekakos, G. and Giaglis, M. (2006). Improving the Prediction Accuracy of Recommendation Algorithms: Approaches Anchored on Human Factors. *Journal of Interacting with Computers*, 18, 410–431.

Liang, T., Lai, H. and Ku, Y. (2006). Personalized Content Recommendation and User Satisfaction: Theoretical Synthesis and Empirical Findings. *Journal of Management Information Systems*, 23(3), 45–70.

Lichtenthaler, U. and Ernst, H. (2008). Intermediary Services in the Markets for Technology: Organizational Antecedents and Performance Consequences. *Organization Studies*.

Liden, C., Wayne, J., Liao, C. and Meuser, D. (2014). Servant leadership and serving culture: Influence on individual and unit performance. *Academy of Management Journal*, 57(5), 1434–1452.

Liferay (2017). *7 Examples of Great Mobile Workforce Apps.* Available at: https://www.liferay. com/blog/en-us/digital-strategy/7-examples-of-great-mobile-workforce-apps [Accessed December 21, 2017].

Liferay (2017). *LGT.* Available at: https://www.liferay.com/resource/lgt [Accessed December 21, 2017].

Lindgren, D. (2011). *The Consumer Data and Information Program: Sowing the seeds of research.* New York: ABC-CLIO.

Lindman, J. (2014). Similarities of Open Data and Open Source: Impacts on Business. *Journal of Theoretical & Applied Electronic Commerce Research,* 9(3), 59–70.

Lindman, J. and Nyman, L. (2014). The businesses of open data and open source: Some key similarities and differences. *Technology Innovation Management Review,* 4(1).

Lindman, J., Rossi, M. and Tuunainen, K. (2013). Open Data Services: Research Agenda *System Sciences (HICSS), 2013 46th Hawaii International Conference,* 1239–1246.

Liu, Y. (2006). Word of mouth for movies: Its dynamics and impact on box office revenue. *Journal of Marketing* 70(3), 74–89.

Liu, Y., Zhang, J., An, B. and Sen, S. (2016). A simulation framework for measuring robustness of incentive mechanisms and its implementation in reputation systems. *Autonomous Agents and Multi-Agent Systems,* 30(4), 581–600.

Liu-Thompkins, Y. and Rogerson, M. (2012). Rising to stardom: An empirical investigation of the diffusion of user-generated content. *Journal of Interactive Marketing,* 26(2), 71–82.

Lu, J., Yao, J. and Yu, C. (2005). Personal innovativeness, social influences and adoption of wireless Internet services via mobile technology. *The Journal of Strategic Information Systems,* 14(3), 245–268.

Lu, J., Yu, C., Liu, C. and Yao, J. (2003). Technology acceptance model for wireless Internet. *Internet Research,* 13(3), 206–222.

Lunden, I. (2015). Smartphone Users Globally By 2020, Overtaking Basic Fixed Phone Subscriptions. Retrieved from http://techcrunch.com/2015/06/02/6-1b-smartphone-users-globally-by-2020-overtaking-basic-fixed-phone-subscriptions/#.l3alh8a:RPIH [Accessed December 29, 2017].

Luo, X., Andrews, M., Fang, Z., and Phang, C. W. (2013). Mobile Targeting. *Management Science,* 60(7), 1738–1756.

Maass, A. and Clark, R.D. (1984). Hidden impact of minorities: Fifteen years of minority influence research. *Psychological Bulletin,* 95(3), 428–450.

Macias, W. (2003). A beginning look at the effects of interactivity, product involvement and web experience on comprehension: brand web sites as interactive advertising, *Journal of Current Issues and Research in Advertising,* 25(2), 31–44.

MacKinnon, A. (2012). User generated content vs. advertising: Do consumers trust the word of others over advertisers. *The Elon Journal of Undergraduate Research in Communications,* 3(1), 14–22.

Madden, M. and Smith, A. (2010). Reputation management and social media.

Magnussum, D. and Torestad, B. (1993). A Holistic View of Personality: A Model Revisited, *Annual Review of Psychology,* 44, 427–452.

Maitland, A. (2009). A to Z of Generation Y attitudes. *Financial times,* Available from: http://www.ft.com/cms/s/0/b147d61a-5b9e-11de-be3f-00144feabdc0.html?ft_ site=falcon&desktop=true#axzz4VSQBiYnj [Accessed January 10, 2018].

Makinson, P., Hundley, S., Feldhaus, C. and Fernandez, E. (2012). Mobile communications anytime, anywhere: The impact on work-life balance and stress. *Frontiers in Education Conference (FIE)*.

Manchanda, P., Xie, Y. and Youn, N. (2008). The role of targeted communication and contagion in product adoption. *Marketing Science* 27(6), 961–976.

Mansfield, E. (1991). Academic research and industrial innovation. *Research Policy,* 20(1), 1–12.

Mansfield, E. (1998). Academic research and industrial innovation: An update of empirical findings. *Research policy,* 26(7), 773–776.

Mansuri, M., Verma, M. and Laxkar, P. (2014). Benefit of cloud computing for educational institutions and online marketing. *Information Security and Computer Fraud*, 2(1), 5–9.

Marston, S., Bandyopadhyay, S. Zhang, J. and Ghalsasi, A. (2011). Cloud Computing—The business perspective. *Decision Support Systems*, 51(1).

Martin, A. (2005). From high maintenance to high productivity: what managers need to know about generation Y. *Industrial and Commercial training*, 37, 29–44.

Maslow, A. (1943). A Theory of Human Motivation. *Psychological Review*, 50, 370–369.

Matei, C and Abrudan, M. (2016). Adapting Herzberg's Two Factor Theory to the Cultural Context of Romania. *Procedia—Social and Behavioural Sciences*, 221, 95–104.

Mathieson, K. (1991). Predicting user intentions: Comparing the technology acceptance model with the theory of planned behaviour. *Information Systems Research*, 2(3), 173–191.

Mayzlin, D. (2006). Promotional chat on the Internet. *Marketing Science*, 25(2), 155–163.

McAlexander, H., Schouten, W. and Koenig, F. (2002). Building brand community, *Journal of Marketing*, 66(1), 38–54.

McCloskey, W. (2006). The importance of ease of use, usefulness, and trust to online consumers: An examination of the technology acceptance model with older consumers. *Journal of Organizational and End User Computing*, 18(3), 47–65.

McKenna, A., Green, S. and Gleason, J. (2002). Relationship formation on the Internet: What's the big attraction? *Journal of Social Issues*, 58(1), 9–31.

McKinsey (2016). *Busting mobile-shopping myths*. Available at: http://www.mikeanthony.me/digital/mobile-marketing-myths-instore-usage/#.W7Yb3GWMDfY [Accessed April 3, 2018].

McLellan, C. (2014). *Enterprise mobility in 2014: App-ocalypse now?* Available from: http://www.zdnet.com/article/enterprise-mobility-in-2014-app-ocalypse-now/ [Accessed December 20, 2017].

Meece, M. (2011). *Who's the Boss, You or Your Gadget?* New York Times. Available at http://www.nytimes.com/2011/02/06/business/06limits.html [Accessed December 2, 2017].

Meeker, M. and Wu, L. (2013). *Internet Trends*. Available from: http://www.kpcb.com/blog/2013-Internet-trends [Accessed December 20, 2017].

Mellon, J. and Prosser, C., (2017). Twitter and Facebook are not representative of the general population: Political attitudes and demographics of British social media users. *Research and Politics*, 4(3), 1–9.

Merz, M., He, Y. and Vargo, S. (2009). The Evolving Brand Logic: A Service-Dominant Logic. *Journal of the Academy of Marketing Science*, 37(3), 328–344.

Messenger (2015). *Features*. Available at: https://www.messenger.com/features [Accessed January 6, 2018].

Messinger, L. (2015). Do time management apps really make people more productive? *The Guardian*. Available at: https://www.theguardian.com/business/2015/aug/18/time-management-apps-work-life-balance-productivity [Accessed December 8, 2017].

Microsoft (2018). What is Power BI. https://powerbi.microsoft.com/en-us/what-is-power-bi/ [Accessed February 9, 2018].

Middelweerd, A., Mollee, S., van der Wal, N. (2014). Apps to promote physical activity among adults: a review and content analysis, *International Journal of Behavioral Nutrition and Physical Activity*, 11, 97.

Midgley, F. and Dowling, R. (1978). Innovativeness: The concept and its measurement. *Journal of Consumer Research*, 4(4), 229–242.

Mikkola, H., McLaren, P. and Wright, S. (2005). Book reviews. *R&D Management*, 35, 104–109.

Mikulincer, M. (1998). Attachment working models and the sense of trust: An exploration of interaction goals and affect regulation. *Journal of Personality and Social Psychology*, 74(5), 1209–1224.

Milgrom, P. and Roberts, R. (1992). *Economics, organization and management*. Englewood Cliffs: Prentice Hall.

Miller, E. (2015). *The most powerful apps for sales and marketing teams | InsightSquared*. InsightSquared. Available at: http://www.insightsquared.com/2015/06/periodic-table-of-appexchange-apps/#integration [Accessed December 28, 2017].

Miller, J. (1992). *Managerial dilemmas*. Cambridge: Cambridge University Press.

Miller-Merrell, J. (2012). The workplace engagement economy where HR, social, mobile, and tech collide. *Employment Relations Today Journal*, 1–9.

Mills, J. and Tancred, P. (1992). *Gendering organizational analysis*. New York: SAGE Publications.

Mills, J. L. (2008). *Privacy: The lost right*. New York: Oxford University Press.

Mintel (2015). The connected consumer. Available at: https://academic.mintel.com/?logon&start=display&id=737211 [Accessed November 29, 2017].

Mintel (2016a). Digital advertising report, March. Infographic Overview http://academic.mintel.com/display/747975/# [Accessed November 2, 2017].

Mintel (2016b). The challenge of optimizing mobile ads. http://academic.mintel.com/display/775978/?highlight [Accessed November 2, 2017].

Mintzberg, H. (1989). *Mintzberg on management*. New York: Free Press.

Mir, A. and Rehman, U. (2013). Factors affecting consumer attitudes and intentions toward user-generated product content on YouTube. *Management & Marketing*, 8(4), 637–654.

Mir, I. and Zaheer, A. (2012). Verification of social impact theory claims in social media context. *Journal of Internet Banking and Commerce*, 17(1), 1–15.

Mishra, P., Heide, B and Cort, G. (1998). Information asymmetry and levels of agency relationships. *Journal of Marketing Research*, 35(3), 277–295.

Mitchell, R. (1982). Motivation: New Directions for Theory, Research, and Practice. *Academy of Management Review*, 7(1), 80–88.

Mobile Marketing Association (2009). MMA updates definition of mobile marketing. Available at: https://www.mmaglobal.com/news/mma-updates-definition-mobile-%20marketing [Accessed April 18, 2018].

Moe, W. and Schweidel, A. (2012). Online product opinions: Incidence, evaluation and evolution. *Marketing Science*, 31(3), 372–386.

Moe, W. and Trusov, M. (2011). The value of social dynamics in online product ratings forums. *Journal of Marketing Research*, 48(3), 444–456.

Moore, C. and Rugullies, E. (2005). *The information workplace will redefine the world of work— At last!* Forrester. Available from: https://immagic.com/eLibrary/ARCHIVES/GENERAL/GENREF/F050601M.pdf [Accessed January 6, 2018].

Moore, G. and Benbasat, I. (1991). Development of an Instrument to Measure the Perceptions of Adopting an Information Technology Innovation. *Information Systems Research*, 2(3), 192–222.

Morgan, L. and Finnegan, P. (2010). Open innovation in secondary software firms: an exploration of managers' perceptions of open source software. *SIGMIS Database*, 41 (1), 76–95.

Morgan, N. and Rego, L. (2009). Brand Portfolio Strategy and Firm Performance. *Journal of Marketing*, 73(1), 59–74.

Morinaga, S., Yamanishi, K., Tateishi, K. and Fukushima, T. (2002). Mining Product Reputations on the Web. *Proceedings of the Eighth ACM SOGKDD International Conference on Knowledge Discovery and Data Mining, ACM*, 2002, 341–349.

Mortazavi, M., Esfidani, R. and Barzoki, S. (2014). Influencing VSN users' purchase intentions: The roles of flow, trust and eWOM. *Journal of Research in Interactive Marketing*, 8(2), 102–123.

Moser, K. (2015). *Wirtschaftspsychologie* (2nd Edition). Berlin, Heidelberg: Springer.

Mueck, M. and Karls, I. (2018). Networking vehicles to everything: Evolving automotive solutions. De|G PRESS.

Muñiz, R. and O'Guinn, T. (2001). Brand community. *Journal of Consumer Research*, 27(4), 412–432.

Muntinga, G., Moorman, M. and Smit, G. (2011). Introducing COBRAs. *International Journal of Advertising*, 30(1), 13–46.

Muthoo, A. (1999). *Bargaining Theory with Applications*. Cambridge: Cambridge University Press.

Naidoo, V. and Hollebeek, L. D. (2016). Higher education brand alliances: Investigating consumers' dual degree purchase intentions. *Journal of Business Research*, 69(8), 3113–3121.

Nam, S., Manchanda, P. and Chintagunta, K. (2010). The effect of signal quality and contiguous word of mouth on customer acquisition for a video-on-demand service. *Marketing Science*, 29(4), 690–700.

Narasimhan, C. (1988). Competitive Promotional Strategies. *J. Business.*, 61(4), 427–449.

Narin, F. and Hamilton, S. (1997).The increasing linkage between U.S. technology and public science. *Research Policy*, 26(3), 317.

Narin, F. and Olivastro, D. (1992). Status report: Linkage between technology and science. *Research Policy*, 21(3), 237–249.

Natwest (2016). *Get our mobile banking app | NatWest*. Available at: http://personal.natwest. com/personal/ways-to-bank/mobile-app.html. [Accessed January 10, 2018].

Naylor, W., Lamberton, P. and West, M. (2012). Beyond the "like" button: The impact of mere virtual presence on brand evaluations and purchase intentions in social media settings. *Journal of Marketing*, 76(6), 105–120.

Negroponte, N. (1996). *Being digital/Nicholas Negroponte*. London: Coronet, 1996.

Neilan, C. (2017). *Hello Dave: Who runs Britain's biggest companies*. Cityam.com. Available at: http://www.cityam.com/212103/ftse-hits-7000-these-are-men-and-few-women- who-run-britains-biggest-companies [Accessed April 25, 2018].

Nelson, D. (1977). Taylorism and The Workers at Bethlehem Steel 1898–1901. *Pennsylvania Magazine of History and Biography*, 487–505.

Nelson, R. and Winter, W. (2005). *An Evolutionary theory of economic change*. Cambridge University Press.

Neuendorf, K. (2002). *The Content analysis*, New York: SAGE Publications, Inc.

Ngai, T., Li, X. and Chau, K. (2009). Application of data mining techniques in customer relationship management: A literature review and classification. *Expert Systems with Applications*, 36(2), 2592–2602.

Nguyen, T., Mia, L., Winata, L. and Chong, K. (2017). Effect of transformational-leadership style and management control system on managerial performance. *Journal of Business Research*, 70, 202–213.

Nicholas, C. (2011). *The shallows: what the internet is doing to our brains*. New York: W.W. Norton.

Niculescu, F. and Whang, S. (2012). Co-diffusion of Wireless Voice and Data Services: An Empirical Analysis of the Japanese Mobile Telecommunications Market. *Information System Res.*, 23(1), 260–279.

Nielsen.com. (2016). *Millennials Are Top Smartphone Users*. Available at: https://www.nielsen.com/us/en/insights/news/2016/millennials-are-%20top-smartphone-users.html [Accessed April 11, 2018].

Nijs, V., Dekimpe, G., Steenkamp, M. and Hanssens, M. (2001). The Category Demand Effects of Price Promotions. *Marketing Science*, 20(1), 1–22.

Nisar, T. M. (2018). Digital advertising's wild west: Deciding which media channel is more effective is the key. *The European Business Review*. http://www.europeanbusinessreview.com/digital, advertisings-wild-west-deciding-which-media-channel-is-more-effective-is-the-key/.

Nisar, T. M. and Prabhakar, G. (2018). Trains and twitter: Firm-generated content, customer relationship management and message framing. *Transportation Research Part A: Policy and Practice*, 113, 318–334.

Nisar, T. M., Prabhakar, G., and Strakova, L. (2018). Social media information benefits, knowledge management and smart organizations. *Journal of Business Research*, DOI: 10.1016/j.jbusres.2018.05.005.

Nisar, T. M. and Yeung, M. (2018). Twitter as a tool for forecasting stock market movements: A short-window event study, *Journal of Finance and Data Science*.

Nisar, T. M., and Prabhakar, G. (2017). What factors determine e-satisfaction and consumer spending in e-commerce retailing? *Journal of Retailing and Consumer Services*, 39, 135–144., DOI: 10.1016/j.jretconser.2017.07.010 2017.

Nisar, T. M., and Prabhakar, G. (2017). Exploring the key drivers behind the adoption of mobile banking services. *Journal of Marketing Analytics*, DOI: 10.1057/s41270-017-0023-5.

Nisar, T. M. and Yeung, M. (2017). Attribution modeling and digital advertising: An empirical study, *Journal of Advertising Research*, DOI: 10.2501/JAR-2017–055.

Nisar, T. M. and Whitehead, C. (2016). Brand interactions and social media: Enhancing user loyalty through social networking sites, *Computers in Human Behavior*, 62, 743–753.

Noble, F. (1986). *Forces of Production*. Oxford: Oxford University Press.

NT, B. (2014). *Advantages and disadvantages of cloud storage*. Available at: http://bigdata-madesimple.com/5-advantages-and-disadvantages-of-cloud-storage/ [Accessed December 4, 2017].

Nunnally, C. and Bernstein, H. (1994). *Psychometric Theory*, 3rd ed. New York: McGraw-Hill.

Nwankpa, K. (2015). ERP system usage and benefit: A model of antecedents and outcomes. *Computers in Human Behavior*, 45, 335–344.

Nytimes.com. (2019). Uber Finds Profits in Leaving Tough Overseas Markets. Available at: https://www.nytimes.com/2018/05/23/technology/uber-finds-profits-in-leaving-tough-overseas-markets.html [Accessed January 6, 2019].

Obermiller, C. and Spangenberg, R. (1998). Development of a scale to measure consumer skepticism toward advertising. *Journal of Consumer Psychology*, 7(2), 159–186.

O'Brien, H. and Toms, E. (2008). What is user engagement? A conceptual framework for defining user engagement with technology. *Journal of the American Society for Information Science and Technology*, 59(6), 938–955.

Office of the Regulator of Community Interest Companies (2013). *Community interest companies: guidance sections*. Available from: https://www.gov.uk/government/publications/community-interest-companies-how-to-form-a-cic [Accessed July 17, 2018].

Onenote.com (2018). *Microsoft onenote*. Available at: https://www.onenote.com [Accessed January 11, 2018].

Open Data Institute (2015). *Public Candidate Database*. Available from: https://docs.google.com/spreadsheets/d/1O3rMngsb3kLGK4lF3UBuyga9mwg8A9CbLprB5FyyCYE/edit#gid=0 [Accessed July 25, 2018].

Open Data Institute *What is open data?* Available from: http://theodi.org/what-is-open-data?cache=1414685955&commit=Preview&edition=1&utf8=%E2%9C%93 [Accessed July 24, 2018].

Open Data Institute *What makes data open?*. Available from: http://theodi.org/guides/what-open-data [Accessed July 24, 2018].

Open Source Initiative *The Open Source Definition*. Available from: http://opensource.org/osd [Accessed July 25, 2018].

Oprescu, F., Jones, C., and Katsikitis, M. (2014). I play at work—ten principles for transforming work processes through gamification. *Frontiers in Psychology*, 5.

Orpen, C. (1979). The effects of job enrichment on employee satisfaction, motivation, involvement, and performance: A field experiment. *Human Relations*, 32(3), 189–217.

Osterwalder, A., Pigneur, Y. and Clark, T. (2010). *Business model generation: A handbook for visionaries, game changers, and challengers*. Hoboken, NJ: Wiley.

Ouye, J. (2011). *Five trends that are dramatically changing work and the workplace*. Available at: https://www.knoll.com/media/18/144/WP_FiveTrends.pdf [Accessed November 19, 2017].

Oxford Dictionary (2018). *Data*. Available from: http://www.oxforddictionaries.com/definition/learner/data [Accessed July 24, 2018].

Oxford Dictionary (2018). *Smartphone*. Available at: https://en.oxforddictionaries.com/definition/smartphone [Accessed July 3, 2018].

Pagani, M. (2004). Determinants of adoption of third generation mobile multimedia services. *Journal of Interactive Marketing*, 18(3), 46–59.

Pai, A. (2016). *Survey: 50 percent of employers use mobile apps to engage employees in their health*. MobiHealthNews. Available at: http://www.mobihealthnews.com/content/survey-50-percent-employers-use-mobile-apps-engage-employees-their-health [Accessed November 30, 2017].

Palmer, A., Koenig-Lewis, N. and Asaad, Y. (2016). Brand identification in higher education: A conditional process analysis. *Journal of Business Research*, 69(8), 3033–3040.

Panepinto, J. (2014). The productivity payoff of mobile apps at work. *Harvard Business Review*, 13 November, Available from: https://hbr.org/2014/11/the-productivity-payoff-of-mobile-apps-at-work [Accessed December 20, 2017].

Panko, R. (2018). *How Customers Use Food Delivery and Restaurant Loyalty Apps | The Manifest*. Themanifest.com. Available at: https://themanifest.com/appdevelopment/how-customers-use-food-delivery-and-restaurant-loyalty-apps [Accessed December 1, 2018].

Park, C., Eisingerich, A. and Park, J. (2013). Attachment–aversion (AA) model of customer–brand relationships. *Journal of Consumer Psychology*, 23(2), 229–248.

Park, S., Nam, M. and Cha, S. (2011). University students' behavioral intention to use mobile learning: Evaluating the technology acceptance model. *British Journal of Educational Technology*, 43(4), 592–605.

Park, T., Shenoy, R. and Salvendy, G. (2008). Effective advertising on mobile phones: a literature review and presentation of results from 53 case studies. *Behavior and Information Technology*, 27(5), 355–373.

Park, W., MacInnis, D., Priester, J., Eisingerich, A. and Iacobucci, D. (2010). Brand attachment and brand attitude strength: Conceptual and empirical differentiation of two critical brand equity drivers. *Journal of Marketing*, 74(6), 1–17.

Parks, R. and Floyd, K. (1996). Making friends in cyberspace. *Journal of Communication*. 46(1), 80–97.

Patterson, A. and Hennessy, L. (2017). *Computer organization and design RISC-V edition: The hardware software interface*. Burlington, MA; Morgan Kaufmann Publishers.

Patterson, R.W. (2018). Can behavioral tools improve online student outcomes? Experimental evidence from a massive open online course, *Journal of Economic Behavior & Organization*, 153, 293–321.

Pavlou, A. and Dimoka, A. (2006). The nature and role of feedback text comments in online marketplaces: Implications for trust building, price premiums, and seller differentiation. *Information Systems Research*, 17(4), 392–414.

Peck, J. (2014). *Business benefits of shifting from paper forms to mobile apps*. Available at: http://www.techradar.com/news/phone-and-communications/mobile-phones/5-business-benefits-of-shifting-from-paper-forms-to-mobile-apps-1252953 [Accessed December 28, 2017].

Peng, F., Chen, Y. and Wen, K.W. (2014). Brand relationship, consumption values and branded app adoption. *Industrial Management & Data Systems*, 114(8), 1131–1143.

Penrose, E. (1959). *The Theory of the Growth of the Firm*, London: Blackwell.

Peter, P. and Olson, J. (2010). *Consumer behavior and marketing strategy*, 9th ed. London: McGraw-Hill.

Pew Research Center (2018). Mobile: Fact-sheet. http://www.pewinternet.org/fact-sheet/mobile/ [Accessed January 4, 2018].

Pitichat, T. (2013). *Smartphones in the workplace: Changing organizational behavior, transforming the future*. Claremont University. Volume 3 issue 1 Available From: http://scholarship.claremont.edu/cgi/viewcontent.cgi?article=1038&context=lux [Accessed January 4, 2018].

Plouffe, C., Hulland, J. and Vandenbosch, M. (2001). Research report: Richness versus parsimony in modeling technology adoption decisions—Understanding merchant adoption of a smart card-based payment system. *Information Systems Research*, 12(2), 208–222.

Plummer, J., Rappaport, S. and Hall, T. (eds.) (2007). *The Online Advertising Playbook: Proven Strategies and Tested Tactics from the Advertising Research Foundation*, 1st ed. John Wiley & Sons.

Pocket-Lint (2014). *Measuring up: How the Apple iPad is changing Clarks shoe shopping - Pocket-lint*. Pocket-lint.com. Available at: http://www.pocket-lint.com/news/128147-measuring-up-how-the-apple-ipad-is-changing-clarks-shoe-shopping [Accessed January 10, 2018].

Porter, E. and Donthu, N. (2008). Cultivating trust and harvesting value in virtual communities. *Management Science*, 54(1), 113–128.

Powell, W. and P.D. Maggio (eds.). (1991). *The new institutionalism in organisational Analysis*. University of Chicago Press.

Prahalad, K. and Hamel, G. (1990). The core competence of the corporation. *Harvard Business Review*. 68, 79–91.

Pratap, U. and Srivastava, K. (2013). Transforming business with mobile enterprise apps. *International Journal of Engineering and Computer Science*, 2, 2057–2066.

Prelec, D. and Loewenstein, G. (1991). Decision making over time and under uncertainty: A common approach. *Management Science*, 37(7), 770–786.

Price, J. (2014). Boost productivity with smartphones, Independent Electrical Contractors. Available at: http://www.ieci.org/newsroom-and-insights/boost-productivity-with-smartphones [Accessed January 5, 2018].

Prins, R. and Verhoef, C. (2007). Marketing communication drivers of adoption timing of a new e-service among existing customers. *Journal of Marketing*, 71(4), 169–183.

Prosser, L. (Ed.) (2010). *UK standard industrial classification of economic activities 2007 (SIC 2007): structure and explanatory notes / editor: Lindsay Prosser; Office for National Statistics*. Basingstoke: Palgrave Macmillan, 2010.

Pugh, S. (1998). *Organisation theory*. Penguin.

Queensland Government (2016). *How businesses use mobile apps | Queensland Government*. Available at: https://www.business.qld.gov.au/business/running/marketing/online-marketing/using-mobile-apps-to-build-your-business/how-businesses-use-mobile-apps [Accessed January 10, 2018].

QuickBooks. (2018). Available: https://quickbooks.intuit.com/uk/accounting-software/ [Accessed January 9, 2018].

Raasch, C., Herstatt, C. and Balka, K. (2009). On the open design of tangible goods. *R&D Management*, 39(4), 382–393.

Rajkumar B., Yeo, S. and Venugopal1, S. (2016). *Market-orientated cloud computing: Vision, hype, and reality for delivering IT services as computing utilities*. Department of Computer Science and Software Engineering, The University of Melbourne, Australia.

Raluca, B. (2013). Web page. Mobile: Native Apps, Web Apps, and Hybrid Apps. https://www.nngroup.com/articles/mobile-native-apps/ [Accessed November 28, 2018].

Ramsaran-Fowdar, R. and Fowdar, S. (2013). The implications of Facebook marketing for organizations. *Contemporary Management Research*, 9(1), 73–84.

Raper, J., Gartner, G., Karimi, H. and Rizos, C. (2007). A critical evaluation of location based services and their potential. *Journal of Location Based Services*, 1(1), 5–45.

Rasel, F. (2016). Combining information technology and decentralized workplace organization: SMEs versus Larger firms. *International Journal of the Economics of Business*, 23(2), 199–241.

Ratchford, T. (1982). Cost-benefit models for explaining consumer choice and information seeking behavior. *Management Science*, 28(2), 197–212.

Rauschnabel, A., Krey, N., Babin, J. and Ivens. S. (2016). Brand management in higher education: The university brand personality scale. *Journal of Business Research*, 69(8), 3077–3086.

Reynolds, K. (2016). *How cultural differences impact international business in 2017 Hult Blog*. Hult Blog. Available at: http://www.hult.edu/blog/cultural-differences-impactinternational-business/ [Accessed December 11, 2018].

Rice, J. (2017). How GE is becoming a truly global network. McKinsey & Company. https://www.mckinsey.com/business-functions/organization/our-insights/how-ge-is-becominga-truly-global-network [Accessed January 2018].

Richardson, P. (1991). *Feedback thought on social science and systems theory*. University of Pennsylvania Press.

Richer, F. (2013). *29% of Americans Use Facebook During Work Hours Every Day Statista*. Available at: https://www.statista.com/chart/1516/website-use-during-work-hours/ [Accessed January 3, 2018].

Riley, S. (2005). *Herzberg's two-factor theory of motivation applied to the motivational techniques within financial institutions,* Eastern Michigan University. Available from: http://commons.emich.edu/cgi/viewcontent.cgi?article=1118&context=honors [Accessed January 8, 2018].

Robbins, S. (2003). *Organizational behavior*. Upper Saddle River, NJ: Prentice Hall.

Robert-Edomi, S. (2015). Mobile technology could be key to workplace happiness. Training Journal. https://www.trainingjournal.com/articles/news/mobile-technology-could-be-key-workplace-happiness-research-claims.

Roberts, J. (2004). *The Modern Firm*. Oxford University Press.

Robertson, S. (1971). *Innovative behavior and communication*. New York, Holt, Rinehart and Winston.

Robey, D. and Cousins, K. (2015). Managing work-life boundaries with mobile technologies. *Information Technology and People*, 28(1), 34–71.

Robson, K. (2015). Is it all a game? Understanding the principles of gamification. *Business Horizons*, 58, 411–420.

Rogers, M. (1983). *The Diffusion of Innovations*, 3rd Edition, Free Press, New York, NY.

Rohm, A., Gao, T., Sultan, F. and Pagani, M. (2012). Brand in the hand: A cross-market investigation of consumer acceptance of mobile marketing. *Business Horizons*, 55(5), 485–493.

Rook, W. and Fisher, J. (1995). Normative influences on impulsive buying behaviour. *Journal of Consumer Research*, 22(3), 305–313.

Ross, E. (2014). Using technology to make your business more efficient: top tips. The Guardian. Available at: http://www.theguardian.com/small-business-network/2014/oct/22/technology-make-your-business-more-efficient [Accessed January 2, 2017].

Rouse, M. (2018). *What is hybrid application (hybrid app)? - Definition from WhatIs.com*. SearchSoftwareQuality. Available at: https://searchsoftwarequality.techtarget.com/definition/hybrid-application-hybrid-app [Accessed November 28, 2018].

Rubygarage.org. (2019). *Why Are Push Notifications So Important?* Available at: https://rubygarage.org/blog/benefits-of-push-notifications [Accessed January 9, 2019].

Ruck, K., Welch, M. and Menara, B. (2017). Employee voice: An antecedent to organisational engagement? *Public Relations Review*, 43(5), 904–914.

Rutter, R., Roper, S. and Lettice, F. (2016). Social media interaction, the university brand and recruitment performance. *Journal of Business Research*, 69(8), 3096–3104.

Rutz, O.J., Bucklin, R.E. and Sonnier, G.P. (2012). A latent instrumental variables approach to modeling keyword conversion in paid search advertising. *Journal Marketing Research*, 49(3), 306–319.

Salber, D., Dey, A. K. and Abowd, G. D. (1999). The context toolkit: aiding the development of context-enabled applications. IN: Proceedings of the SIGCHI conference on Human Factors in Computing Systems, May. ACM, 434–441.

Salesandmarketing.com. (2015). Unexpected Ways Businesses Can Use Smartphones to Drive Profit | SalesAndMarketing.com. Available at: https://salesandmarketing.com/content/5-unexpected-ways-businesses-can-use-smartphones-drive-profit [Accessed December 22, 2017].

Salesforce (2018). Salesforce. Available at: https://www.salesforce.com/uk/cro/sem/salesforce-products/?r=https%3A%2F%2Fwww.google.co.uk%2F&r=https%3A%2F%2F.

Salesforce. (2015). *Why move to the cloud? 10 benefits of cloud computing*. Available at: https://www.salesforce.com/uk/blog/2015/11/why-move-to-the-cloud-10-benefits-of-cloud-computing.html [Accessed November 29, 2017].

Sarker, S., Xiao, X., Sarker, S. and Ahuja, M. (2012). *Managing employees' use of mobile technologies to minimize work-life balance impacts*. MIS Quarterly Executive.

Sasaki, T. (2014). The evolution of cooperation through institutional incentives and optional participation. *Dynamic Games and Applications*, 4(3), 345–362. Available from: https://link.springer.com/article/10.1007/s13235-013-0094-7 [Accessed January 8, 2018].

Schawbel, D. (2015). *5 ways to make your employees happier and more productive*. Entrepreneur. Available at: https://www.entrepreneur.com/article/247817 [Accessed November 8, 2017].

Schiffman, G. and Kanuk, L. (2008). *Consumer behavior*, 9th ed. Harlow: Pearson.

Schilit B., Adams N. and Want R. (1994). Context-aware computing applications. In: First International Workshop on Mobile Computing Systems and Applications, 85–90.

Schivinski, B. and Dabrowski, D. (2016). The effect of social media communication on consumer perceptions of brands. *Journal of Marketing Communications*, 22(2), 189–214.

Schlee, C. (2013). Targeted Advertising Technologies. In: The ICT Space. Springer Fachmedien vWiesbaden, 1–7.

Scholz, M., Dorner, V., Landherr, A. and Probst, F. (2013). Awareness, interest, and purchase: the effects of user-and marketer-generated content on purchase decision processes. *Paper presented at 34th International Conference on Information Systems*, Milan, December 15–18.

Schouten, J. and McAlexander, J. (1995). Subcultures of consumption: An ethnography of the new bikers. *Journal of Consumer Research*, 22(1), 43.

Schubert, P. and Ginsburg, M. (2000). Virtual communities of transaction: The role of personalization in electronic commerce. *Electronic Markets*, 10(1), 45–55.

Scotland, F. (2017). *The impact of technology on work/life balance*. Available at: https://www.firstpsychology.co.uk/files/Research-report-FULL-technology.pdf [Accessed April 7, 2018].

Seigneur, J. M. and Jensen, C. D. (2004). Trading privacy for trust, *Lecture Notes in Computer Science*, 2995, 39–107.

Seitz, V. and Aldebasi, N. (2016). The effectiveness of branded mobile apps on user's brand attitudes and purchase intentions. *Review of Economic and Business Studies*, 9(1).

Senecal, S. and Nantel, J. (2004). The influence of online product recommendations on consumers' online choices. *Journal of Retailing*, 80(2), 159–169.

Shanafelt, T., Hasan, O., Dyrbye, L., Sinsky, C., Satele, D., Sloan, J. and West, C. (2015). The changes in burnout and satisfaction with work-life balance in physicians and the general US working population between 2011 and 2014, *Mayo Clinic Proceedings*, 90(12), 1600–1613.

Shankar, V., Venkatesh, A., Hofacker, C. and Naik, P. (2010). Mobile marketing in the retailing environment: Current insights and future research avenues. *Journal of Interactive Marketing*, 24(2), 111–120.

Shugan, M. (2004). The impact of advancing technology on marketing and academic research. *Marketing Science*, 23(4), 469–476.

Simon, A. and Shaffer, S. (2008). *Data warehousing for consumer-to- consumer and consumer-to-business models.* Data Warehousing and Business Intelligence for E-Commerce, 61–73.

Small Business Trends (2011). *What the Heck is an "App"?* Trends. Available at: https://smallbiztrends.com/2011/03/what-is-an-app.html [Accessed January 10, 2018].

Smith, A. (2014). *Older adults and technology use.* Pew Research Center: Internet, Science and Tech. Available at: http://www.pewInternet.org/2014/04/03/older-adults-and-technology-use/ [Accessed December 8, 2017].

Smith, A. (1776). *An inquiry into the nature and causes of the wealth of nations.* London: W. Strahan.

Sonnier, P., McAlister, L. and Rutz, J. (2011). A dynamic model of the effect of online communications on firm sales. *Marketing Science*, 30(4), 702–716.

Sorauren, F. (2000). Non-monetary incentives: Do people work only for money? *Business Ethics Quarterly*, 10(4), 925–944.

Sørensen, C. F., Wu, M., Sivaharan, T., Blair, G. S., Okanda, P., Friday, A. and Duran-Limon, H. (2004). *A context-aware middleware for applications in mobile adhoc environments.* IN: Proceedings of the 2nd workshop on Middleware for pervasive and ad-hoc computing. ACM, 107–110.

Sordo-Garcia, M., Dias, B., Li, M., El-Deredy, W. and Lisboa, G. (2007). Evaluating retail recommender system via retrospective data: Lessons learned from a live-intervention study. *Proceedings of the International Conference on Data Mining*, 197–203.

Spiekermann, S., Rothensee, M. and Klafft, M. (2011). Street marketing: how proximity and context drive coupon redemption. *Journal of Consumer Marketing*, 28(4), 280–289.

Stamford, C. (2013). *Gartner says that by 2017, 25 percent of enterprises will have an enterprise app store.* Available from: http://www.gartner.com/newsroom/id/2334015 [Accessed December 20, 2017].

Stanley, R. (2015). *Mobile apps in the workforce: Overcoming challenges to reap the benefits of a fully mobile workforce.* Available at: http://blogs.clicksoftware.com/index/mobile-apps-in-the-workforce-overcoming-challenges-to-reap-the-benefits-of-a-fully-mobile-workforce/ [Accessed December 28, 2017].

Statista (2016a). *Statistics and facts about YouTube.* Available from: http://www.statista.com/topics/2019/youtube/ [Accessed June 12, 2018].

Statista (2016b). *Statistics and facts about Smartphones.* Available from: http://www.statista.com/topics/840/smartphones/ [Accessed July 5, 2018].

Statista (2017). *Number of apps available in leading app stores as of March 2017.* Available: https://www.statista.com/statistics/276623/number-of-apps-available-in-leading-app-stores/ [Accessed January 9, 2018].

Statista (2018). Global smartphone shipments forecast. Available at: https://www.statista.com/statistics/263441/global-smartphone-shipments-forecast/ [Accessed January 9, 2018].

Statista (2019). Number of smartphone users worldwide 2014–2020 | Statista. Available at: https://www.statista.com/statistics/330695/number-of-smartphone-users-worldwide/ [Accessed January 4, 2019].

Statista (2019). Revenue per employee of leading tech companies 2017 | Statistic. Available at: https://www.statista.com/statistics/217489/revenue-per-employee-of-selected-tech-companies/ [Accessed January 4, 2019].

Stawarz, K., Cox, L., Bird, J. and Benedyk, R. (2013). I'd sit at home and do work emails: How tablets affect the work-life balance of office workers. *Proceedings of the 2013 Conference on Human Factors in Computing Systems (CHI-2013), Extended Abstracts*, 1383–1388. New York: ACM.

Steenkamp, M., Hofstede, F. and Wedel, M. (1999). A cross-national investigation into the individual and national cultural antecedents of consumer innovativeness, *Journal of Marketing*, 63(2), 55–69.

Stephens, J. and Allen, J. (2013). Mobile phone interventions to increase physical activity and reduce weight: a systematic review. *Journal of Cardiovascular Nursing*, 28(4), 320–329.

Stephens, K. (2008). Optimizing Costs in Workplace Instant messaging Use. *IEE Transactions on Professional Communication*, 51(4), 369–380.

Stolovich, H. (2010). Incentives, motivation and workplace performance: Research and best practices. Available at: http://theirf.org/research/incentives-motivation-and-workplace-performance-research-and-best-practices/147/ [Accessed June 10, 2018].

Strategicgrowthconcepts.com. (2016). Increase productivity and profitability with mobile technology. Available at: http://www.strategicgrowthconcepts.com/growth/increase-productivity--profitability.html [Accessed July 2, 2017].

Straub, D., Keil, M. and Brenner, W. (1997). Testing the technology acceptance model across cultures: A three country study. *Information & Management*, 33(1), 1–11.

Straz, M. (2015). *4 Ways to Use Technology In the Workplace to Motivate Employees*. Available at: http://www.entrepreneur.com/article/242961 [Accessed December 30, 2018].

Sultan, F., Rohm, A. and Gao, T. (2009). Factors influencing consumer acceptance of mobile marketing: A two-country study of youth markets. *Journal of Interactive Marketing*, 23(4), 308–320.

Symantec (2014). Mobile apps in the workplace: Balancing freedom with protection. Available at: https://www.symantec.com/content/en/us/enterprise/white_papers/b-mobile-apps-in-the-workplace-norton-mobile-insight-WP-21344085-en-us.pdf [Accessed December 21, 2017].

Taivalsaari, A. and Mikkonen, T. (2015). From apps to liquid multi-device software. *Procedia Computer Science*, 56, 34–40.

Tam, Y. and Ho, Y. (2005). Web personalization as a persuasion strategy: An elaboration likelihood model perspective. *Information Systems Research*, 16(3), 271–291.

Tam, Y. and Ho, Y. (2006). Understanding the impact of web personalization of user information processing and decision outcomes. *MIS Quarterly*, 30(4).

Tateishi, K., Ishiguro, Y. and Fukushima, T. (2001). A reputation search engine that gathers people's opinion form the internet. *Technical Report NI-144-11, Information Processing Society of Japan*, 75–82.

Tatley, N. (2017). *Top five small business apps to help you streamline in 2017*. Available at: http://smallbusiness.co.uk/top-five-small-business-apps-help-streamline-2017-2536531/ [Accessed December 2, 2017].

Taylor, S. and Todd, P. (1995a). Understanding information technology usage: a test of competing models. *Information Systems Research*, 6(2), 144–176.

Taylor, S. and Todd, P. (1995b). Assessing IT usage: the role of prior experience. *MIS Quarterly*, 19(4), 561–570.

Teece, J. (1986). Profiting from technological innovation: Implications for integration, collaboration, licensing and public policy. *Research Policy*, 15, 285–305.

Tesoriero, R., Tebar, R., Gallud, J. A., Lozano, M. D. and Penichet, V. M. R. (2010). Improving location awareness in indoor spaces using RFID technology. *Expert Systems with Applications*, 37(1), 894–898.

Thaler, R. (2015). *Misbehaving: The making of behavioral economics*, New York: W.W. Norton.

The Economist (2012). *Slaves to the smartphone. The Economist.* Available from: http://www.economist.com/node/21549904 [Accessed January 4, 2018]

The Economist (2015). *Digitial Taylorism.* [Available at: http://www.economist.com/news/business/21664190-modern-version-scientific-management-threatens-dehumanise-workplace-digital [Accessed December 29, 2017].

The Guardian (2015). 1983 to today: a history of mobile apps. Available at: https://www.theguardian.com/media-network/2015/feb/13/history-mobile-apps-future-interactive-timeline [Accessed December 22, 2018].

The Guardian (2016). Mobile banking on the rise as payment via apps soars by 54% in 2015. Available at: https://www.theguardian.com/business/2016/jul/22/mobile-banking-on-the-rise-as-payment-via-apps-soars-by-54-in-2015 [Accessed December 24, 2018].

The Guardian (2017). Monzo? Might it just be the future of banking. Available at: https://www.theguardian.com/money/blog/2017/sep/09/monzo-future-of-banking-smartphone-tom-blomfield [Accessed December 27, 2018].

The Guardian (2018). *How mobile enterprise apps allow micro-moments of productivity at work* [online] Available at: https://www.theguardian.com/media-network/media-network-blog/2014/jun/19/mobile-enterprise-productivity-apps [Accessed January 11, 2018].

The Linux Information Project (2004). *Source Code Definition.* Available from: http://www.linfo.org/source_code.html [Accessed July 25, 2018].

Thelwall, M., Buckley, K., Paltoglou, G., Cai, D. and Kappas, A. (2010). Sentiment strength detection in short informal text. *Journal of the American Society for Information Science and Technology*, 61(12), 2544–2558.

Thomas, M. and Tsai, I. (2012). Psychological distance and subjective experience: How distancing reduces the feeling of difficulty. *Journal of Consumer Research*, 39(2), 324–340.

Thomas-Aguilar, B. (2015). *23 Disturbing Statistics about Mobile Security.* Available from: http://blogs.air-watch.com/2015/10/23-disturbing-statistics-mobile-security/#.WHKNzbaLTJw [Accessed December 20, 2017].

Thompson, S., Kim, M. and Smith, K. (2016). Community participation and consumer-to-consumer helping: Does participation in third party-hosted communities reduce one's likelihood of helping? *Journal of Marketing Research*, 53(2), 280–295.

Tidd, J. and Trewhella, J. (1997). Organizational and technological antecedents for knowledge acquisitions and learning. *R&D Management*, 27(4), 359.

Tirunillai, S. and Tellis, G. (2012). Does chatter really matter? Dynamics of user-generated content and stock performance. *Marketing Science*, 31(2), 198–215.

Tiwana, A. and Bush, A. (2000). Peer-to-peer valuation as a mechanism for reinforcing active learning in virtual communities: actualizing social exchange theory. *In Proceedings of the*

33rd Hawaii International Conference on System Sciences—Volume 1. Maui, Hawaii: IEEE Computer Society.

Tode, C. (2013). Location targeting more than doubles performance of mobile ads: Report. Mobile Marketer (February 6). Available at: http://www.mobilemarketer.com/cms/news/research/14731.html [Accessed August 15, 2018].

Tornatzky, L. and Klein, K. (1982). Innovation characteristics and innovation adoption-implementation: A meta-analysis of findings. *IEEE Transactions on Engineering Management*, EM-29(1), 28–45.

Torode, C. (2011). The realities of consumerisation: Christina Torode takes a shop-floor look at Ford's bring-your-own-device program. *Computer Weekly*, 14, 8.

Torrevillas, M. (2016). *The best iPhone and iPad apps for employee management.* Available from: http://www.apppicker.com/applists/3939/the-best-iphone-and-ipad-apps-for-employee-management [Accessed January 6, 2018].

Totaltelecom (2007). *Location based services.* Available from: http://www.totaltele.com/View.aspx?ID=91162&t=4 [Accessed June 20, 2018].

Trello. (2018). Available at: https://trello.com/about [Accessed January 9, 2018].

Trope, Y. and Liberman, N. (2010). Construal-level theory of psychological distance. *Psychological Review*, 117(2), 440–463.

Trott, P. (2008). *Innovation management and new product development / Paul Trott.* Harlow, England: Financial Times, Prentice Hall, 2008.

Trusov, M., Bucklin, E. and Pauwels, K. (2009). Effects of word-of-mouth versus traditional marketing: Findings from an Internet social networking site. *Journal of Marketing*, 73(5), 90–102.

Tumarkin, R. and Whitelaw, F. (2001). News or noise? Internet postings and stock prices. *Financial Analysts Journal*, 57(3), 41–51.

Tweedie, S. (2014). *Timeful, the app that thinks for you, has hired a key data scientist from LinkedIn.* Available at: http://www.businessinsider.com/timeful-app-hires-linkedin-data-scientist-gloria-lau-2014-10?IR=T [Accessed December 4, 2017].

Urban Airship. (2017). *New Urban Airship Study Reveals App Publishers that Don't Message Users Waste 95 Percent of their Acquisition Spend.* Available at: https://www.urbanairship.com/company/press-releases/new-urban-airship-mobile-app-retention-study [Accessed January 9, 2019].

Valet, V. (2015). *More than two-thirds of U.S. employers currently offer wellness programs,* Forbes. Available at: http://www.forbes.com/sites/vickyvalet/2015/07/08/more-than-two-thirds-of-u-s-employers-currently-offer-wellness-programs-study-says/#ccd7e336c7b8 [Accessed December 1, 2017].

Venkatesh, V. and Davis, F. (2000). A theoretical extension of the technology acceptance model: Four longitudinal field studies. *Management Science*, 46(2), 186–204.

Venkatesh, V. and Morris, M. (2000). Why don't men ever stop to ask for directions? Gender, social influence, and their role in technology acceptance and usage behavior. *MIS Quarterly*, 24(1), 115.

Ventola, L. (2014). Mobile devices and apps for health care professionals: Uses and benefits. *Pharmacy and Therapeutics*, 39(5).

Vijayasarathy, R. (2004). Predicting consumer intentions to use on-line shopping: The case for an augmented technology acceptance model. *Information and Management*, 41(6), 747–762.

Vodanovich, S., Sundaram, D. and Myers, M. (2010). Digital natives and ubiquitous information systems. *Information Systems Research*, 21(4), 711–723.

Volkmann, W., Landherr, M., Lucke, D., Sacco, M., Lickefett, M and Westkämper, E. (2016). Engineering apps for advanced industrial engineering. *Procedia CIRP,* 41, 632–637.

Von Hippel, E. (1988). *The sources of innovation*. New York; Oxford; Toronto and Melbourne: Oxford University Press.

Von Hippel, E. (2005). *Democratizing innovation*. Cambridge, MA: MIT Press.

Wagner, V. (2013). *7 apps to organize your meetings*. Available at: https://www.americanexpress.com/us/small-business/openforum/articles/7-apps-toorganize-and-streamline-your-meetings/ [Accessed December 4, 2017].

Wall Street Journal (2014). *Should companies monitor their employees' social media?*

Wang, C. (2015). *Do people purchase what they viewed from YouTube? The influence of attitude and perceived credibility of user-generated content on purchase intention*, Master's thesis, Florida State University. Available from: http://diginole.lib.fsu.edu/islandora/object/fsu:253059/datastream/PDF/view [Accessed July 2, 2018].

Watson, A., Viney, H. and Schomaker, P. (2002). Consumer attitudes to utility products: a consumer behaviour perspective. *Marketing Intelligence & Planning*, 20(7), 394–404.

Welbourne, L., Blanchard, L and Boughton, D. (2009). Supportive communication, sense of virtual community and health outcomes in online infertility groups. *In Proceedings of the 4th International Conference on Communities and Technologies*. University Park, PA: ACM Press, 31–40.

Wen, Z. and Lin, Y. (2010). Towards finding valuable topics. *SIAM International Conference Data Mining* (SIAM, Philadelphia), 720–731.

West, J. and Bogers, M. (2014). Leveraging external sources of innovation: A review of research on open innovation. *Journal of Product Innovation Management*, 31(4), 814–831.

West, J. and Gallagher, S. (2006). Challenges of open innovation: the paradox of firm investment in open-source software. *R&D Management*, 36(3), 319–331.

White, K. (2015). *How to create enterprise apps employees will actually use*. Available from: http://www.cio.com/article/3005597/mobile-development/how-to-create-enterprise-apps-employees-will-actually-use.html [Accessed January 29, 2018].

Wicker, S. (2018). Smartphones, contents of the mind, and the fifth amendment. *Communications of the ACM*, 61(4), 28–31.

Widhiastuti, H. (2012). The effectiveness of communications in hierarchical organizational structure. *International Journal of Social Science and Humanity*, 2(3), 185–190.

Williamson, O. (1985). *The Economic Institutions of Capitalism: Firms, Markets, Relational Contracting*, New York: Free Press.

Wilson, E and Elliot, E. (2016). Brand meaning in higher education: Leaving the shallows via deep metaphors. *Journal of Business Research*, 69(8), 3058–3068.

Wilson, H., Schenone, S., Escolin, T., Christopher, S. (2014). *Software-based tool for digital idea collection, organization, and collaboration*. Sticky Storm, LLC. U.S. Patent Application 14/213,147.

Wolf Street (2019). Uber loses shares to Lyft. Available at: https://wolfstreet.com/2018/04/30/uber-loses-share-to-lyft-both-crush-rental-cars-and-taxis/ [Accessed January 4, 2019].

Wong, Y., Khong, W. and Chu, K. (2012). Interface design practice and education toward mobile apps development. *Procedia—Social and Behavioral Sciences*, 51, 698–702. Available from: http://www.sciencedirect.com/science/article/pii/S1877042812033654 [Accessed January 5, 2018].

Wu, H. and Wang, C. (2005). What drives mobile commerce? An empirical evaluation of the revised technology acceptance model. *Information and Management*, 42(5), 719–729.

Xiaobao, P., Wei, S. and Yuzhen, D. (2013). Framework of open innovation in SMEs in an emerging economy: firm characteristics, network openness, and network information. *International Journal of Technology Management*, 62(2/3/4), 223–250.

Xu, X., Venkatesh, V., Tam, Y. and Hong, J. (2010). Model of migration and use of platforms: Role of hierarchy, current generation, and complementarities in consumer settings. *Management Science*, 56(8), 1304–1323.

Yan, D. and Sengupta, J. (2013). The influence of base rate and case information on health-risk perceptions: A unified model of self-positivity and self-negativity. *Journal of Consumer Research*, 39(1), 931–946.

Yang, X., Hsee, K., Liu, Y. and Zhang, L. (2011). The supremacy of singular subjectivity: Improving decision quality by removing objective specifications and direct comparisons, *Journal of Consumer Psychology*, 21, 393–404.

Yarmosh, K. (2015). How much does app cost? https://savvyapps.com/blog/how-much-does-app-cost-massive-review-pricing-budget-considerations [Accessed January 9, 2018].

YouTube (2016). Statistics. Available from: https://www.youtube.com/yt/press/en-GB/statistics.html [Accessed June 12, 2018].

Yu, G., Carlsson, C. and Zou, D. (2014). Exploring the Influence of User- Generated Content Factors on the Behavioral Intentions of Travel Consumers. *Paper presented at 25th Australasian Conference on Information Systems*, Auckland, December 8–10.

Yuan, R., Liu, M., Luo, J and Yen, D. (2016). Reciprocal transfer of brand identity and image associations arising from higher education brand extensions. *Journal of Business Research*, 69(8), 3069–3076.

Zaglia, E. (2013). Brand communities embedded in social networks. *Journal of Business Research*, 66, 216–223.

Zetlin, M. (2015). *These 5 apps help your employees become a team*. Available at: http://www.inc.com/minda-zetlin/5-easy-to-use-apps-that-turn-your-employees-into-a-team.html [Accessed December 27, 2017].

Zhang, X. (2009). Retailers' multichannel and price advertising strategies. *Marketing Science*, 28(6), 1080–1094.

Zhang, Z. (2010). Feeling the sense of community in social networking usage. *IEEE Transactions on Engineering Management*, 57, 225–239.

Zhao, Z. and Balagué, C. (2015). Designing branded mobile apps: Fundamentals and recommendations. *Business Horizons*, 58(3), 305–315.

Zhu, F. and Zhang, X. (2010). Impact of online consumer reviews on sales: The moderating role of product and consumer characteristics. *Journal of Marketing*, 74(2), 133–148.

Zhu, R., Dholakia, M., Chen, L. and Algesheimer, R. (2012). Does online community participation foster risky financial behavior? *Journal of Marketing Research*, 49(3), 394–407.

Zikopoulos, P. and Eaton, C. (2011). *Understanding Big Data Analytics for Enterprise Class Hadoop and Streaming Data*. New York: McGraw Hill.

Zuiderwijk, A., Helbig, N., Gil-García, R. and Janssen, M. (2014). Special issue on innovation through open data - A review of the state-of-the-art and an emerging research agenda, *Journal of Theoretical & Applied Electronic Commerce Research*, 9(2), I–XIII.

Zuiderwijk, A., Janssen, M. and Davis, C. (2014). Innovation with open data: Essential elements of open data ecosystems. *Information Polity: The International Journal of Government & Democracy in the Information Age*, 19(1/2), 17–33.

Index

DOI 10.1515/9781547400546-012